THE STRUGGLE FOR CATALONIA

RAPHAEL MINDER

The Struggle for Catalonia

Rebel Politics in Spain

HURST & COMPANY, LONDON

First published in the United Kingdom in 2017 by
C. Hurst & Co. (Publishers) Ltd.,
41 Great Russell Street, London, WC1B 3PL
© Raphael Minder, 2017
All rights reserved.
Printed in the United Kingdom by Bell and Bain Ltd, Glasgow

The right of Raphael Minder to be identified as the author
of this publication is asserted by him in accordance with the
Copyright, Designs and Patents Act, 1988.

A Cataloguing-in-Publication data record for this book
is available from the British Library.

ISBN: 9781849048033

This book is printed using paper from registered sustainable
and managed sources.

www.hurstpublishers.com

For Ian

'Every nationalist is haunted by the belief that the past can be altered.'

George Orwell

CONTENTS

ACKNOWLEDGEMENTS

Many of those who have made this book possible feature in its pages. I hope that I have done justice to the care and the time that they spent sharing their memories, views and predictions about Catalonia. Other people asked not to be mentioned in this book, but I am certainly grateful for their contribution.

My special thanks go to Jordi Alberich and Josep Ramoneda for their friendship and guidance since we first met over dinner in October 2010. They opened many doors for me in Catalonia and always left their own doors open while I worked on this book. Salvador Garcia-Ruiz made me understand early that separatism was changing Catalonia. I thank him for his help, as well as the friend who put us in touch, the late Edward Hugh, a British economist with a profound love for Catalonia. More recently, Xevi Xirgo shared with me his passion for Girona and convinced me that understanding Catalonia required frequent travel beyond Barcelona. Olga Grau helped me connect the dots in the Catalan story, with the insight of a Barcelona journalist who previously worked for Madrid-based newspapers. Jimmy Burns, a great '*culé*' and football expert, reviewed a draft chapter on F.C. Barcelona. While reporting for *The New York Times*, I worked alongside outstanding Catalan photographers, who opened my eyes to the beauty and complexity of Catalonia. I would like to thank in particular Arnau Bach, Edu Bayer and Samuel Aranda.

Some of my closest friends in Madrid are fellow correspondents. Marianne Barriaux provided invaluable encouragement and help, including great advice to make this book understandable to foreign readers. Fiona Govan reviewed a draft civil war

ACKNOWLEDGEMENTS

chapter—and then kindly put up with having to discuss its content almost line by line.

In Barcelona, Joan Picanyol offered to turn his flat into my second home on the day that I told him about this book. I thank him for his incredible hospitality and friendship. Joan also made me discover some of the more remote corners of Catalonia.

I finished this book at the Carey Institute in upstate New York, on a Logan fellowship. I'm grateful to all the outstanding people at the institute and to Jonathan Logan for believing in the value of nonfiction writing.

I also thank Kirk Kraeutler, my editor at *The New York Times*, for making it easier for me to dig deep into Catalonia.

I would never have written this book without my publisher, Hurst. I thank Michael Dwyer, Jonathan de Peyer and Alasdair Craig for commissioning this book and for showing faith in my reporting and writing. Rachel Halliburton not only painstakingly edited the manuscript but also rightly pushed me to insert more of my own voice and views into the text.

FOREWORD

We live in a world that is obsessed by the politics of boundaries. In Africa and the Middle East, it is all too easy to see the toxic legacy of lines drawn on the map by imperialists. In America, President Donald Trump's promise to build a wall between Mexico and the United States has become the hallmark of his protectionism. In the European Union, a refugee crisis is straining a post-war project that was partly built upon the idea of dismantling rather than reinforcing Europe's internal borders. And in Scotland and Catalonia, debates over whether to redraw boundaries are stirring up issues of pride, sovereignty and identity that both challenge the status quo and point the way to an uncertain future.

Like many people, I first became aware of Catalonia through football. I was a boy, it was 1982, and FC Barcelona's world-famous team had come to Geneva to challenge the minnows playing for my home team, Servette. I lobbied my father to take me to the stadium, even though he really didn't care about football. There we watched a depressing match, in which Servette got swept aside by mighty Barcelona, 1–4. Yet despite our gloom, it was impossible not to be impressed by the brilliant attacking skills of a little guy with frizzy black hair, whom my father—with misplaced excitement—initially believed to be playing on our side because he had become confused by the maroon flags in the stands. (Barcelona is called the *blaugrana* team, because of its blue and maroon shirt, while the Servette players are nicknamed '*grenats*', or maroons, also because of their shirt colour.) I had to correct my father that the 'little guy' was Barcelona's Argentine star, Diego Maradona, whose record-setting transfer fee to the team had made him the world's most valuable footballer.

Football is just one reason why people are drawn to Catalonia. What has consistently struck me while researching this book is quite how many aspects of Catalan culture resonate around the globe. As part of my journey I crossed landscapes that inspired Salvador Dalí, Pablo Picasso and other great artists of the twentieth century. At one point I visited a monastery that had proved a focus for Heinrich Himmler's Nazi fanaticism and search for the Holy Grail. I heard about a falling out between Ferran Adrià and Santi Santamaria, two celebrity chefs who redefined gastronomy and made Catalonia a major pilgrimage destination for foodies. I also learnt about divisions over how to complete what should eventually become the world's tallest church, the Sagrada Família designed by Antoni Gaudí.

On a more intimate level, I found people worried about their future, but others equally anxious to revisit the past, including secret archives kept by Franco's police in Salamanca—part of the troubled legacy of the Spanish civil war. I heard from people caught up in very different kinds of disputes: about water along the shores of the mighty Ebro river; about football in Barcelona's Camp Nou stadium; and about how to celebrate unique medieval festivals, like the Patum in Berga.

The issue of why the Catalans are so exercised about nationality fascinates me as an adult, not least because I found the idea of strict national boundaries confusing as a child. I grew up in Switzerland, but my family had mixed East European origins. Where we lived—in Geneva—we were only one mile from the border, so physically I could see France from my bedroom window. My father used to work at CERN, the European nuclear research organisation that operates the world's largest particle accelerator, in an underground tunnel right below the Franco-Swiss border. So borders seemed malleable—almost meaningless to me. My only worry concerned the wine that my father sometimes bought in our neighbouring French town, since I didn't know if he was observing the Swiss customs restrictions on importing alcohol.

Soon enough, however, I discovered the often terrifying importance of territorial borders and national identity. I switched to an English boarding school when the country was still celebrating victory in the Falklands War. This was also the time when England was suffering repeated attacks from the IRA. As I grew up, I realised more and more the extent to which questions concerning boundaries could become tied up with matters of life and death. Even in peaceful Western Europe, I lived in some countries—Britain, Belgium and now Spain—where families could be arguing and generations split because of concerns surrounding borders.

So many factors affect the way people define themselves on a map, but my research has highlighted the extent to which the economic situation impacts on concepts of national identity. The more scarce resources are, the more people tend to bolster their self-esteem through national pride. I have no doubt that one of the reasons I became immersed in this story is that I arrived in Spain in April 2010, when the consequences of the financial crisis were really beginning to bite. Within weeks of my arrival it became clear that the economic situation in other euro-based economies—Greece, Ireland, and Portugal—was threatening to be one of the great financial disaster stories of our time.

In May 2010, Greece won approval for an international bail-out. That same month, Spain's goverment had to make its first budgetary cuts, following the bursting of a decade-long construction boom that left many Spanish banks with unsustainable mortgage losses. For my American editors, the priority was then to establish whether a sovereign debt crisis that started in Greece would extend to the Iberian peninsula and derail Europe's financial stability. At that stage, Spain's territorial tensions were of international interest only in as far as they could further weaken Spain's finances, since regions needed to make their own spending cuts.

FOREWORD

Seven years later, the situation has changed. The government in Madrid is no longer in the eye of a European financial storm, but the ongoing Catalan separatist challenge was without doubt linked to the financial crisis. So volatile is this challenge that it raises wider questions about the future of the European Union.

It would be foolish to predict what will occur next in either Madrid or Barcelona. Instead I have used this book to reflect the sheer complexity of what is happening in this extraordinary and beautiful part of the world. I conducted more than 200 interviews to write the book, both on and off the record, which I hope allows a true sense not just of the issues but of the humanity involved. As the book's appendix should show, I have worked hard to counterbalance what I heard in the seats of political and corporate power with the views of people for whom politics and business are almost swear words.

Some of these people belong to a generation that is sadly disappearing, including the last survivors of the civil war. They gave me not only a fascinating oral account of history but also often unbelievably detailed and personal stories. On the second occasion that I met Alfons Cànovas, a lifetime resident of the Barceloneta neighbourhood in Barcelona, he was close to celebrating his ninety-ninth birthday. But he could still remember the names of members of his swimming club in the early 1930s, as well as those of soldiers he then fought alongside in the civil war. 'I've got no problem remembering the details of the past, but I probably can't tell you exactly what I did yesterday,' he said.

It is partly in tribute to extraordinary people like Cànovas, who are the guardians of the history of Catalonia and Spain, that I wrote this book.

But this project has been mostly motivated by my desire to understand the forces that shape our identity, what makes so many people want to dig deep into the past and their cultural roots in a world that is increasingly driven by digital technology and other global forces that override boundaries.

FOREWORD

I would like to highlight just three of the challenges involved in writing such a book. First, Catalan secessionism is a fast-evolving story unfolding in an unpredictable political landscape, in Spain but also beyond. Between 2015 and 2016, Spain's longstanding two-party system was fragmented into four. The structure of the European Union has also been thrown into turmoil by British voters opting to leave the EU in a referendum in 2016. Whatever direction politics takes next, changes on such a scale and at such a pace mean this account is necessarily hostage to future events.

Second, for all my interviewing and travelling, I have not been able to grasp some of the passions that Catalonia arouses in people. On many occasions, I have found myself fruitlessly seeking rational answers to attitudes that come from the heart rather than the head.

But such an emotional shortfall can also be a source of strength. This book is that of a correspondent for an American newspaper who has spent seven years reporting on Spain. Yet it is also that of a Swiss citizen who believes he can understand the concept of creating a state of 7.5 million people in Catalonia, since it is almost the same size as Switzerland. Switzerland provides an interesting counterpoint to Catalonia, because it has found strength in diversity and neutrality, combining different languages, cultures and religions without trying to break anything apart. The examples of Switzerland and Catalonia suggest that there is no one-size-fits-all model for any given society, particularly none that can be simply imported from outside. I am not interested in falling down on one side of the fence or the other, but I am interested in understanding why there are fences and why some people find them unacceptable.

Third, wherever I have worked as a correspondent over the past twenty-four years, I have faced the challenge of trying to write for an international audience while also considering local readers interested in an international perspective on their own country. This balancing act risks oversimplifying things for

FOREWORD

some readers, while going into too much detail for others. But I have done my best to keep a broad audience in mind or, at the very least, avoid leaving readers as confused as my father was on that football night in Geneva.

CREATING STATEHOOD ON THE STREETS

On 11 September 2012, Catalans celebrated their Diada, or National Day, as never before. Record crowds filled the centre of Barcelona.

Earlier that year, the city had been the scene of violent protests against economic austerity policies. During one demonstration, vandals had ransacked shops, smashed the windows of bank offices and burnt down a Starbucks café.

By contrast, the Diada of 2012 was peaceful, and really felt like a Catalan public holiday. Young parents pushed along prams covered in Catalan flags while students walked to the beat of drums, soaking in the sunshine and the carnival-like atmosphere. By around 6pm, so many people had assembled that the march had turned into a human traffic jam. Nobody appeared to know what would happen next but everybody seemed to enjoy the occasion—sensing that this would be a historic event. The chants for independence became louder and louder. As a journalist, I found it almost impossible to interview anybody against the noise. The density of the crowd also collapsed the wireless network, so that I could not reach my editor to tell him why this particular Diada was going to justify an article.

The scale of the demonstration meant that there was the constant danger that violent anarchists would show up, and that the police would intervene. Yet somehow trouble did not occur. Even though such a huge turnout had not been anticipated, Barcelona managed to host the most significant demonstration in its history—and almost certainly the largest in Europe that year—without anybody to spoil the occasion.

Even the frail and elderly took part. Sitting that day in her wheelchair in the crowd, Nuria Capdevila explained that she had insisted that her family take her to the rally to defend Catalonia's rights, even if she felt uncomfortable and stranded amid so many people. 'If Catalan independence wasn't important to me, I can assure you that I would have stayed at home,' the eighty-six-year old told me.

It was striking, therefore, that many Catalan politicians did stay at home that afternoon. The most prominent absentee was Artur Mas, who had been elected as leader of the Catalan government in late 2010. A polyglot and economist by training, Mas was among a generation of budding conservative businessmen who had switched to politics after Jordi Pujol had founded his centre-right Catalan party, Convergence, as part of Spain's democratic transition following the death of General Francisco Franco in 1975.

Pujol was key in turning Convergence into the dominant political force in Catalonia. He led Catalonia's government from 1980 to 2003, winning several elections on a platform of moderate nationalism. While demanding (and often obtaining) more autonomy from Madrid, Pujol in return pledged allegiance to successive Spanish governments, as well as to the Spanish constitution that was ratified in 1978.

As a result Pujol became the grand patriarch of Catalan politics. He also acted as the buffer between politicians in Madrid and the minority of more radical Catalan separatists. Pujol sought more Catalan autonomy but never independence, particularly not at a time when secessionism became a dirty word in Spain, owing to the violent separatism of ETA, the Basque terrorist group. The year that Pujol took charge of Catalonia—1980—was the year that ETA killed the most people in Spain.

Pujol also led Catalonia through the transformation of Spain's economy, particularly after Spain joined the European

Union in 1986, which opened new doors for Spanish exports. With the help of massive European subsidies, Spain then upgraded its industrial and farming infrastructure and expanded its transport networks.

So Mas had a hard act to follow. When he finally succeeded Pujol as party leader, he quickly discovered that Catalan voters did not put the same faith in him as they had in the party's founder. On two occasions he failed to get enough votes to become regional leader, in 2003 and 2006, kept out of office by reinvigorated Socialists and other left-leaning politicians.

In November 2010, he was finally elected. But now Spain's economic situation had taken a sharp turn for the worse amid the world financial crisis. A decade-long property bubble had burst, pushing the country deep into recession and to the edge of a banking crisis. Like the other governing politicians of Spain, Mas had to keep public finances afloat. He introduced both deep spending cuts and tax increases, at the risk of incurring the wrath of the voters.

When the Diada was held in 2012, citizens took to the streets because they were upset by rising unemployment and budgetary squeezing, but mostly because they were galvanised by the belief that independence could somehow brighten Catalonia's economic future. Many demonstrators wanted to underline their faith in the European Union rather than in Spain. There were EU flags and the dominant slogan of the demonstration was 'Catalonia, new state of Europe.'

From a chain to an arrow

After staying away from the Diada, Mas jumped on the separatist bandwagon the following morning. In a public address, he challenged Madrid to grant more fiscal sovereignty to Catalonia. Departing from the more cautious line followed during Pujol's years in office, Mas pledged to lead Catalonia out of Spain should Madrid not answer his fiscal demands. And in a poignant reference to Spain's return to democracy after Franco's dictatorship, Mas declared that morning that 'Spain made its transition—and now it is our turn.'

But did Mas overestimate the separatist show of force of the Diada?

Almost every aspect of the Diada remains a source of disagreement, including the precise turnout in 2012. The organisers of the rally claimed two million attendees. Local police estimated 1.5 million, but the central government in Madrid countered that 'only' 600,000 Catalans took to the streets on that day. Yet even the lowest estimate represented a sizeable proportion of the 7.5 million residents of Catalonia.

Whichever figure was correct, the Diada raised the separatist pressure on Mariano Rajoy, Spain's prime minister, at a critical moment. Rajoy was in the throes of a major Spanish banking crisis. However, he refused to succumb. Whatever the size of the Diada and the pressure from Mas, Rajoy was not going to offer Catalonia a more advantageous fiscal treatment just when Spain was worrying about a debt default. So the game was upped. From that point, the Diada became an annual show of force by Catalan separatists, which took a different format each year.

In 2013, the demonstrators formed a human chain that crossed Catalonia. It copied the chain formed in August 1989 by the inhabitants of the Baltic republics of the Soviet Union, to demand their independence from Moscow. In 2014, the Diada took the shape of a seven-mile-long 'V' for 'vote' down two of the main avenues of Barcelona. In 2015, the Diada march resembled a human arrow. In 2016, separatists held smaller demonstrations in five cities, rather than just Barcelona.

But no matter what form it took, the Diada never impressed the unionist politicians in Catalonia. When the human chain was formed in 2013, Alicia Sánchez-Camacho, the then leader of the Catalan branch of Spain's governing Popular Party, held an alternative event. She reminded attendees of their glorious Spanish inheritance, including the triumphant return of Christopher Columbus to Barcelona after he discovered America. 'Here Spain understood that it was the greatest country in the world,' said Sánchez-Camacho.

Critics of the Diada demonstrations have claimed that the street rallies have been manipulated and subsidised by separatist politicians. But they have rarely addressed the more important question, which is why so many people would use their last summer public holiday to protest in Barcelona rather than go to the beach.

'The fact that such large protests have taken place without leading to more widespread violence in Catalan society is admirable, no doubt about it,' José Álvarez Junco, a Spanish historian, told me.

The Diada demonstrations have been coordinated since 2012 by two citizens' associations—Òmnium Cultural and the Catalan National Assembly (known by the Catalan acronym ANC). Founded in 1961, Òmnium Cultural was briefly closed down by Franco's regime. It worked to keep the banned Catalan language alive and gave clandestine training to a new generation of teachers, 'so that when democracy finally arrived, they would be prepared to teach Catalan in schools,' said Elena Jiménez, an official from Òmnium Cultural.

In 2010, Òmnium made its first foray into politics and joined a mass street protest in Barcelona, after Spain's constitutional court ruled against a statute granting Catalonia greater autonomy. The court's ruling demonstrated that Madrid did not believe in half-way autonomy, leaving independence as the only alternative, said Jordi Cuixart, the packaging machinery entrepreneur who is Òmnium's president.

Even so, Cuixart insisted that Òmnium had embraced secessionism without wanting to be tied to any of the main separatist parties. 'We try to keep them as far away from our organisation as possible,' he said. 'We are also victims of their mistakes and their corruption.'

He talked of the ANC as 'our sister organisation'. But the ANC is a much younger sibling, started in 2012, less than a year after anti-austerity demonstrators occupied Puerta del Sol, the thriving heart of Madrid.

The indignados

Sol's occupation began on 15 May 2011. Overnight, the Madrid square became the epicentre of a nationwide, youth-led movement—the 'indignados' (indignants)—whose members wanted to overhaul Spanish institutions. Sol was turned into an agora, where anything could be debated in public. It also became a bustling camp at the heart of Spain's capital, maintained by donations of food, fuel and even items like computers. At a time of austerity, the spirit below the tarpaulin covers of Sol was one of conviviality and solidarity.

The Sol occupation is worth a mention because it was a precursor to similar movements that would spring up worldwide, not least Occupy Wall Street in New York later that year. In many ways, the secessionism of the ANC and Òmnium tapped into the same resentment about social and economic inequalities provoked by the financial crisis and government austerity cuts.

Copycat versions of Sol first took shape in other Spanish cities, including on the Plaça de Catalunya in Barcelona. For several weeks, people met in such places to demand the uprooting of traditional parties and institutions and a return to a less corrupt and more balanced society.

As Josep Ramoneda, a political columnist and philosopher, told me around the time of the historic Diada, secessionism added a more positive dimension to the feelings of frustration expressed earlier in Sol, Wall Street and elsewhere. Catalan independence offered 'the only optimistic message in a Spain that is in crisis.' In other words, secessionism promised change and prosperity in a new Catalan state, instead of stagnation in a rotten Spain.

Because of the financial crisis, many of the demonstrators in the Diada in 2012 were not dreaming of secession, but attending out of despair. Mònica Soriano, the owner of a communications and branding agency, joined the Diada just as she was cutting staff, losing clients and struggling with debts. Separately, her father's furniture company was filing for bankruptcy.

During the Diada, she told me, 'I joined the pack on the streets because I was feeling very, very lost. I was finding it hard to get motivated and get up to work every morning. I had debts and I didn't see where the light would come from, so I wanted to protest, say that enough is enough.'

She attended the next Diada, in 2013, but then stopped going. She realised she had grown cynical about many separatist politicians and frustrated that they had not tabled concrete proposals about how to build an independent Catalonia. 'Perhaps independence is a really good plan, but nobody has explained to me just why,' she said.

Indeed, this has proved the Achilles heel of a secessionist project led by politicians whose commonality is limited to the goal of seceding from the rest of Spain. On social and economic issues, the main separatist parties find more reasons for disagreement than consensus. Separatist politicians have sought to brush their differences under the carpet until their statehood project matures, but voters have the right to receive a clearer roadmap before deciding in which direction Catalonia should go. Otherwise, secessionism risks losing plenty more adherents like Soriano.

Podemos, a promise of change within Spain

As a result of similar social and economic tensions, the rise of Catalan secessionism coincided with the emergence of Podemos, a far-left party backed by many of the militants who had occupied Sol. The chain reaction is that of 'an economic crisis that becomes a crisis of politics and values in which people look for an exit from the current system,' said Marina Subirats, a sociologist. 'The Catalan solution is to say that we should get out of the Spanish system, as opposed to the Podemos answer, which is to say that we should overturn the system.'

Both Catalan secessionism and Podemos have attracted younger voters who form part of the first post-war generation facing worse job and financial prospects than their parents. Subirats said her own generation also had high expectations in the 1960s, but based on a very different experience of politics. On the one hand, it was 'the most dangerous kind of politics,' she said, rooted in clandestine opposition to Franco's regime. On the other hand, the political militancy of the 1960s involved 'a level of debate that was sometime excessively theoretical, steeped in our readings of Marx, Gramsci and others.'

A group of politics professors from Madrid's Complutense university launched Podemos in January 2014. But the party's academic leadership—embodied by Pablo Iglesias, Juan Carlos Monedero and Iñigo Errejón—was not addressing an audience immersed in 1960s political theory. In fact, the founders of Podemos previously cut their teeth not only in Sol but also as consultants to far-left politicians in Latin America, in countries like Ecuador, Bolivia and Venezuela. After starting Podemos, they also turned to a new role model in southern Europe, Syriza, another far-left party that had managed to overhaul Greek politics on an anti-austerity programme.

In January 2015, Podemos celebrated its first anniversary, which coincided with the electoral triumph of Syriza in Greece. Podemos organised 'a march of change' and more than 100,000 people walked to Sol, the public square and spiritual home of Spain's anti-austerity movement. After the crowd chanted his name, Iglesias, the pony-tailed leader of Podemos, told them that 'the wind of change is beginning to blow in Europe' and would also soon uproot Spain's establishment. Iglesias then listed the economic and social changes made by Alexis Tsipras, the Syriza leader, during his first days in office as Greek prime minister—and even inserted into his speech a few words of Greek for good measure. Iglesias promised social justice, but most of his speech concerned Spain's financial woes and rising economic imbalances. To the delight of his audience, he blamed crony capitalism for a financial crisis that, he said, hit ordinary people but safeguarded impunity for ruling politicians and their financiers.

In many ways, Iglesias was reading from an old book of grievances. But for many of the young people in his audience, his message hit a raw nerve. Each generation confronts similar problems from its own perspective.

'We were following political models that this new generation doesn't have at all,' Subirats said. 'We now have young adults who were born in democracy, who have a high level of education, but no real experience of politics and no real understanding of class struggles. These are young people who have grown up with a sense of limitless opportunities and the belief that their dreams must be converted to reality. They don't want to be delivering pizza when they thought that they could govern the world.' The 2012 generation of pro-independence protesters is also different from the movement which took to the streets of Barcelona in the 1970s, in the aftermath of Franco's dictatorship.

Manel Armengol, a Catalan journalist, witnessed a violent episode in Spain's political transition that also changed his life. On 1 February 1976, Armengol was sent by his weekly publication *Hoja del Lunes* (The Monday Sheet), to cover a street protest. Franco had died two months earlier, but Spain was more than a year away from democratic elections, and part of the political and cultural censorship of the dictatorship was still in place. The demonstrators were calling for freedom, an amnesty for all political prisoners, and the establishment of a statute of autonomy for Catalonia. The overriding concern, Armengol said, was 'really to make sure that the death of Franco meant freedom for everybody, that decades of opposition to Franco would now bring change and that his death didn't somehow mean that the dictatorship was not also dead.'

As more protesters gathered in downtown Barcelona, the police suddenly blocked their path. The protesters sat on the ground, but the police charged, wielding truncheons and firing rubber bullets. Armengol put away his notebook and picked up his camera. The photos he took are considered among the most powerful reminders of the social unrest that followed Franco's death.

Armengol knew that no publication in Spain would print photos of police violence. So he headed for a newsstand and jotted down addresses from the mastheads of foreign newspapers. He sent one of the photos to several foreign publications, along with a photo caption and his name and address. He also attached a note, written in faulty English, to ask for his name not to be published, as he feared the Spanish authorities.

Two weeks later, Armengol received a yellow envelope containing a *New York Times* clipping of an article illustrated by his photo, as well as a cheque for $150. The photo did carry his name, however. 'My English was so bad that they probably didn't understand my note,' Armengol said. Major publications reprinted his photo, like *Der Spiegel* in Germany and *Paris-Match* in France. Over a year later, the photo finally returned to Spain and was printed by *Interviú*, a new magazine which then hired Armengol as its photographer and sent him to New York for a year.

The photos of the 1976 protest 'changed my life and made me switch from journalism to photography,' Armengol said. What did he feel about the recent Diada protests in favour of independence?

After a long silence, Armengol responded that he could understand why Catalans had once more taken to the streets, against a 'government in Madrid that really doesn't care about us.' But as to whether the protests of 1976 had anything to do with the Diada demonstrations four decades later, Armengol shrugged his shoulders. He said that he had felt strongly about Franco's death, but then never joined any political party, nor felt any inclination to embrace the independence movement.

'I don't understand independence and I have not even managed to become independent of myself,' he said with an enigmatic smile. 'The photographer should let the photo speak on his behalf.'

I have heard others express a similar wariness that the politics of independence should trump other issues. Those who no longer live in their homeland are often more inclined to provide this sense of perspective.

Antoni Muntadas is a Catalan multi-media artist who both exhibits in the United States and has worked as a professor at the Massachusetts Institute of Technology. He returns every summer to Catalonia, but is determined to keep the secessionist debate at arm's length. 'The artist should let his work speak for itself, but I also see a failure of dialogue here, a situation created by certain groups of people and the media, in part built on Romantic notions that seem to have little to do with living in 2016,' Muntadas said. 'If Catalan identity has to be understood in bellicose and conflictive terms, it doesn't interest me.'

The separatist converts

Nobody knows exactly how many Catalans converted to secessionism after the start of the financial crisis. But politicians and sociologists generally agree that about half of those who voted for separatist parties in 2015 did not support secessionism a decade earlier. In the Catalan election of 2015, 48 per cent cast their ballot in favour of separatist parties, which was enough for separatists to gain a parliamentary majority.

Separatists presented the electoral result as proof that they were advancing, after several demonstrations, starting with the mass protest in 2010 that followed the constitutional court's ruling against a Catalan statute of autonomy.

However, there were other triggers for embracing secessionism before the financial crisis. Xavi Giménez, a Catalan cinematographer, dates his separatist switch to 2003, when José María Aznar, Spain's then prime minister, joined the American-led military coalition that occupied Iraq. Aznar's decision divided Spanish society and led to street protests across the country. During a protest against the Iraqi invasion, 'I felt for the first time a profound feeling of impotence before the Spanish state, the incapacity to change anything in Spanish politics,' said Giménez. 'The protester in Madrid stands up to his own state, while those of us in Barcelona felt like we were confronting a government beyond our reach.'

In the absence of any official referendum, opinion polls are an important barometer. In June 2012, separatists welcomed the first poll in which a majority of 51.1 per cent of respondents said they wanted independence. Since then, the *Centre d'Estudis d'Opinió*, an official Catalan agency, has published several polls showing something akin to a technical draw, with small oscillations. By November 2016, the same poll had swung back slightly against the secessionists, with 45.1 per cent against independence, versus 44.9 per cent in favour.[1] Still, Catalan polls have continued to show strong support for an independence referendum—to help resolve the secessionist conflict, whichever way the result might go.

The sociologist Subirats forecasts that support for secessionism would drop if Spain's job market and economy improved significantly. But she warns that 'if young people continue to struggle to find work, they will also continue to look for that exit path, which means independence will remain very appealing.'

As in other countries, economic inequalities have widened in Spain as a result of the financial crisis. Since 2013, unemployment has declined—from a crisis peak of 27 per cent to 18 per cent in early 2017—but the debate has now shifted to the quality of the work contracts, as well as the dwindling financial support for the most vulnerable. 'With the financial crisis, the map of poverty suddenly changed, with some people really struggling who could never have imagined becoming poor before,' said José Martí Gómez, a radio journalist for Cadena Ser. 'The people who have fallen into poverty are often those who have also really become the most politically radical.'

Yet while the economic crisis has helped push secessionism and left-wing social militancy into each other's arms, they have not always been perfect bedfellows. The ANC was born shortly after the occupation of Sol, but the two movements 'initially looked at each other with quite a lot of scepticism,' said Marcelo Exposito, a member of the Spanish parliament who represents En Comú Podem, a far-left party. For left-wing militants, secessionism looked suspiciously like an attempt by the Catalan establishment—represented by the Convergence party—to reclaim its political leadership. For the secessionists, however, a left-wing movement that had originated in a Madrid square 'looked like the Trojan horse sent by Madrid to destroy all pro-independence claims,' he said.

The ANC and Òmnium also sparked their own suspicions of a 'Trojan horse infiltration'. They claimed to be citizens' movements, but also had leaders connected to politics. Muriel Casals became president of Òmnium Cultural in 2010, then left Òmnium's presidency to win a seat in Catalonia's regional parliament in 2015. (She died in early 2016 after being hit by a cyclist.)

When the Diada was held in 2013 and protesters joined hands to form a human chain that crossed Catalonia, 'the parking lots were filled with BMWs and it really looked as if the Catalan bourgeoisie was having a fun day out,' said Manel Manchón, the editor of *Economía Digital*, an online publication. 'It keeps being said that this is a revolution and a grassroots movement led by ordinary people and workers, but the ANC is also filled with former politicians.'

Indeed, Carme Forcadell, the feisty former president of the ANC who helped transform the Diada into a mass demonstration, has repeatedly switched between elected political office and street activism. A fervent defender of Catalonia and its language, Forcadell worked as a television journalist and a teacher. She entered local politics, but then suffered an election setback and turned her attention instead to civil society and the ANC. On the back of her success with the ANC, Forcadell then returned to mainstream politics. She became president of the Catalan Parliament in October 2015.

A year earlier, I interviewed Forcadell in a windowless, neon-lit office of the ANC, shortly after watching her lead another impressive Diada. Standing on a podium, she had then promised the Diada's large crowd that 'we will vote and we will win,' and had raised her hand above her head to form the 'V' sign of victory. Her message was to the point, devoid of any grand statements.

Forcadell initially combined her ANC leadership with her teaching duties. But she then took unpaid leave from teaching to help organise Catalonia's independence movement. Forcadell told me that the movement owed nothing to Barcelona's political establishment. Her own roots, she said, were embedded in the Catalan countryside, in Xerta, the village where she still has a home and where her father once combined a small transport business with agricultural work because he could not 'earn enough just from the land'.

Forcadell used 'a simple approach and a power to bring people together that most politicians don't have,' said Pere Martí, a journalist who published a book on the ANC. 'She speaks the way normal people speak, without adding any intellectual flourish.'

At the time of writing, Forcadell was presiding over a Catalan parliament led by a coalition of separatist parties committed to holding an independence referendum. However, Carles Puigdemont, who succeeded Mas as Catalan government leader, had not clarified how such a referendum could possibly take place amid fierce opposition from the Spanish government and courts.

The Catalan government's road map toward independence was 'presented almost as if it was as inevitable as the law of gravity, but it has turned out to be more complex,' said Miquel Iceta, the leader of the Catalan Socialist Party. 'One of the mistakes of the independence movement is to think that this had to happen very quickly,' he added. 'But when you consider that the problem dates back 300 years, five years is very little.'

Another problem is that the separatist coalition has been strained by internal tensions. The rise of the ANC and Òmnium Cultural coincided with a fight for Catalan political hegemony between the Convergence party founded by Pujol and the left-leaning Esquerra Republicana party. Esquerra had history on its side, since it was already the leading separatist force in the early 1930s, before the onset of Spain's civil war. Convergence, on the other hand, had no such past. Instead, in 2015 Convergence lost its smaller but longstanding coalition partner, the Democratic Union of Catalonia, because the leaders of this Union party did not embrace secessionism. Secessionism also created tensions within other parties. It even split the Catalan Socialist party 'into two souls', according to Antón Costas, an economist. Some Catalan Socialists took their cue from the Socialist party's central administration in Madrid, which never pushed for Catalan independence, while the others moved closer to the separatist movement in Barcelona.

After the giant Diada rally of September 2012, Mas faced a critical choice. He could either distance his conservative Convergence party from the separatist grassroots movement led by the ANC and Òmnium, or instead reposition Convergence as the leading separatist party, ahead of Esquerra Republicana. Costa recalled warning Mas not to lose sight of his conservative electorate, and telling Mas that 'any radical turn could make him lose the centralism of Catalan politics.' 'He answered that I was wrong,' Costas told me, 'that this centralism was already in the streets.'

Mas made 'a political bet,' but the alternative would have been just as risky, according to José Antich, editor of *El Nacional*, an online publication. Had Mas rejected secessionism, 'the next demonstration could have been against Mas,' he suggested.

The next generation

The Diada brings all generations together. But the most important participants are probably the teenagers who will soon get the chance to vote in Catalonia. 'The younger you are, the more importance you attach to the future rather than the past,' Oriol Junqueras, the leader of the Esquerra party, told me. 'A true Catalan is not someone who has always been Catalan but someone who wants to be Catalan forever.'

In fact, ever since 2012, the Diada has helped forge the seces-sionist voters of tomorrow. Children grow up looking forward to the excitement of taking to the streets on Catalonia's national day, just as they prepare to watch their first football match at Barcelona's Camp Nou stadium.

Since 2012, I have frequently asked adolescents why they want Catalonia's independence. They have given some thought-ful and emotional responses. Sometimes, though, the teenagers have sounded as if they are reciting some form of Catechism. They simply list a series of Catalan grievances, including one against a Spanish tax redistribution system judged to hurt Catalonia—a complex fiscal issue that would normally not be taught in a European secondary school.

'We don't want Spain to keep all our money,' says Leire Díaz, a fourteen-year-old, who has a Catalan flag painted on her cheek for the Diada and who flashes a big smile that shows the braces on her teeth. 'We give a lot of money and only get a little back.' Others sound like a budding generation of free-dom fighters.

'We want to be free to do all that we want to do,' says Enric Mumbardó, a twelve-year-old draped in a Catalan flag. How-ever, he struggles to list his freedom deprivations, so his mother comes to his help: 'And what does Spain say when Catalonia asks to do something?' she asks. Enric shouts out his answer with glee: 'No!'

Manchón—the economics editor I had talked to earlier—told me he was 'very cautious' about discussing independence with his twin teenage daughters. 'Independence has reached the school yard,' he said. 'Children want to find out who went to the Diada and who didn't.'

The media have also played their part. Mumbardó's parents explained to me that their son had mostly learnt about the harmful impact of Spain on Catalonia by watching *Polònia*, a television programme of political satire.

Admittedly, the carnival element of the celebration has a universal appeal that goes beyond politics. Many young Catalans embrace the Diada almost like Halloween. María del Mar Azemar, a fourteen-year-old, recounts her excitement at selecting her own face paint and her two Catalan flags, ahead of the Diada. Still, when she grows up, she says she certainly would not want to join politics. 'There are too many problems with politicians,' she declares.

Why are the young here so into independence, when everybody travels and has friends everywhere? asked Joan Tarrida, the owner of Galaxia Gutenberg, a publishing company. There is probably no single answer, he continued, but both globalisation and job scarcity have made local identity more important. On the other hand, 'it seems Spain isn't a reality that young Catalans now really think much about,' he argued. 'If a young person wants to be successful and can't find the dream job in Barcelona, the next step is no longer necessarily to search in Madrid, the capital—it could just as well be Edinburgh or Shanghai.'

With so many factors in the balance, maybe it is no surprise that some Catalans have turned their backs on the secessionist dreams of their youth. Joan Planas made a documentary and a book about the impact of the financial crisis on ordinary citizens. He crisscrossed Spain for two months and interviewed strangers in bars. 'I found lots of people around Spain who were worse off than most people seemed to be in Catalonia,' he said. 'It was clear that we all shared the need to make things better.' Planas left Catalonia as a secessionist and ended his trip opposing independence. He returned to Barcelona on 9 November 2014, when Catalonia was holding a non-binding independence vote. Planas voted that day against independence. 'I just realised that my beliefs in independence didn't really make sense,' he said. 'There was still room to improve Spain as a whole.'

El País, Spain's leading newspaper, published a profile of Planas that highlighted his U-turn on secessionism. In Catalonia, this quickly provoked a backlash. 'Many people reacted badly and some Catalan media even lied about me, saying that I was a political militant,' he said.

One of the problems—as Planas discovered on his trip—was 'a clear breakdown in communications' across Spain. 'I started with the feeling that anything that was from Catalonia was rejected outside, but the truth is that most people are just really badly informed,' he said. In Asturias, Planas interviewed a miner who considered Catalans were really 'not people', certainly not the kind of men willing to work in a coal mine.[2] Planas also came across tensions between the inhabitants of other parts of Spain. In the Rioja region, for instance, people were upset with the Basques over job relocations.

Finding a place in Europe

Still, an anti-establishment sentiment has grown throughout Spain and is now widespread across Europe. In countries like the Netherlands and France, it is coupled with a xenophobic and more aggressive form of nationalism, which has helped far-right politicians make headway. In other parts of Europe, however, far-left parties have driven the anti-establishment movement, as demonstrated by Syriza in Greece. In the United States, voters elected a political outsider, Donald Trump, as their president. Trump built his victory upon a promise to return power to ordinary Americans and end the hegemony of Washington's political elite.

The shortcomings of the European Union—stretching from the mishandling of the euro debt crisis to the 2016 decision by British voters to leave the EU—have also influenced the Catalan debate.

'The European Union made a very serious mistake, identifying national and cultural identity with its member states rather than with its people,' said Ignasi Guardans, a former lawmaker from the European Parliament. 'Part of the debate in Catalonia is identical to that in France or Britain, because it is about people wanting to regain control.'

In Spain, 2016 was a year of unprecedented deadlock, as politicians feuded over who should form the next government, following two inconclusive elections. The politicians claimed to fight for the general interest of Spain, but they indulged instead in cloak-and-dagger manoeuvres. The Socialists even ousted their own leader, Pedro Sánchez, before unexpectedly re-electing him in 2017. The spectacle left voters deflated, including those who backed two new parties—Podemos and Ciudadanos—that had promised to overhaul politics. In early 2017, Podemos was weakened by an intense leadership battle between Iglesias and Errejón, former friends and university colleagues. Iglesias eventually prevailed, but the bruising encounter showed voters that Podemos could not maintain its lofty political goals above personal ambitions and rivalries. The bickering over Catalan secessionism similarly provoked a mix of apathy, frustration and distrust.

'The victimisation of the Catalan people doesn't interest me, nor do the claims in Madrid about the dire consequences of a break-up of Spain,' said Perico Pastor, a painter whose studio was filled with canvases depicting the peaceful shades of blue of the sea and the sky. 'I don't care if Catalonia is a nation or a post office box.'

Cristian Segura is a journalist who has followed the secessionist debate for three newspapers, most recently *El País*. The polarisation in politics, he argued, had actually left many Catalans stuck in a no man's land, uninterested or unsure about where they belong. Some were probably raised in families like his, speaking Catalan but originating from other parts of Spain.

In 2012, Catalan secessionism rose to the top of Spain's political agenda. The unprecedented Diada also reshaped politics within Catalonia, once Mas endorsed a secessionist movement that his party's founder, Pujol, had kept on the sidelines. And such change was achieved without anybody breaking a shop window.

But to redraw boundaries and replace institutional structures, secessionism still acts as a battering ram that is difficult to control. The drive for statehood divides a society, reopens old cracks and sometimes creates new fractures. To have any chance of success, a secessionist movement must reach a critical size and then maintain its momentum, which is also why separatists have attached such importance to the annual staging of the Diada. The Diada is a forceful demonstration of secessionist feelings, but not an indicator of voting intentions. People also stay away from the Diada for different reasons, some of which have nothing to do with their love of Spain. Some simply prefer a holiday on the beach. Others are upset about the Diada itself, because they feel Catalonia's national day has been usurped by the secessionists. For many Catalans, independence will never turn into their raison d'être because they do not wish to define their identity in terms of a given citizenship.

Segura is such a person. He doesn't anticipate Catalonia's independence, but he acknowledges that his Catalan education has made him lose any special feelings for Spain. 'For me, somebody from Albacete or any other place in Spain feels no closer than somebody from Bordeaux or Naples,' he said.

While hundreds of thousands join the Diada rally every year, Catalan politicians should not forget that secessionism has instead left some people feeling '*apátrida*', Segura said. In other words, stateless.

2

CELEBRATING A DEFEAT

The year 1714 is to Catalans what 1776 is to Americans or 1789 to the French—a turning point in history that is now marked by national celebration.

Curiously, however, Catalonia commemorates a crushing defeat rather than a successful revolution. On 11 September 1714, at the end of the War of Spanish Succession, Barcelona fell to the troops of Philip V, the first Bourbon king of Spain. Earlier in the war, Barcelona had come under the control of Archduke Charles of Austria, who had been accepted as the new monarch. But in the summer of 1713, the Bourbon troops had fought back by besieging Barcelona. When Philip won after just over a year, he took revenge, suppressing Catalonia as a political entity and asserting absolute power.

George Orwell, the British writer, was among the foreign volunteers who enlisted in Barcelona more than two centuries later to fight Franco during Spain's civil war. He wrote in an essay that 'every nationalist is haunted by the belief that the past can be altered.'[1] In Catalonia's case, that moment from the past is the 1714 defeat. It has become the historical wrong that needs to be challenged for Catalonia to assert its nationhood.

The date of the commemoration—September 11—is internationally more notorious for the attack on America's World Trade Center. Yet in Catalonia, the siege of Barcelona in 1714 remains the prime preoccupation, and since 2013 has been showcased in the Born Cultural Centre, which some might describe as the ground zero of the Catalan secessionist move-ment. Located in a building of glass and cast iron that once served as a major food market, the cultural centre generated controversy long before its opening.

The market was initially meant to be turned into a public library, but that idea was shelved once the construction work revealed archaeological remains below the ground. They con-stitute 'perhaps the best preserved remains from the eighteenth century in all of Europe,' according to Miquel Calçada, who was the commissioner for the commemorations of the 300th anniversary of the Barcelona siege, in 2014. 'There is no other place where you can see exactly how the streets were laid out,' he claimed.

Not everybody in Barcelona agrees. The excavated streets are a nice reminder of the past, but not that valuable, according to Perico Pastor, a Catalan artist who lived in the Born district for twenty years.

Pastor compared the way the Catalan secessionist movement preserved these eighteenth-century streets with the way earlier Catalan politicians had destroyed Roman ruins and Islamic remains during work on another infrastructure project in the Born district.

He told the story of how workers had stumbled by chance upon the ruins of a Roman necropolis in 1991, during the construction of a parking lot. The authorities only granted archaeologists seventy-four days to study the site before the parking lot's construction resumed. During their excavations, the archaeologists also found about thirty skeletons positioned to face Mecca. This discovery was unique evidence that a mosque probably stood in the Born during the brief Arab occupation of Barcelona. In their final report, the archaeolo-gists lamented the lack of time they were given to explore an area of such historic relevance.[2]

At the time, however, Barcelona was preparing for the 1992 summer Olympics and scrambling to upgrade the city's infra-structure. Barcelona wanted to be a modern host city for the

Olympics far more than it cared about archaeology and its own ancient history.

'In order to create a parking lot, they destroyed a Roman necropolis, which seems to me a fair bit more important than some streets' from the eighteenth century,' Pastor said, with a wry smile.

Quim Torra, the former director of the Born Cultural Center, responded that the parking project was indeed 'an absolute disaster' in terms of archaeological preservation, but the city had also needed to give utmost priority to the Olympics. He told me that even if the city had mishandled the parking lot's construction, Barcelona later made amends by taking the greatest care in preserving the old streets of the Born. The current archaeological exhibition, he said, gave viewers an extraordinary insight into how the district was developed and then destroyed by the Bourbon monarchy after 1714.

'The value of the Born is that stones don't lie—the truth can't be manipulated,' he continued. The cultural centre presents Catalan history 'with a narrative that a minority doesn't like, but one that is in line with that of the great Catalan historians'.

In 2015, the Born welcomed almost 1.5 million visitors, which meant it had more than doubled its intake since its 2013 opening. But it is hard to know whether tourists flock to the Born mainly because of its striking structure and lay-out, with passageways above the street excavations, or because of its narrative and didactic value. The museum has few original exhibits from the period, apart from an eclectic display of broken pottery. Instead, it relies on texts, drawings and a slide show to explain how Barcelona heroically resisted the Bourbon troops.

After conquering Barcelona, King Philip remodelled the city. He also closed Catalonia's parliament and universities, and prohibited Catalan as an administrative language. Until early 2016, the Born Centre housed an exhibition devoted specifically to the War of Spanish Succession, whose slogan was that 'nothing was ever the same' after 1714. It portrayed

Barcelona as an idyllic city until the siege and the destruction caused by Philip V.

The permanent exhibition also gives the sense of Barcelona enjoying a Golden Age before the Bourbon oppression. At the start of the eighteenth century, Barcelona had 'an abundance of yards and ornamental vegetable gardens, the latter, equipped with one or more waterwheels, were sources of food but also places of relaxation and leisure, with a great variety of flowers from local places or from all over Europe,' according to one of the explanatory panels. Yet after the war, Philip V demolished nearly a fifth of Barcelona—including its Born district.

As an outsider, it seemed to me that the War of Spanish Succession exhibition overidealised life in Barcelona before Philip's arrival, and it also brushed over the precise context in which the city fell. The siege was one of many episodes in a lengthy, complicated, pan-European war. Charles II, Spain's Habsburg monarch, died in 1700 without an heir. The fight for his succession provoked war in many other parts of Europe, from Antwerp to Naples, as different countries sided with the two pretenders to the throne. Many feared an over-powerful France, since Philip V was the grandson of Louis XIV and had been born in the Palace of Versailles. Others, however, became alarmed about the rising influence of Archduke Charles, who had become Holy Roman Emperor, under the title of Charles VI, following the death of his elder brother Joseph I, in 1711. The series of treaties that settled the conflict—signed in Utrecht, Rastatt and finally Baden—redrew the map of Europe and beyond, since Britain also took over French claims in North America.

Making wrong choices

As a result, the eighteenth century was marked by several European conflicts in which Barcelona and the Catalans often suffered the misfortune of picking the losing side. Before being overrun in 1714, Barcelona had already endured two major

sieges by the French, during the War of the League of Augs-
burg, in which a European coalition fought against King Louis
XIV of France. The second French assault on Barcelona was so
devastating that 'there are no known precedents of such an
intense siege,' according to the exhibition in the Born museum.

It's interesting to realise now that the Diada only became a
Catalan national day in 1886, when a commemoration Mass
was celebrated in Barcelona's church of Santa María del Mar.
Ferran Mascarell, a Catalan historian and politician, explained
that Catalan intellectuals and politicians had intense debates
over the choice of 1714. Some Catalan nationalists wanted to
celebrate 1640 instead as Catalonia's special year. That was the
year that marked the start of the 'War of the Reapers', a peasant uprising triggered by the suffering endured during a previous conflict, Europe's Thirty Years' War. During this lengthy
war, Catalan peasants had been forced to house and feed about
40,000 Spanish soldiers. The impoverished peasants eventually
linked up with city dwellers to overthrow and kill Dalmau de
Queralt, the viceroy of Catalonia, and install a Catalan Republic, under the leadership of Pau Claris. The Republic was short-
lived, but it established Claris, who had been a lawyer and
clergyman, as a heroic character in Catalan history. Streets are
named after him across the region.

However, Claris also sided with King Louis XIII of France
against Philip IV, the Spanish monarch. It was an ill-fated
choice. When Franco-Spanish hostilities ended, Catalonia lost
both its autonomy and part of its territory, as France took over
the Catalan region on the north side of the Pyrenees. France's
territorial gains and new border with Spain were then for-
malised in the 1659 Treaty of the Pyrenees.

Ironically, the fighting in Catalonia also helped Portugal
regain independence from Spain—after a period of Iberian
union between the Spanish and Portuguese crowns. This was
because Spanish troops left the western side of the Iberian
peninsula in order to provide reinforcement for those fighting
in northeastern Spain. Portuguese noblemen seized this

opportunity and started their own insurrection in 1640 with far more success than the Catalan reapers. In 1668, Spain recognised the House of Braganza as Portugal's new and independent ruling dynasty.

Yet it is the terrible defeat of 1714 that has been etched into the collective memory of Catalans, rather than the major loss of territory to France in the previous century. The importance of 1714 resides as much in the fourteen months of Barcelona's siege as in the repression that ensued under Philip, Spain's first Bourbon monarch.

Historians differ in their interpretations of the year-long siege of Barcelona and its aftermath. The defenders of Barcelona held firm to the bitter end. They turned down a last offer to negotiate their surrender a week before they were forced into unconditional capitulation. The resistance during the siege of Barcelona was 'heroic, no doubt, but also obsessive and suicidal,' according to a book that Gabriel Tortella, an economic historian, co-wrote with other academics.[3]

The repression after Barcelona's fall was deplorable, according to Tortella, but 'absolutely not surprising,' given the practices of the time. A similar repression, for instance, took place in Scotland following the Jacobite uprising of 1745.

The Born 'should have been the greatest library of Barcelona and instead it has become this incredible effort to create identity,' said Pere Rusiñol, a Catalan journalist and magazine editor. 'It has become the ground zero of the Spanish genocide of Catalans, when it is in fact the starting point for the construction of a Catalan narrative.'

Catalans sometimes recount a spectacular twist in the story of the surrender of Barcelona, which they believe symbolises both the bravery and the resilience of the city's defenders. On 13 September 1714, two days after the final assault, the Bourbon troops led by the Duke of Berwick finally entered Barcelona. There they found the city's inhabitants not just burying their dead, but also getting back to work, with all the shops already reopened.

The shop reopening account might be 'a half-truth, which we have magnified,' Jordi Pujol, the former leader of Catalonia, told me. 'But the people understood that the war was lost and another different war had to start, based on hard work.'

A Romantic rebirth

Fast-forward three centuries and many of Catalonia's historians and archivists are also busy reviewing their past. Some openly acknowledge that their role is to defend Catalonia's historic patrimony against manipulation by the politicians and historians from Madrid. One of their number is Joan Boadas, a Catalan archivist with a white drooping moustache who is also a former president of the Spanish federation of archivists.

'I'm an archivist because I'm interested in the future rather than in the past,' he told me. Some scientists, he continued, had established that human beings use the same part of the brain either to remember things or to imagine the future, 'so if we translate this to a social context, we can say that a society that can't remember its past also cannot imagine its future... So that is why, after every war, the victor always tries to destroy all archives, not only to destroy the past but also to make sure the loser can never again write his future. The Spanish, as well as the French, tried to do that to us Catalans.'

Yet the destruction was never completed, Boadas explained, in part because Catalonia had an army of notaries, who oversaw its complicated property rules and hence also produced a mountain of written records. 'In Catalonia, the notary as a public registrar had huge importance, which is why we have millions of documents dating from the fourteenth century,' Boadas said. 'Our archives are different not only in their content and language to those of other places, but also in the care that we have shown for documents.'

When I first visited Josep Fontana, a veteran historian, I apologised that I hadn't read his latest book on Catalonia, *The Formation of an Identity: a History of Catalonia*, which was published in Catalan in early 2016. I promised to make amends and get a copy once the book was made available in Castilian Spanish.

To my surprise, however, Fontana said that he didn't plan to translate his book into Castilian, even though the book was already a bestseller in Catalonia. 'I really wanted to write it for the readers of this country,' he said.

Fontana is one of the most influential Spanish historians of his generation, the author of a dozen books covering Spain, but also the Cold War and different aspects of social and economic history. But the chasm between Madrid and Barcelona over Catalonia's independence has taken on such proportions that Fontana, aged eighty-four, sitting in his book-stacked apartment, had lost interest in reaching a non-Catalan speaking audience.

Despite this attitude, he was cautious in his views. He criticised separatist politicians for trying to rush independence, rather than manage the process carefully. His latest book on Catalan history, he said, was designed in part 'to remind people to take things calmly.' He described the idea of a strict timetable to achieve independence as 'absurd', not least the one of eighteen months set by Catalonia's governing politicians in 2015. (At the time of writing, separatists were scheduled to hold an independence referendum on 1 October 2017.)

Asked why he was firmly committed to Catalan independence, Fontana turned the question on its head. 'What preoccupies me now is not so much the fight for independence but the fight against dependence, which is another question altogether, and which is part of a broader fight against all kinds of abuses,' he said.

As part of my research, I went to the bookshop of Blanquerna, a cultural centre in Madrid run by the Catalan government. There the sales attendant offered advice about the book that I was planning to buy. The book was selling well, she said, but it was 'probably not really objective' about Catalonia's history.

Her warning was meant to be helpful. But it was further evidence of the deep divisions that a project like independence generates. Alongside other academics, the main historians of Catalonia have either taken sides or been pigeon-holed as unionists or secessionists by others. Similar situations occur whenever a territorial dispute becomes intractable, as anybody writing about the Arab–Israeli conflict can vouch.

The book in question was *Historia mínima de Cataluña* ('A Minimal History of Catalonia'), published in 2015. Its author, Jordi Canal, is a Catalan historian who teaches in Paris, after a long stint at the university of Girona. In his prologue, Canal stressed the difficulty of writing such a history since 'Catalonia is a society contaminated by the past.'

His main aim was to dismantle what he labels as the myths of Catalan history, including the idea that Catalonia was a nation in medieval times, even if it then was formally part of the Kingdom of Aragón.

'Before the twentieth century, there was no nation called Catalonia,' he wrote. 'Nationalists embarked in the late 1890s on the project of building a nation and nationalising Catalans.'[4]

Romanticism was a cultural movement that spread across Europe starting in the late eighteenth century. Once Romanticism reached Catalonia, its impact was accentuated by Catalonia's own linguistic dilemma. Fascinated by the Romantic portrayal of a lost, mystical but also more natural past, a group of writers and poets took on the task of reviving the Catalan language, which was by then widely considered to be 'doomed' and irrelevant.[5]

This Catalan cultural rebirth, or *Renaixença*, started around 1832, with the publication of *Oda a la Pàtria*, or Ode to the Fatherland. Written by Bonaventura Carles Aribau, the ode made a passionate defence of Catalonia's language, feelings and traditions. In the following years, several other authors published patriotic writings. They often drew their material from the accounts and legends of medieval Catalonia, inspired by the historical novels of authors like Sir Walter Scott. The *Renaixença* in turn spawned a new generation of nationalist politicians, determined to gain more autonomy for

Catalonia. Simultaneously Catalonia was leading Spain's industrial revolution, which added an economic dimension to the notion of rebirth, as well as a new social subclass—a Catalan industrial bourgeoisie.

According to Joaquim Nadal, a Catalan historian, the *Renaixença* reinterpreted the facts of history, but it also helped solidify the concept of a Catalan identity long before there was any political separatism.

Mutual ignorance

As political tensions have built up, some Catalan historians have complained about how their Madrid counterparts treat Catalonia in their narrative about Spain. 'The history of Catalonia is completely ignored by Madrid historians,' said Arnau Gonzàlez i Vilalta, a history professor at the Autonomous University of Barcelona. In Madrid, he claimed, 'our books aren't read by anybody-it's as if they were written in Swahili or Papuan.' The reverse situation would be unimaginable, he said: 'I read all the Spanish, English and other books' available.

Joan Tarrida, the Barcelona-based publisher, said he was struck by how often 'I have discussions with Madrid historians who don't seem to have come here a lot and really need to widen their focus.' Even living in Barcelona, he added, 'the independence movement is so complex that there are parts I really find hard to understand.'

Gonzàlez i Vilalta acknowledged that 'there are times when Catalan historians fall into the trap of demonising Spain,' but he maintained that such transgressions were minor compared to the mistreatment of Catalonia from Madrid. Spanish historians, he said, failed to recognise that 'Catalans had contributed a great deal to Spanish history.'

He gave examples from Spain's twentieth century historical narratives that failed to feature the role of Catalonia properly. Worker movements in Barcelona, he said, shaped the rise-and-fall of the Second Republic, which ended with civil war. They also played a key role in the political transition that followed Franco's death in 1975, eventually eclipsing the Communists, even though Communists had led the opposition to Franco's dictatorship.

'There would have been no Second Republic without the anarchists of Barcelona,' Gonzàlez i Vilalta said.

Borja de Riquer, another Catalan historian, argued that even if there are divergent opinions over Catalonia's past and its place in Spanish history, historians should consider why Spanish nationalism has not had a more positive impact on Spanish society. He suggested that perhaps it was because Spanish nationalism has looked backwards rather than to the future, glorifying Spain's past rather than presenting a modern and progressive Spanish project.

Spain's right-wing politicians and academics have shaped the country's historical narrative, he continued. They have 'infused the national project with right-wing elements'—which has meant showcasing Catholicism and the monarchy. For all their efforts, Spain's left-wing thinkers never managed to challenge the history and 'homogeneity imposed by the right'.

One aspect that particularly upset him is the importance attributed to the region of Castile in many accounts of Spanish history. Castile was the home of the Catholic Queen Isabella in the fifteenth century. Her reign and marriage to Ferdinand II, the king of Aragón, are often presented as the moment of Spain's transition from medieval to modern history. They laid the foundations of the Spanish nation that remains to this day. Ferdinand, whose kingdom encompassed Catalonia, outlived Isabella. From Niccolò Machiavelli's perspective, Ferdinand was the example of 'a new prince'. Machiavelli described him as a ruler transformed 'by fame and glory, from being an insignificant king to be the foremost king in Christendom.'

Yet within Spain, Isabella's legacy overshadowed Ferdinand's. This bias created a history in which 'in effect only Castile is really Spanish, while the rest of Spain is in a second-tier category,' de Riquer said. This narrative of a unique Castilian nation, however, provoked Basque and Catalan backlashes in the late nineteenth century, especially when coupled with the Romantic literature of the time. Basques and Catalans got 'the feeling of being excluded from a Spain that didn't recognise diversity,' he told me. Spain developed as a nation of diverse people, but with a Castilian bias and without any concept of a pluralist society. If the same had happened in Great Britain, de Riquer argued, it would be like 'the English telling the Scots that only the English are really British.'

Spain's prime minister, Mariano Rajoy, and other conservative politicians draw their historic references from this biased account of Spanish history, which comes almost straight from the textbooks of Franco's regime, he continued. Rajoy and other conservatives refer to Spain as Europe's oldest nation— based on an inaccurate definition of the nation state that also exaggerates the political union that resulted from the wedding of Isabella and Ferdinand. While the two Catholic monarchs defeated the Moors together and eventually also expelled the Jews in 1492, each kept their own kingdom.

'Rajoy always repeats that Spain is the oldest nation in Europe, but that is nothing more than a speech drawn straight from Franco's historians, an idea that no serious modern historian can possibly defend,' de Riquer told me. Rajoy and others 'seem to think that the wedding of two sovereign rulers is the foundation of a nation, but since when does a wedding create a single nation or identity?' he continued.

The arguments over Catalonia's origins and place in Spanish history are convoluted, and not eased by the growing split between historians in Madrid and Barcelona. In response to de Riquer's claims, one academic bluntly told me that 'the problem is that he's now working for independence.'

But national identity is rooted in history, which is why so much importance is attached to celebrating one event rather than another, or elevating one monarch over a consort. And when there is serious disagreement over the past, it becomes even harder to agree over the present, let alone the future.

3

CATALONIA'S HAZY BORDERS

Tomàs Molina has been the weatherman on Catalan public television since shortly after the network was launched in 1983. Before that year, no TV channel had been devoted entirely to Catalan-language programmes. Now TV3—which is based in the region's capital, Barcelona—can be seen across the region and beyond, and the more established it has become, the more Molina's fame has grown. His over-polished style of delivery is impersonated on a satirical programme, and he often gets stopped on the street by people wanting to pose for selfies with him.

However, Molina uses a weather map that cannot be found in a conventional atlas. It shows the so-called *Països Catalans*, or Catalan Countries, a term used for an area that stretches beyond the modern borders of Catalonia to include other regions where Catalan is spoken. Some see it as controversial, criticising it as a manifestation of Catalan expansionism.

Yet Molina has asserted that the map was selected for practical rather than political considerations. 'I show the weather for our audience—this is about proximity,' he told me. The rest of Spain isn't completely ignored, he added, since 'Spain appears in the map of Europe' that also features in his weather presentation.

Even so, it is almost impossible to avoid politics when referring to the Catalan Countries. In 2012, Oriol Pujol, who was then the secretary general of the governing Convergence party, defended the weather map. The purpose of Catalan public television, he argued, was to serve 'the lands, people and nations that speak Catalan.'[1]

In practice, however, viewers in neighbouring regions did not always have a chance to see Molina's weather presentation. The areas where Catalan television can broadcast have long been disputed. In this case a row sprang up when the conservative Popular Party governed in Valencia, which is immediately to the south of Catalonia. The conservative party claimed that the free-to-air broadcast was illegal, and fined the association that set up the relay stations for Catalan television. The signal to Valencia was cut off in early 2011.

The Spanish Supreme Court ruled against Valencia's conservative government eighteen months later, forcing it to annul the fines. But the conflict was not fully resolved till 2016, after left-wing politicians replaced the conservatives in Valencia.

Such a broadcasting dispute might sound puerile and out of place in a democratic country, where viewers can surely decide for themselves what to watch. In the age of online streaming, it also seems anachronistic to dismantle TV relay stations. Yet it is perhaps precisely because information has become so readily available, also distributed for free on the internet, that politicians get even more obsessed—and upset—about what gets seen and heard where.

Border tensions

The television controversy highlights just a few of the questions raised when dealing with Catalan speakers outside Catalonia itself. There are Catalan speakers in seven different places, who share other aspects of Catalan culture, but mostly distance themselves from Catalonia's politics, especially when it comes to the question of secession.

As well as in Valencia, just south of the region's border, there are Catalan speakers in the Franja d'Aragó (the Strip of Aragón) to the west. In the principality of Andorra, which is wedged in the mountains between France and Spain, Catalan is the official language. On the French side of the Pyrenees mountains, Catalan is the second language, after French, in the *département* of Pyrénées-Orientales. Out on the Mediterranean, variants on Catalan are spoken in the Balearic Islands, as well as in the city of Alghero, on the Italian island of Sardinia.

Catalan-speaking regions have a total population of 13.5 million, which is almost double the number of people who reside in Catalonia itself. About 11 million people understand Catalan while 9.1 million people speak it, according to a government study.[2]

To add to the complexity, not everybody agrees on what kind of Catalan is spoken where. In Valencia, for instance, residents call their language 'Valenciano', which some have sought to label as linguistically separate from Catalan. This has been part of a largely moribund debate that has shifted depending on which party has been in power. In 2015, a new left-wing regional government said the place should be renamed as València, introducing a grammatical accent that is not used in standard Castilian Spanish, but is common in Catalan. Predictably, unionist politicians voiced outrage.

As in so many other parts of the world, the modern borders of Catalonia do not mark the precise limits of a cultural identity that inevitably became more widespread through migration. After Christians defeated the Moors, many people emigrated to Valencia from what is now the western edge of modern Catalonia, around Lleida. They took with them their way of speaking, which is slightly different to that spoken along the eastern coastline.

'I call it Valenciano but it is historically part of the same linguistic system as Catalan,' Pere Soler Martínez, a librarian in the town of Altea, told me, as he reorganised a pile of recently-returned books. 'To assert anything else would be like a Colombian arguing that his Colombian language has nothing to do with the Spanish conquest.'

The debate, he said, should have ended when Spain returned to democracy, after Franco died in 1975. It should also have been settled by academics, rather than left in the hands of politicians who sometimes do not even speak Valenciano themselves.

That, of course, does not mean that there are not language variations even within a region like Valencia. As an example, Soler Martínez said anybody shopping for beans would ask for '*bajoques*' in Altea. But if they used the same word in the town of Alcoi, forty miles away, they would be sold peppers.

Returning to their roots

Indeed, in the Catalan Countries, travelling a few miles in any direction can make a world of difference. This became clear to me during a journey in the summer of 2016 across the strip of Aragón, a thinly-populated and remote area of Spain mostly ignored by tourists, despite its well-preserved medieval villages and unusual rock formations, like those around Horta de Sant Joan, which inspired Pablo Picasso to start painting Cubist landscapes.

In 1909, during his second stay in Horta, Picasso also became the village's unofficial photographer, snapping some of the earliest portraits of the residents there. However, the relationship between the liberal artist and this traditional and rural community could be tense, not least because he travelled to Horta with Fernande Olivier, who was his lover as well as his model. One day, local women threw stones at the balcony of their hostel, to protest against the presence of an unmarried couple. Infuriated, Picasso came out with a pistol, which he fired in the air, according to documents in Horta's Picasso centre. Horta and the surrounding villages have modernised significantly since Picasso's visits. But the area does sometimes feel almost frozen in time, with ageing residents whose rugged faces bear the evidence of a tough life spent working the land.

In August, however, almost every village is decked out in the colours of Spain and Aragón, to celebrate the *fiestas grandes*, the weeklong summer festivities. These fiestas are a sight to behold.

The evening normally starts with a performance of the *jota*, a Spanish folk dance, but then ends as a modern village party. At this point the clicking of castanets and playing of flutes is replaced by the beat of Latino and disco music blaring from loudspeakers.

Above all, the fiestas mark the return of people who were born in this stretch of Aragón but then migrated to Barcelona and other cities. It has become a time of unofficial pilgrimage across the Iberian peninsula, in which families reunite in their village of origin for the fiestas.

In the village of Maella, I met a group of pensioners sitting at the terrace of a café, close to a statue of Pablo Emilio Gargallo. Born in Maella in 1881, Gargallo left Aragón to become a sculptor in Barcelona. There, he befriended painters including Picasso and another famous Cubist, Juan Gris.

Just like Gargallo, most of these pensioners left Maella to find work around Barcelona. They settled easily in Barcelona— some would say because they already spoke Catalan. However, the pensioners begged to differ. Their language, they said, is 'Maellano', which is linked to Catalan but is subtly different.

'The fact that we speak a language derived from Catalan doesn't mean that we ever want to be dominated politically by Catalonia,' said Miguel Ángel Catalán Barceló, a sixty-nine-year-old pensioner with a soft voice but forceful ideas. With a cheeky grin, he suggested that, if anything, other Catalan speakers should recognise 'Maellano' as 'the mother of the Catalan language'.

Such is the desire of each village to underline its own identity that each claims to speak a language slightly different from that in the other villages. Opening his mouth far wider, Catalán Barceló said he could tell somebody from the neighbouring village of Fabara, because Fabara's inhabitants elongate vowels to make their village sound like 'Faabaaaaraaaa.'

I didn't visit Fabara to check whether he was exaggerating. Despite his assertions, Catalán Barceló is the embodiment of conflicted identity within the area. Even as he declares the right to independence from Catalan politics and traditions, his own names reveal family origins that tie him to the very heart of Catalan culture and Barcelona. Indeed, he retired to Barcelona after working for a savings bank there. He left Maella as a sixteen-year-old, 'because I had clearly reached the age to start working and I had no interest in agriculture, which was the only thing around here,' he said.

Catalonia was reshaped by people like Catalán Barceló. Barcelona became a modern European city largely because it led Spain's industrial revolution, and this prompted a surge of migrants from the countryside. Maella's fortunes, on the other hand, declined still further following the battle of the Ebro in 1938. It was the last—ultimately unsuccessful—attempt by Republican forces to turn around the Spanish civil war and defeat Franco. Once the battle ended after 115 days of fighting, many farmers could not replant their devastated fields and instead became scrap metal pickers, searching for utensils and military equipment abandoned by soldiers.

Yet in Maella, the oldest inhabitants do not allow such dark memories of war to overshadow the fiestas. Their reunions remain an opportunity to reaffirm a specific cultural identity, mostly opposed to Catalan secessionism. 'If Catalonia became independent, the first thing that people would do in Maella is put up a barrier on the road,' Catalán Barceló told me.

For the second round of drinks, Catalán Barceló was joined at the table by an old friend, Miquel Vaquer, whose family is from Batea. The village is only a few miles away, but significantly lies on the other side of the regional border, in Catalonia. Vaquer was happy to visit Maella, which he also remembered fondly from his youth. 'The dances in Maella always had very nice girls,' he said, with a twinkle in his eye.

Yet even if his moves on the dance floor were once persuasive, Vaquer's separatist views were no longer going to win him admirers in Maella. Once the discussion around the table moved to politics, Vaquer was the only one to defend Catalonia's independence.

'Don't try to mend what doesn't need fixing,' said Miguel Lacueva, who also left Maella as a youngster to find work in Catalonia. 'Catalonia has always been a part of Spain and has actually prospered within Spain, so why not continue that way?'

Like Catalán Barceló, Lacueva has a complicated relationship with Aragón. He remembered travelling from Maella to take school exams in Zaragoza, the regional capital of Aragón, and getting mocked there for his Catalan accent, alongside Maella's other schoolchildren. 'We of course had our accent, so we were always just treated as the *Polacos*,' he said, using a demeaning term to describe Catalans. (*Polaco* means Polish in Spanish, but academics are divided over why it became used to describe Catalans as foreign.) 'We all feel that we've always been in a situation of abandonment, the inhabitants of the last villages, left to God's will and in a antediluvian situation.'

The divisions between the two regions became more marked in 2013. As secessionism gathered strength in Catalonia, the regional authorities of Aragón adopted a controversial law to underline the linguistic differences between the 1.2 million inhabitants of Aragón and the 7.5 million people living Catalonia.

The resulting new names were acronyms that sounded as if they had been inspired by science fiction. The 60,000 Catalan speakers in Aragón were labelled as speaking Lapao, an acronym that roughly translated as the 'Aragonese language specific to the Oriental area'. Aragonese, the indigenous language of the region, was relabelled Lapapyp. Despite the determined opposition of left-wing parties, the law was pushed through by lawmakers from the nationalist party of Aragón and the conservative Popular Party.

However, in a perfect demonstration of ongoing tensions, it was removed after a change of government in Aragón in 2015. Javier Lambán, the new leader of Aragón, said the law had provoked 'the most frightening ridicule across the whole of Spain.'[3]

In the Catalan villages of Aragón, residents also scoffed at the rules imposed by politicians in Zaragoza, the region's capital. When I asked whether he had noted the change to Lapao,

Catalán Barceló was derisory. '*Ni puto caso*,' he declared, a colourful phrase that essentially means that he ignored it.

The invention of Lapao is a striking example of how far politicians can become disconnected from their own voters and people—all in the name of forging a stronger common identity. As in other parts of the world, politicians rarely worry about the ridicule or the absurdity of their decisions, if such decisions also turn them into flag bearers for a nation, region or city.

But it also struck me that almost every Catalan village of Aragón seemed to be caught in a political no man's land, struggling with a feeling of neglect that is perhaps one of the most common characteristics of peripheral communities worldwide. Most villagers opposed Catalan secessionism, but also appeared slightly uncomfortable within their own region of Aragón, in part because of the language divide. There were also the—perhaps inevitable—splits within Aragón itself. One political dispute had led to the proposal to remove the commune of Matarraña from Aragón's association of communes.[4]

All too often the feelings I encountered were a curious mix of love and hate. Perhaps unsurprisingly, football sparked some of the strongest contradictions.

José Antonio Arguera was the co-founder of Maella's only club of football supporters, for fans of FC Barcelona. A jovial and chubby retired businessman, Arguera told me how he left his own Barcelona fan club 'on the day that I saw that Barça had handed out flyers in the stadium saying that Catalonia isn't Spain.' Yet he continued to follow Barcelona's team, not least because of his admiration for its star player, Lionel Messi. 'Unfortunately, when I watch Messi play, I just can't help myself and always love what I'm seeing,' he said.

A week later, on a sweltering afternoon in Valderrobres, in south Aragón, I started a conversation with three old ladies seated side-by-side on a steep and cobbled street leading up to the castle and church that dominate the town. The three women were old friends, although two of them had moved from

Valderrobres to Barcelona during the economic downturn that followed the civil war.

Clutching old-fashioned fans in their hands, the three women sat on wooden chairs, opposite the house where one of them—Hortensia Alvesa, now an eighty-seven-year-old widow—had lived with her husband. The couple had left the house soon after their wedding, when a brutal winter destroyed the olive trees that Alvesa's husband had been farming.

'I can hardly believe how much easier life here has become in only half a century,' Alvesa said. Even before that terrible freeze, she said, 'every day was a struggle, working this difficult land without the help of a single tractor.'

Many destitute farmers headed straight to Barcelona. Alvesa's husband found a job in the district of Poblenou, in a factory that produced vermouth, a fortified wine that is popular in Catalonia.

Alvesa still lives in Barcelona, as do her children, but she returns every summer to Valderrobres for the fiestas. Even after sixty years spent in Barcelona, her fondness for Catalonia has its limits. She said that she would never vote in any Catalan independence referendum.

'We have lived through so many hard times that I can't understand why politicians would now want to complicate things again,' she said. Valderrobres, she explained, remained the place that best defined her. 'We are meant to die as we were born,' she said, with an enigmatic smile. I waited to hear more. Instead, she adjusted her hair, rearranged her flowery dress over her knees, and then switched topic.

The French exception

'The Catalan Countries, in political terms, is now more of an invention than reality,' Joaquim Nadal, a Catalan historian and former politician told me. 'There is a broader Catalan language community, but I have seen this concept generate more rivalry than consensus.'

To explore this further, a few weeks later I travelled to the 'centre of the world', the name given by Salvador Dalí to the train station of Perpignan, in southwestern France. Nowadays, the artist's description is still painted in white on the main platform. After returning from the United States in 1948, Dalí used Perpignan as a transport hub, to send paintings to American collectors while circumventing export restrictions imposed by Franco's regime.[5]

Perpignan has lost much of its economic importance since Dalí's transport scheme, but it remains the capital of the département of Pyrénées-Orientales, the French territory that is home to about 450,000 French Catalans.

By coincidence, I visited at a moment when the Catalan identity crisis was being hotly debated. In 2016, France merged and renamed several regions, as part of an administrative reform. The Catalans of the North, as the French Catalans call themselves, were fighting to prevent the area from being renamed as Occitania.

Occitania is a cultural rather than political term that dates to the Middle Ages. It refers to a vast stretch of territory in southern Europe where the main language was once Occitan, which like Catalan is a Romance language. While Occitan is no longer widely used, people continue to speak the language and its different variants in parts of France, Spain and Italy.

In one political outburst, I watched Hugues Di Francesco, a local singer, interrupt his concert in Le Cannet (a seaside resort near Perpignan) to grab the Catalan flag. Dressed in white from head to toe, he then waved his red-and-yellow flag vigorously while calling on the audience to stand up against the name change. 'We have our identity and culture, so don't erase us from the map,' he told the crowd, before launching into the protest song that became a local hit that summer. The crowd joined in to sing the chorus: 'We're not Occitans, we're Catalans, we won't change our accent or the colour of our blood.'

After French, Catalan is the second language in the Pyrénées-Orientales. Occitan is only spoken in a tiny fraction of the territory. France absorbed the Catalans in a 1659 peace treaty signed by King Louis XIV, which shifted France's border with Spain down to the Pyrenees mountains. The modern dispute over Occitania suddenly revived the feelings of Catalan identity in southwestern France.

But strong as these feelings are, I found very few French Catalans willing to break away from Paris. Ironically, many wanted more interventionism from the capital instead, but in the shape of Manuel Valls, France's then prime minister. Valls was born in Barcelona and speaks Catalan, but he stayed on the sidelines of the Occitania dispute. 'Can you imagine a Frenchman going to Quebec and fighting against the recognition of French culture there? That is just what Manuel Valls has done here,' grumbled Brice Lafontaine, a local politician.

In Perpignan, which was once an important military stronghold town, those resisting Occitania wanted at the very least to force a compromise by rebranding their enlarged region as 'Occitanie—Pays Catalan.' Others suggested that the new name should avoid referencing either Occitan or Catalan altogether. Instead, they proposed 'Pyrénées-Méditérranée', a name that is culturally neutral and instead highlights geographic features.

As the deadline for the reform approached, Catalans held a large street protest in Perpignan, while some Catalan mayors put up alternative road signs to identify their towns as Catalan. Yet amid the tensions over the new region of Occitania, I didn't hear people debate the essence of France's administrative reform, which was to reduce the country's regions to thirteen from twenty-two. The overhaul was driven by economics, rather than cultural or political priorities. The rationale was that France would gain competitiveness if its regions got larger, and would therefore be better equipped either to challenge or cooperate with their counterparts in other parts of Europe. The reform's goals were debatable, particularly since cities have recently taken the lead in organising international networks, rather than regions.

But nobody in Perpignan seemed to have the energy and time to worry about this economic rationale. Similarly, many inhabitants of historic regions like Alsace and Lorraine were most incensed by the loss of their names (in this case they were regrouped into a new region called Grand Est—or Big East). They were far less worried about whether it would really give them an advantage over neighbouring Germany. So what's in a name change? When it comes to defining identity, the answer is often everything.

Sex, Lies and the Estelada

As French Catalans fought over a name, some of the more radical among them flew the Estelada—otherwise known as the Catalan separatist flag. The Estelada was designed in 1918 by Vicenç Albert Ballester, a Catalan who had lived in Cuba and Puerto Rico and was inspired by their successful independence wars against Spain. He therefore drew a flag that combined Catalonia's traditional red-and-yellow stripes with a star contained in a triangle, similar to the stars on the flags of Cuba and Puerto Rico. Since 2012, as separatism has gathered pace, the Estelada has increasingly been flown as an alternative to the official striped Catalan flag, the Senyera.

Jacques Font, a fourth-generation owner of cinemas in Perpignan, hangs his Estelada from the balcony of his attic apartment, in full view of the Castillet, a medieval gate that is a remnant of Perpignan's fortified past.

Font owns the Castillet cinema, which is a monument itself. Opened in 1911, this building, painted mustard yellow and partly built in the Catalan Modernist style, is considered the oldest cinema operating in France.

Font's grandfather, Joan Font, wanted to start his own cinema business after working alongside his father in Barcelona's Marítim cinema, opened in 1905. So he built his Castillet cinema on a plot of land left vacant by the destruction of Perpignan's historic ramparts. Before the cinema's inauguration, Perpignan's local newspaper, *L'Indépendant*, wrote a hostile article, deriding his building as a 'masterwork of Spanish bad taste.'

Despite this, the inauguration proved a triumph. Joan Font spent lavishly on the opening night. Spectators watched a live operetta, followed by newsreels and then a movie.

However, his son, Antoine, wanted to leave Perpignan and applied to the French foreign office for a job. But in 1934 the French government passed a law preventing naturalised French citizens from working in the ministry. Unable to fulfil his diplomatic ambitions, Antoine instead enrolled in the French army. During the Second World War, he spent almost five years as a prisoner-of-war of Nazi Germany.

'My father never showed any rancour towards France, but I can't forgive France for how it treated him,' Font said. His father, he argued, exemplified the history of humiliation suffered by Catalans in France. 'The repression in Spain was brutal, applied by a dictatorship. But here it has taken the form of a soft repression by a democratic state, a method that can be even more effective.'

After the war, Antoine returned to the family's cinema business. He was still running it in the early 1970s, when Perpignan saw a boom in cinema revenue for somewhat disreputable reasons. Because of censorship under Franco's regime, Spaniards crossed into France to watch movies banned in their own country, particularly erotic films.

One of the films was *Emmanuelle*, which told the story of a French diplomat's wife who embarked 'on a voyage of sexual discovery'. Released in 1974, the movie was screened at the Castillet for two years. 'My father kept the main screen in the Castillet to show Jean Gabin and the other great French actors, but the seats there were normally three-quarters empty while the cinemas around Perpignan that showed porn were always full,' Font told me.

I noticed Font's Estelada while admiring the cinema's ornate exterior. I asked a cinema employee to help me speak to the flag's owner. When I phoned him, Font invited me to return later and ring a doorbell at the back of the building, from where an industrial lift took me to the attic. His apartment overflowed with contemporary paintings and other artwork, including a video installation in his open kitchen that showed surreal, computer-animated images.

After Spain's return to democracy, one of the more unexpected consequences was a reverse in the flow of the sex business. Because the rules prohibiting prostitution are stricter in France than in Spain, to this day French visitors cross the border to fulfill their sexual cravings, just as Spaniards travelled to France to avoid Franco's cinema censorship.

In 2010, the Paradise nightclub opened in the Catalan border town of La Jonquera. It was also considered the largest brothel in Europe, with room for as many as 160 prostitutes. While it has since faced legal problems, it continues to operate among a dozen brothels located within a short drive from the French border.

Should it be a surprise that sex is among the few industries that encourages mass travel backwards and forwards across the border? Aside from this, fewer than a thousand residents cross the border daily to go to work on the other side, a fragment of the numbers crossing other French border posts, such as those into Switzerland, even though the Swiss are outside the European Union.

Josep Puigbert is the director of the representative office of Catalonia in Perpignan, which also houses small exhibitions about Catalan culture on its ground floor. Puigbert forecasts that an independent Catalonia would boost cross-border investments.

'Nobody can now open a new road here without the authorisation of Paris and Madrid, two capitals that are 900 kilometres from the border,' he said.

During my visit, I talked to Brice Lafontaine, a politician who was then thirty-three and the assistant to the mayor of Perpignan. He also asserted that Perpignan would profit from an independent Catalonia in the same way that Mulhouse, a city in eastern France, has benefited from strong links with the Swiss region around Basel.

Lafontaine did not grow up obsessing about Catalan politics. On the contrary, he decided to become a fireman, a rescue profession that he chose after his father died in a car crash. Now, however, he thanks Jacques Chirac, the former president of France, for involuntarily turning him into a politician. In 2005, Lafontaine took part in a television show in which citizens asked Chirac about the European Constitution, ahead of a French referendum. Afterwards Lafontaine talked with Chirac backstage and asked whether Europe's Constitution would boost Catalan and other minority languages in France. Chirac mocked his question, according to Lafontaine, and advised sarcastically that Lafontaine might as well ask for Catalan independence.

'I took him at his word,' Lafontaine said. Back in Perpignan, Lafontaine started evening classes in Catalan. In the French municipal elections of 2014, he was elected as a candidate for Unitat Catalana, a local party.

Lafontaine's story shows how misplaced words or an unfortunate gesture can impact on politics. How often have Catalans explained their secessionism by quoting the arrogant or insulting words of a Madrid politician talking about Catalonia?

The complex emotions surrounding Catalan independence are also in evidence in the frontier towns on the other side of the French border. One of these is Portbou, which has a long history of receiving people struggling to escape persecution and war. Here the railway station has a century-old customs room, which has kept the long, U-shaped tables on which passengers escaping France's Nazi occupation once had their luggage checked. Others chose instead to cross the mountains along the same steep paths used by Franco's opponents to flee Spain in the spring of 1939.

Portbou, however, was not a safe haven for everybody. Walter Benjamin, the German Jewish philosopher and literary critic, crossed from France into Portbou in September 1940. When he was found dead in his hotel room, the official story was that he had committed suicide with an overdose of morphine. The documents relating to his tragic stay—including his registration form and an extremely detailed inventory of the belongings found in his room—can still be seen in Portbou. It is also possible to see the serial numbers of the French franc and dollar bills that he carried, as well as descriptions of his nickel-plated glasses and his pipe, with a nozzle made of amber.

Most speculate that after checking into his hotel, Benjamin was informed by the Spanish authorities that he had in fact arrived illegally. He reached Portbou just after Franco's police had tightened its visa policy and started sending back more people who had hoped to transit through Spain. At the time, he was carrying a permit to enter the United States, which had been delivered by the American consulate in Marseille.

His death itself is shrouded in mystery. So are the whereabouts and content of a manuscript that Benjamin allegedly carried with him. Some researchers believe Benjamin was killed by Stalinist agents, while others attribute his death to Franco's collaboration with a Nazi regime that had helped him win Spain's civil war. Of particular note is the fact that Benjamin's hotel is within a stone's throw of a supermarket that was at the time used as an office of the Gestapo.

Almost half a century later, in 1986, Spain's entry into the European Union reduced Portbou's importance as a transit hub. Since then, the town has relied on tourists rather than transiting train passengers.

These days, Portbou is run by Convergence, the conservative party that embraced separatism in 2012. However, when I talked to Portbou's deputy mayor, Toni Sánchez Serra, who is also a customs broker, he seemed uninterested in secessionism, joking that he would prefer an independent republic of Portbou to a republic of Catalonia.

But as we traced Benjamin's footsteps around Portbou, Sánchez Serra became more sombre. Our final stop was a memorial built in Benjamin's honour, next to a cemetery that overlooks the Mediterranean. Dani Karavan, the Israeli artist who created the memorial, split it into different elements, including a tunnel and a flight of steps that almost reach the water. But I found the walk inside the cemetery more poignant, as I meandered among the white niches and evergreen cypress trees whose colours contrast with the deep blue of the sea. As I was taking in the beauty of Benjamin's final resting place, I saw a rusty plaque, inscribed with a few sentences that he had written in Portbou, after he understood that he would never start a new and better life in America. The original of his note was later destroyed. But Benjamin allegedly wrote, 'It is in a small village in the Pyrenees where no one knows me that my life will come to a close'.

As we returned from the cemetery, Sánchez Serra declared that borders can create pointless suffering. Portbou, he said, should make every effort to be valued for its openness to all people, whatever Catalonia's political future.

'We've always been a place of transit, open to the world and everybody,' said Sánchez Serra. 'It makes sense for all frontier towns to be flying all possible flags, whether on this side of the border or in France.'

An outpost in Italy

Alghero, a city at the northwestern tip of the island of Sardinia, has no concerns over land borders and is too far east of Barcelona to fit onto Molina's television weather map. Alghero is also a place over which Catalans lost any political influence centuries ago. But it remains a unique bastion of the Catalan language in Italy. The first Catalans reached Sardinia in the fourteenth century, when the troops of King Peter IV of Aragón sailed from the eastern coast of Spain as part of an expansion into the Mediterranean.

Alghero proved very hard to control. After residents slaughtered the troops garrisoned in Alghero during an uprising, King Peter expelled most of the city's Genoese and Sardinian inhabitants and instead brought in a significant number of Catalans from the mainland. Many were convicts, prostitutes and other so-called 'undesirables'.

The Catalan repopulation of Alghero explains to this day why Alghero uses a language spoken only within the confines of its ancient fortified walls.

However, the language is struggling to survive. It is hardly spoken among younger people and barely taught in Alghero's schools. Only about one quarter of the 43,000 inhabitants of Alghero use Catalan as their main language, according to local officials. A century ago, 80 per cent of the population were native Catalan speakers, according to a census conducted in 1921, and everybody spoke at least some Catalan.

'You can organise conferences, publish books and do many other things, but speaking is the only thing that really keeps a language alive,' said Sara Alivesi, a local journalist.

After the Turin-based House of Savoy took over over Sardinia in 1720, the Catalan language virtually disappeared on the island. It has also since been lost in families that married outside Alghero, like that of Maria Giovanna Fara, who works for a local tourism foundation. Her mother came from the non-Catalan town of Uri, which is only about ten miles from Alghero.

In 1999, Italy adopted a law to protect Catalan and eleven other historic minority languages. Local officials, however, sounded despondent about Catalan's future in Alghero—and even more so about the sidelining of minority languages within the Italian education system.

'For a certain period, they faked it, because it was politically correct to say that you wanted to enhance languages,' said Francesco Ballone, a local linguist, who has a doctorate in applied phonetics from the Autonomous University of Barcelona. 'Now that period is finished.'

José Álvarez Junco, a Spanish historian, respects efforts to preserve languages, but is dismissive of any initiative that harkens back to the times of imperialism and territorial expansion. The Catalan Countries are 'part of an old imperialist dream dating to a time when Barcelona, Valencia and Palma controlled a large part of the Mediterranean, but that reminds me of what we were taught at school under Franco, about the golden age when Spain controlled the Americas and had the greatest empire ever,' he said. Some Catalan separatists probably hope that Catalonia's independence would encourage fellow Catalan speakers to follow suit, but 'to speak now about the Catalan Countries is like speaking about the music of angels,' he said. In other words, pie in the sky.

4

REMEMBERING THE CIVIL WAR AND FRANCO

In July 2016, a crowd sat and watched a ninety-three-year-old man shuffle towards a podium. Once he had reached it, Catalan officials handed him booklets and photos that had been confiscated from his Republican family during the Spanish civil war. 'This is a very unexpected and happy moment,' he said afterwards, holding back the tears.

The ceremony took place in the Catalan archives in Sant Cugat del Vallès, on the outskirts of Barcelona. The old man—Pere Bartolomé—wore a dark green suit for the occasion. He used a cane and needed a rest after receiving his documents. But his thoughts and memory were clear enough for him to recall how Franco's victorious soldiers had ransacked his village and confiscated documents from his family. As he spoke, Bartolomé made great sweeping gestures with his arms to illustrate the way soldiers had thrown furniture around his home.

For Bartolomé and others involved, the ceremony brought relief, surprise, and sadness. But there was also frustration that it had taken so long to recover documents that had been hidden in a massive police archive. As Franco had started to push back his Republican opponents in the war, he had created a special unit to seize documents that could eventually help identify and punish his opponents. The unit had stored any confiscated material in a building in Salamanca—a university city that became Franco's military headquarters. Now the files carry its name.

Bartolomé was among the very few attendees who had actually lived through the horrors of the war. Most of the fifty or so people who collected grey boxes containing seized documents did so on behalf of deceased grandparents and other missing relatives. Some hoisted the boxes above their head as if they were trophies, to rapturous applause from the audience.

Like several other aspects of the civil war and the resulting Franco dictatorship, the so-called Salamanca Papers have done more to stir controversy than provoke reconciliation. Even after Spain's parliament agreed to return documents to Catalonia in 2005, the process continued to be mired in both legal and technical difficulties.

Catalonia's efforts to recover the Salamanca papers are part of a broader push to explore the history of the civil war and the resulting dictatorship, an effort that has not been equalled elsewhere. Catalonia has more civil war museums than any other region of Spain.

During the ceremony at the Catalan archives, Santi Vila, the official in charge of culture within Catalonia's regional government, condemned Franco's repression. But Vila also pointed out ugly echoes between past and present. He attacked Jorge Fernández Díaz, then Spain's Interior Minister. The minister had triggered outrage in Catalonia in mid-2016 after he had been heard in a leaked recording trying to dig up dirt to incriminate Catalan political opponents.

Joan B. Culla, a leading Catalan historian, was among the first academics to gain access to the documents. He visited Salamanca in November 1975, just as Franco died. Drawing his own comparison, he suggested that returning documents stolen from Republican families was like restituting paintings seized from Jews by the Nazis.

'The fact that we're still having such a debate shows that, even forty years later, there is no sense of shame felt in defending the Franco period,' he argued. 'Could a town in Germany now be saying that something shouldn't leave because Hitler had put it there?'

REMEMBERING THE CIVIL WAR AND FRANCO

I first found out about the Salamanca documents during a chance encounter on Sant Jaume Square, in the heart of Barcelona. A group of demonstrators were standing outside the headquarters of the Catalan government, holding signs protesting against Franco's legacy.

Some were victims of Franco's repression, like Felipe Moreno, who said he had been tortured by Antonio González Pacheco, an officer in Franco's police who was known as 'Billy the Kid' because he liked to show off his gun. Moreno was protesting against the Spanish government's refusal to extradite González Pacheco to Argentina, where a judge was investigating Franco's crimes. Josep Cruanyes, a lawyer, was also attending the protest. Cruanyes first became interested in Salamanca's police files while researching the history of his own grandfather, a lawyer who fled to France after the war. As a result he decided to help retrieve every Catalan document stolen by Franco, a mission that put him at the heart of tortuous negotiations between Madrid, Barcelona and Salamanca.

Spain's other regions did not try to help Catalonia recover the Salamanca files. The Socialist government also got cold feet once the Salamanca issue triggered a conservative backlash. As a result, when the first documents were eventually withdrawn from Salamanca's archive in 2006, they were wheeled out on small carts around 5 am almost in secrecy.

Cruanyes said to me, 'It looked like a criminal dawn raid rather than what should have been a historic moment. In France or any other place, whenever a painting stolen by the Nazis is found, it's a special event, but clearly that isn't possible in Spain.'

In 2014, a lawyer and historian called Policarpo Sánchez created an association to lobby for Salamanca to become a state archive. He believes that Catalonia's bid to dismantle the archive was part of a vendetta, driven by 'ideological hatred' for Spain rather than by sympathy for the victims of Franco. Catalan separatists, he claimed, 'want to declare independence and therefore need to erase the collective and historical memory of

Spain.' He acknowledged that in Salamanca Franco had created something akin to the Stasi police files used in Communist East Germany. But since Spain's return to democracy, he told me, the archive had been overseen by Spain's Culture ministry and had provided a treasure trove for historians.

In 2016, Sánchez came to international attention when he found the press accreditation of Antoine de Saint-Exupéry, the author of *The Little Prince*, who had covered the civil war for French newspapers. 'Documents can be found in Salamanca that the Library of Congress or any other archive would kill to have,' he declared. 'Can you imagine breaking up the Prado museum, leaving perhaps only copies in Madrid and taking back each painting to its place of origin?' He and his association also filed a lawsuit against the Catalan authorities for allegedly mishandling documents, as well as removing some papers that originally came from other regions.

But in fact, few of the documents returned to Catalonia in 2016 held major historic value. One exception was the boardroom minutes book of the association created in 1926 by Pau Casals, the world-famous cellist. The book contained details relating to concerts for factory workers and their families. The document showed Casals was not only striving for personal success but he 'also wanted to allow workers to listen to quality music in the same places as the bourgeoisie,' explained Jordi Pardo, the director general of the Casals foundation.

Pardo anticipated that the boardroom minutes would shed light on a solidarity network formed around one of Europe's greatest musicians. Casals was so vehemently anti-Franco that, after his victory, he left Spain and refused to play in any country that supported Franco's regime. For Franco, however, once the book had been seized it may have helped establish the political links of several music lovers. So the document is also a chilling reminder of how the same information can serve diametrically opposed purposes when it switches hands.

Many of the relatives I met at the ceremony struggled to work out exactly what they had received. Most of the original document owners have long been dead. María Isabel Salazar Bertran could not decipher the dedication written into a book about Catalonia that had belonged to her grandfather, Joan Bertran i Llopart, a former Republican town mayor. However, she had found out about her grandfather's book on the day that her own mother had died. It was a poignant coincidence.

'For me, this book is in itself a symbol of the history and the dignity of my family who, like so many others, didn't deserve to be persecuted for holding a different ideology,' she said.

In July 2016, Barcelona commemorated the eightieth anniversary of the start of the civil war. The city authorities held a concert in the sumptuous Palau de la Música and hung anniversary banners from Barcelona's public buildings. 'Memory isn't a duty but a civil right that has to be protected,' said Ricard Vinyes, a historian and city hall official who had organised the commemoration. Vinyes contrasted Barcelona's efforts with the longstanding silence in Madrid, dating to the Socialist government's attempt in 1986 to ignore the fiftieth anniversary of Franco's uprising. At the time, the Socialist administration declared that the civil war 'no longer has, and should not have, a living presence in the reality of a country whose moral conscience is based on the principles of freedom and tolerance.'[1]

Indeed, a visitor to Spain's capital will nowadays struggle to find evidence of Madrid's key role in the war. There is no war museum or even a plaque next to the few structures that remain from the conflict, like the fortifications of the Parque del Oeste, or Madrid's western park. In Madrid's Museum of History—a pink building filled with displays about the Napoleonic occupation and other wartime events—the city's history stops in its tracks about a decade before the civil war.

Beheading Franco

On 20 November 1975, Franco died in a Madrid hospital at the age of eighty-two. He received a state funeral, with huge queues of supporters lining up to pay their last respect at his open coffin, in the chapel of Madrid's royal palace. 'Franco would never have lasted forty years without a very high level of social acceptance,' Francesc Homs, the leader of the Convergence party in the Spanish Parliament told me. Franco's funeral and the outpouring of grief that followed it, he added, isn't typical of 'how dictatorships normally end.'

With his dark eyebrows and thick mass of greying hair, Homs became a recurring face on Catalan television in 2010, after Mas chose him as his government spokesman. With Mas's support, Homs eventually switched to the Spanish parliamentary arena to represent Catalonia's interests in Madrid. But in 2017, he became one of the first Catalan separatist politicians sentenced for civil disobedience, for helping coordinate an unauthorised independence vote eight years earlier. At the time of writing, Homs remained as a lawmaker, pending an appeal against the sentence, which would ban him from holding political office for one year.

In 1977, Spain tried to shut the door on attempts to rake over the past, adopting an amnesty law that covered the crimes of both the civil war and the dictatorship. But thirty years later, the Socialist government passed a very different kind of legislation, known as the law of historical memory, to condemn Franco and help recognise silenced victims. This law also encouraged the search for mass graves, at the same time as calling for the removal of any remaining symbols of Franco from public spaces.

But the historical memory law has proved extremely hard to apply. A case in point is the divisive debate over whether to maintain the Valley of the Fallen, the giant mausoleum and basilica that Franco built in the mountains near Madrid, using prisoners as forced labour.

Secessionism, in some ways, has added a fresh layer of controversy. In October 2016, Barcelona held an exhibition about Franco's legacy in which the centrepiece was an outdoor statue of the general. The equestrian statue was pelted with eggs, splashed with paint and decorated successively with separatist flags, a blow-up doll and a pig's head. Vandals finally knocked down the statue, just four days after it was put on display. 'It's extraordinary to think that we spent four decades not protesting or disrupting anything to do with Franco, but that he manages to provoke us into destroying his statue four decades after his death,' said Josep Ramoneda, a philosopher and political columnist.

The exhibition was held at the Born Cultural Centre. Protesters sent a petition to Barcelona's mayor, Ada Colau, urging her to cancel the 'public exhibition of a murderer' in a cultural centre that is 'the main symbol of resistance, struggle and suffering of the Catalan nation.' Olga Amargant, a Catalan lawyer challenged her, asking: 'Can you imagine German politicians deciding to show Hitler statues next to the Jewish Museum in Berlin?'

Franco's equestrian statue was originally commissioned in 1963 for a military museum that had been inaugurated by Franco in the Montjuïc castle that overlooks Barcelona. The statue remained in Montjuïc's courtyard until 2008, when it was moved to a warehouse. Five years later, the statue was mysteriously beheaded while in storage. The Born Cultural Centre exhibition was not designed to pay homage to his dictatorship but instead to recall the convoluted history of his public artwork, not least the difficulties in 'banishing the Franco regime' from places like the Montjuïc castle. The exhibition was also used as a platform for denouncing lawsuits against modern artists who have criticised Franco.

Rosa Maria Muga, is a culture official in L'Hospitalet—a city next to Barcelona—which has a bust of Franco in the local history museum. When I talked to her about the incident, she replied, 'Whether we like it or not, Franco is part of our past. I don't see why any effort to explain our history can ever be bad.'

In recent years Barcelona has been building up a video archive of testimonies from the last survivors of the civil war. The city has also opened some bunkers and other war sites of relevance to the public. There are some smaller Catalan towns with impressive civil war museums, too, like Gandesa, whose exhibits focus on the battle of the Ebro. A museum in La Jonquera, which opened in 2008, recounts how half a million Spaniards fled to France and other countries when Franco won the war.

After Franco's death, Catalan historians began a campaign to reinsert Catalonia into the history of Spain. 'Our study books ended in the nineteenth century and the twentieth century just didn't feature—especially not Catalonia,' said Ferran Mascarell, who co-founded a history magazine, *L'Avenç*, in 1977. Their campaign remains a work in progress, not least at Montjuïc castle, which is now a tourism attraction in stark contrast to its function as a political prison a century earlier. On summer evenings, one of the castle's moats is turned into an outdoor cinema. As filmgoers laugh at Billy Wilder's *Some like it hot*, it's unclear how many realise that the screen is next to the wall where Lluís Companys, the former Republican president of Catalonia, was executed by a firing squad in 1940.

In a moat on the other side of the Montjuïc castle, a monument is dedicated to the 'heroes and martyrs of the glorious National movement.' It was built in 1940, on the spot where supporters of Franco's uprising were executed. Until 2015, a far-right association, called 'Friends of the Castle,' held a catholic Mass there every July. When Barcelona's city hall became left-wing, it cancelled the Mass and expelled the association from the castle.

The historian Vinyes is one of those who have been working on drawing 'a red line' under Franco's dictatorship. 'The government of this city wants to preserve the memory of historic events on these streets—with the exception of what happened under the dictatorship,' he told me. Yet a number of symbols of Franco's dictatorship remain in Catalonia. For example residents in Tortosa, a city in the south, voted in May 2016 to keep a huge Franco monument. When I got there, the hotel provided a city map on which the monument was strikingly absent, even though the map pinpointed the city's thirty-two other landmarks. 'It's a bit sensitive, really,' the receptionist explained. She then helpfully drew a cross to mark the spot where it stands.

In fact, nobody needs a map to spot Franco's two-pronged monument. It stands in the middle of the river Ebro, on the pillar of a former bridge that was destroyed during the war. Franco inaugurated the monument on the twenty-fifth anniversary of his victory in the battle of the Ebro. At the same time he was also made honorary mayor of Tortosa. The honorary title wasn't removed till 2016, 'a week after we realised he had still kept it,' said Tortosa's most recent conservative mayor, Ferran Bel.

After Franco's death, Tortosa's first democratic mayor removed the most offensive symbols of his dictatorship, including the Fascist arrows that adorned the monument.

Once Bel became mayor in 2007, he found himself under pressure from far-left politicians to remove Franco's monument altogether. To stop the issue from festering, the mayor organised a local referendum. The vote's result, Bel said, showed that 'the monument forms part of our skyline.' Bel argued that every city had to understand that its identity, however modern it claims to be, will comprise both the negative and positive aspects of its past. He mentioned another example in Tortosa, which has a district still known as '*tretze de gener*' or the thirteenth of January, the day when Franco captured Tortosa.

Bel suggested that some of the residents who voted to maintain Franco's monument were upset by Barcelona's politicians meddling in Tortosa's affairs. 'People don't like to be lectured, especially not after forty years of nobody showing any interest,' he said.

He told me he had received personal attacks from radical separatists, even though he is the deputy head of the Catalan association of pro-independence mayors. 'I've been accused of being a Fascist mayor and all sorts of other stupidities,' Bel said. 'There are some people who can't bear the idea that a pro-independence mayor should do something like this.'

THE STRUGGLE FOR CATALONIA

Collaboration and survival

Secessionism has tended to airbrush some of the more complex nuances of the dictatorship by presenting Franco as an outsider who oppressed Catalonia from Madrid.

In 2013, the lawmakers of the Catalan Parliament approved a declaration of sovereignty, in defiance of the government in Madrid and Spanish courts. The preamble to the declaration states that 'the dictatorship faced active resistance from the people and government of Catalonia.' That same year, Catalonia commemorated the fiftieth anniversary of a famous act of defiance by Aureli Maria Escarré, the abbot of the Montserrat monastery. In 1963, Escarré demanded more rights for Catalonia during an interview with the French newspaper *Le Monde*. 'Catalonia is a nation among the Spanish nationalities,' Escarré said. 'The Spanish regime calls itself Christian but it doesn't obey the basic principles of Christianity.' Two years later, he went into exile in Italy, marking himself out as a Catalan symbol of resistance to Franco.

'The Church has never exerted a major influence on Catalan politics—apart from Escarré,' said Ricard Lobo i Gil, a writer and former monk of Montserrat. 'Escarré never wasted an opportunity to denounce regime abuses, until Franco finally pressured the Vatican to have him expelled from Catalonia,' he continued.

However, there is a different perspective on this story, which raises age-old questions about the relationship between the church and totalitarian regimes. Lobo spent two decades in Montserrat, where he overlapped with Hilari Raguer, a monk and historian who has extensively studied the clergy's role during the Civil War. Raguer has a more provocative take on the 'heroic' abbot. When I visited him in the monastery infirmary, he told me that Escarré did not oppose Franco, but demanded instead that the monks show allegiance to his regime. Escarré forbade anybody from joking about Franco, 'not even about his wife,' Raguer said. He eventually changed his stance, Raguer claimed, not out of personal conviction but because he lost his own influence over Montserrat's Benedictine monks.

Escarré spoke to *Le Monde* in 1963 after he had been sidelined and replaced as the spiritual leader of Montserrat by another monk, Gabriel M. Brasó. The frustrated abbot gambled that he could provoke his own expulsion from Montserrat and then later make a triumphant comeback at the helm of the Catalan Church, once Franco's dictatorship was over. 'He thought Franco's regime would come to an end shortly, and the Vatican would put their trust in him,' claimed Raguer.

When I told Raguer what Lobo had said about Escarré, Raguer said that the portrayal of Escarré as a resistance leader was a 'myth' spread by 'a powerful lobby' within Catalonia. In fact, he said, most clerics had welcomed Franco's victory, after suffering persecution throughout the war from anarchists and far-left militants. In 1936, twenty-three of Montserrat's monks were killed. 'In my own family home, we spent the whole war praying with our rosaries for Franco's victory,' Raguer said. He told me that Franco had visited Montserrat five times. During his first visit, a power cut interrupted the dinner. 'When the lights finally came back on, everybody in Franco's entourage was crouching under the table, except for Franco, who hadn't moved one inch,' Raguer said.

Franco's admiration for Montserrat probably shaped his decision to set up a new Benedictine monastery near Madrid, in what became the Valley of the Fallen and the symbol of the religious nationalism of Franco's regime. Montserrat did not send over monks, but Escarré selected some decorations for Franco's new monastery, according to Raguer.

The prior of Montserrat, Ignasi Fossas, backs Raguer's point of view. During Franco's dictatorship, the Catholic Church 'played with the advantage that Franco was a Catholic who could not become the enemy of the Vatican,' he said. However, he continued, some members of the clergy witnessed a far more brutal brand of Fascism outside Spain that made them also fearful of Franco. The civil war forced many monks to flee

Spain—only to find themselves then in Germany and other European countries occupied by the Nazis. When they eventually returned to Montserrat, 'they had come to know Nazism and a Fascist ideology that repelled and worried them,' he said.

Money and Resistance

Catalonia's industrial bourgeoisie also had mixed feelings about Franco's regime, even those who pushed for greater Catalan autonomy before the civil war. Francesc Freixas Miquel started his business career in the cosmetics company owned by the family of his wife, Carme Cortès Lledó. Their factory made a skin cream to remove freckles. The couple were Catalan patriots who voted for the Lliga Regionalista, the nationalist movement led by Francesc Cambó after 1917. Cambó and his party advocated greater autonomy for Catalonia, but Cambó was also a minister in different Spanish governments and an ardent defender of conservative values against anarchism and Communism, particularly following the creation of the Soviet Union.

During a trip to England, Freixas discovered pyjamas and opened a workshop in Barcelona to promote this exotic bedroom attire. On the back of this inspired entry into Catalonia's thriving textile industry, Freixas also became the first owner of a car in Lloret de Mar, the seaside resort where he built his holiday home.

But in 1936, Franco's military uprising plunged Barcelona into turmoil. During the uprising, Freixas's own workers took over his factory. As a result Freixas spent most of the war holed up in Lloret. In early 1939, Freixas joined the crowd watching Franco's troops parade through Barcelona. As he watched, he repeatedly shouted Franco's name—so loudly that his wife kept elbowing him to get him to calm down.

'My very liberal grandparents, who had been reading Stefan Zweig and Aldous Huxley and never went to Mass, completely endorsed Franco's regime, along with all of their friends. They did so mostly without enthusiasm or fanaticism, but with the feeling that it was a return to the values of property, law and order,' said Laura Freixas, a writer who is also the granddaughter of Freixas Miquel. During Franco's dictatorship, Freixas' grandparents put their bourgeois values above their Catalan patriotism. Even though they were atheists, they pretended to espouse the Catholicism of Franco's Spain, she said. Freixas' grandmother would wear a traditional mantilla and carry a novel disguised with a black cover, so that it looked like a prayer book.

Aligning with Franco proved extremely profitable. Freixas reclaimed his confiscated business, which had a dozen workers before the war, and transformed it into Unyl, a company that employed 700 workers at its peak, making shirts and blouses. Everything went well till the 1980s, when the business went bankrupt—along with many other textile companies—as Spain's return to democracy also opened up its market to competition from cheaper clothing imports.

Under any authoritarian regime, people have to make stark choices. Some put their political and moral convictions ahead of their survival instincts and economic interests. But from Argentina to Communist Eastern Europe, history has taught the grim lesson that relatively few are prepared to risk death or imprisonment for insubordination. Military dictators, on the other hand, generally know how to secure the loyalty of their troops. They also understand the importance of sharing some of the spoils of victory with their supporters in order to stay in power.

In Spain's case, any evaluation of the opposition to Franco's dictatorship is complicated by the mass exodus that took place before he secured power. Many of his fiercest opponents escaped in the final months of the civil war, at the point when Franco's victory became inevitable but before he could control the border with France. Eventually, many Republicans decided to leave Europe altogether, for Mexico and other Spanish-speaking countries, swelling the ranks of the Spanish diaspora in Latin America.

Others joined another war—against Nazi Germany—in the hope that, after defeating the Nazis, the Allies would oust Franco so as to complete the removal of Fascism from Europe. The Allies, however, had other plans. After the war, bereft of international support, Franco's weakened and exiled opponents spent more time bickering among themselves than coordinating Franco's overthrow. By the early 1960s, former Republican fighters stopped launching sporadic incursions into Spain from over the French border.

Culla, the Catalan historian, estimates that between 3,000 and 4,000 people were shot in Catalonia between 1939 and 1942, as part of Franco's purges. 'He didn't have to shoot more because so many of his opponents had already gone into exile,' he said.

Freixas understands both her grandfather's relief at the end of the war, and her father's support for Franco's regime once he took over the family clothing business. What she does not accept is the way some separatist politicians have been rewriting the dictatorship's history to fit their narrative of Catalonia as a longstanding beacon of resistance to any control from Madrid. Under Franco, the Catalan bourgeoisie 'did very well socially and economically. They were neither revolutionaries nor the martyrs that some of the new Catalan elite now want to pretend they were,' she told me.

In 2014, Freixas wrote a column for the newspaper *El País*, shortly after the publication of the diaries of Joan Estelrich, which, she claimed, 'allow us to understand a political evolution that at first sight is difficult to understand, but that nonetheless affected a large part of a generation.'[2] Estelrich had been the secretary of Cambó, the leader of the Lliga, but he then spent the war in Paris, running Franco's press office. In his diaries, Estelrich explained how he switched sides less than two months after Franco's uprising, because 'the victory of the military seems the lesser of two evils,' compared with Communism or anarchism.

REMEMBERING THE CIVIL WAR AND FRANCO

In 2014, an inheritance court battle put the spotlight on Julio Muñoz Ramonet, a tycoon who bequeathed his mansion to his city, Barcelona. After the war, Muñoz Ramonet became one of Spain's richest men, with assets ranging from textiles to insurance. In 1946, in a lavish ceremony held in Bilbao, Muñoz Ramonet married the daughter of a leading Spanish banker, thereby strengthening his ties to Franco's financiers. Once Franco's regime ended, however, he ran into problems and eventually fled Spain after being targeted in a major insurance fraud investigation. He died in a luxury hotel in Switzerland in 1991.

Two decades later, Barcelona's city hall accused his daughters of surreptitiously removing their father's art collection before the city took over his mansion. The alleged loot amounted to some 200 paintings that included masterpieces painted by Rembrandt, El Greco and Goya, as well as Flemish tapestries and other objects. At the time of writing, the court case between the daughters and the city was ongoing. Even though it had none of the artwork, the mansion and its gardens were reopened to the public in 2015, offering a peak into Muñoz Ramonet's grand lifestyle. In the wine cellar, some dust-covered bottles of 1969 Dom Pérignon champagne were among the leftovers of the sumptuous dinners that he once hosted.

Should Barcelona celebrate Muñoz Ramonet today or highlight his questionable past? 'I'm not here to judge the contradictions in the life and work of Muñoz Ramonet, but to make sure that the city gets full usage of the incredible gift that he left for his city,' said Jaume Ciurana, then Barcelona's city councillor for culture.

José Álvarez Junco, a Spanish historian, told me that Catalonia was torn apart by the civil war like the rest of Spain. An added complication was that, in all likelihood, still more people were executed in Catalonia (by left-wing militants) in the run-up to and during the war than after Franco won. The churches and homes of the bourgeoisie were ransacked to such an extent that wartime Barcelona became 'a paradise for art dealers and antiquarians,' flocking from all over Europe to buy looted art-work, he said.

Franco found plenty of support among Catalonia's elite, starting with Cambó himself, who fled Barcelona after the onset of the war and ended up in Buenos Aires, where he died in 1947. For all his earlier commitment to an autonomous Catalonia, Cambó mostly feared anarchism and the radical left, and so 'he gave orders to put his money and influence at the service of Franco', said Álvarez Junco. Santi Vila, a historian and politician, told me that Franco offered Catalans the chance to join his 'project of assimilation.' Those who joined Franco, he said, 'paid the price of renouncing their identity.'

In the final stage of Franco's dictatorship, however, some members of the Catalan bourgeoisie took up the fight against Franco in earnest—with support from the Catalan church. As a young man, Pere Portabella became what he called 'the very, very black sheep' within his establishment family. Portabella resisted his father's advice that he should join one of his family's companies, as well as his warnings not to oppose Franco's regime. In 1970, Portabella campaigned instead to get six captured members of ETA, the Basque separatist group, to face a civilian rather than a military court. Together with another left-wing militant, he travelled to Madrid to see Manuel Díez-Alegría, Franco's chief of staff, presenting him with a folder of evidence to show that ETA's captured members deserved a fair trial. Díez-Alegría dismissed them, without any reprimand but also without opening their file. Fearing that they would soon find themselves in prison, Portabella and about 300 other militants sought refuge later that year in Montserrat's monastery.

The Montserrat standoff helped bridge the gap between the intellectuals and the working class militants who resisted Franco, particularly those from the Catalan Communist Party, or PSUC, Portabella told me. When the militants left the monastery, after Montserrat's abbot secured a promise from Franco's regime that they would not be imprisoned, 'the new message was that artists and intellectuals could achieve success' in opposing Franco, Portabella said.

Jordi Pujol, Catalonia's former leader, told me about his own dealings with the church when, as a sixteen-year-old, he publicly called on the Archbishop of Barcelona, Gregorio Modrego, to preach in Catalan rather than Castilian Spanish. Pujol eventually joined his father's bank, while also increasing his activism against Franco's regime.

In 1960, he was arrested and sentenced to seven years in prison for 'subversive' activities, including writing a pamphlet that criticised Franco. After serving almost half of that sentence, 'I was no longer a banker but a banker who went to prison—and that gives you a certain notoriety,' Pujol recounted. Once Spain returned to democracy, Pujol made political headway by combining his anti-Franco track record with his opposition to the far-left ideology for which most other political militants were jailed under the dictatorship. This allowed Pujol to occupy a political space also left vacant by the exiled opponents of Franco.

At the end of the civil war, 'the intellectuals left but the financiers stayed and started to find ways to make more money under Franco,' the historian Culla told me. When Franco visited Catalonia, 'they would all put on their tail coats and go to shake his hand,' he said. As Franco headed back to Madrid, however, 'they would joke about him and laugh about his economic ignorance.'

World upside down

Even among artists there were multi-faceted responses to Franco. Not least from Salvador Dalí.

Dalí designed his own museum, in his hometown of Figueres, in a former theatre where he had once displayed his work as a teenager. He decorated every wall and corner of his museum both with his artwork and collected objects, including a black Cadillac received from General Motors. One of the ceilings depicts the soles of his own feet alongside those of his wife, Gala, as part of an enormous fresco in which the couple is seen ascending to heaven as Dalí's artwork and money trickle down onto Figueres. Dalí correctly predicted he would make Figueres wealthy. His museum opened in 1974 and is nowadays the most visited art museum in Catalonia, drawing about 1.3 million people a year.

Yet he maintained an ambiguous relationship with the political authorities—even after his death. When he died in 1989, Catalonia's politicians were stunned to find that, in his will, Dalí had bequeathed his artwork to the Spanish state rather than Catalonia. Fortunately, to avoid fuelling political tensions, Jorge Semprún, Spain's then culture minister, agreed that the collection in Figueres need not be transferred to Madrid.[3]

During his lifetime, Dalí had designed posters for Franco's regime and had painted a portrait of Franco's daughter. A few months before Franco's death, the ever controversial artist even sent a telegram to congratulate him for the latest death sentences carried out under his dictatorship. Joan Manuel Sevillano Campalans is the managing director of the Gala-Salvador Dalí foundation, which oversees Dalí's estate and whose office overlooks the white egg statues that line the roof of the Figueres museum. Dalí was more interested in business than politics, he explained to me, and 'wanted his works to get recognition and sell well.' After the civil war and a long spell in America, he continued, 'Dalí wanted to return home, to the Catalonia that had been the fountain of his creative energy, and he was willing to adapt to the political circumstances to do that.'

In yet another example of Dalí's contradictions, in 2016, Josep Playà Maset, a culture journalist, worked out that he had more honourable political motivations when he sold a painting to an American industrialist. The proceeds were to cover the debts of Josep Tarradellas, a Republican opponent of Franco's, who later returned from exile to lead Catalonia.[4]

A clean sweep

After her 2015 election as mayor of Barcelona, Colau decided she wanted to erase the remaining symbols of the Franco regime, as well as some linked to the Spanish monarchy. New left-wing mayors in cities like Madrid and Valencia did likewise.

Colau targeted prominent Catalans who had collaborated with Franco, notably Juan Antonio Samaranch, who started his career in Franco's officialdom. Yet at that point Samaranch was turning his passion for an obscure sport—roller hockey—into a surprisingly successful career path that would propel him to the pinnacle of sports governance. He went on to join the International Olympic Committee in 1966, became its president in 1980 and then helped bring the Olympic games to his native Barcelona in 1992.

Despite his Olympic contribution to the development of his city, Colau's administration decided in 2016 to remove an inscription honouring Samaranch from an allegorical statue within Barcelona's city hall, because of his connections with Franco. Eventually, however, opposition parties came together to overturn her decision.

'I can't stop anybody from looking into my father's past and interpreting his career one way or another,' said Juan Antonio Samaranch, a Madrid-based financier who has followed in his father's footsteps to become vice-president of the International Olympic Committee. 'There are people who think he is marvellous and others who denounce him for being bad or not respectable.' Today Catalan politicians obsess about Samaranch's ties to Franco, but his son pointed out that, 'my father was also accused many times of being a KGB agent.' This was because he had been Spain's ambassador in Moscow during the Cold War.

Gonzalo Rodés, a lawyer and president of Barcelona Global, a business association, said he favoured removing any symbols linked to Franco, but 'the case of Samaranch is an exception,' not least given his contribution to Barcelona. Samaranch joined

Franco's administration because it 'was just part of the normal opportunism of those times,' Rodés argued.

When I worked previously in Paris as a correspondent, I often found myself wrestling with the contorted accounts that came out of Germany's wartime occupation of France. The French collaboration with the Nazis had long been considered a taboo subject. It was only in 1995 that Jacques Chirac, the French president, officially apologised for the role of the French authorities in the mass roundup of Jews in Paris in 1942, a desperate and tragic event known as the *Rafle du Vel' d'Hiv*.

Spain too faces an ongoing struggle to come to terms with the darker chapters of its recent history. It is a society that remains deeply divided over the legacy of Franco's dictatorship, whether in practical aspects like where to put Franco's remains or questions about renaming his monuments.

From a worldwide perspective, the 1936 civil war put Spain at the heart of the European struggle between Fascism and Communism, at the same time as turning the country into a laboratory for new forms of warfare, particularly the use of aerial bombing.

Within Spain itself, however, the conflict also unleashed several 'wars within the war,' rooted in the class and ideological struggles that preceded Franco's military uprising. Not everybody fought for the same reasons. In the run-up to the war, conservative politicians in Madrid like José Calvo Sotelo had urged the military to intervene against 'the twin threats of Communism and separatism'.[5] The uprising was thwarted in Barcelona, but the anarchists, Communists and other forces lost time and energy—as well as human lives—settling old scores rather than pooling their resources to fight a civil war. Ultimately, such disputes among left-wing Republicans greatly facilitated Franco's victory.

More than forty years after Franco's death, as historians continue to research the different aspects of the war, what they discover continues to be distorted by politicians and others determined to use history to push forward their politics. Sometimes, new facts help confuse the historical record rather than add accuracy and objectivity.

Cristian Segura, a journalist for newspaper *El País* in Barcelona, recounted how his own grandfather, Francisco Arasa, was a famous doctor and Republican supporter, who 'changed shirt once he realised that the regime would last.' He even had personal meetings with Franco. 'There is a healthy side to the recovery of the memory of the civil war in Catalonia, but I feel there is also an unhealthy one, which is this attempt to equate Spain with Franco,' said Segura. In Catalonia, 'the memory of the civil war has unfortunately mainly served to teach that Spain was bad—and remains so today.'

5

REVIVING A LANGUAGE AFTER DICTATORSHIP

Catalonia and England share the same patron saint. But in Catalonia the feast of Sant Jordi (St George) comes with a sweep of literary and romantic traditions that mark it apart from the celebrations associated with his Anglo-Saxon incarnation.

While men have traditionally offered roses, women have bought them books in return—though the march of modernity means that books and flowers are more evenly distributed between the sexes these days. Barcelona, and the other cities where it is celebrated, are transformed for the occasion. Bookstands line the main streets along with flower stalls. Children run around with buckets filled with roses, earning pocket money by selling flowers that are often tied together with a red-and-yellow ribbon to evoke the flag of Catalonia.

Charming though it is, the books tradition is a more modern innovation than it first appears. Sant Jordi is a feast that dates back to medieval times, but the sale of books was introduced only in the 1930s by business-savvy publishers, according to Ignasi Aragay, a culture journalist for *Ara*, a Catalan newspaper. April 23 coincidentally marks the anniversary of the deaths of both William Shakespeare and Miguel de Cervantes, giving publishers a great excuse to promote literature on that day. Nowadays, the festival is also treated as a second Catalan national day—which allows it to act as a counterbalance to the highly politicised Diada, with its emphasis on street demonstrations. 'One hundred per cent of Catalans celebrate Sant Jordi,'

Aragay said. 'We keep the political issues for 11 September,' the day of the Diada.

Not surprisingly, the feast also allows readers to meet their writers. Established authors organise book-signings, while début writers will aim for the release of their work to coincide with Sant Jordi in an effort to jumpstart sales. Like other literary festivals, Sant Jordi has no problem pulling in big names, including English-language novelists such as John Banville, Ken Follett and James Ellroy. Each year a guest writer opens the festival and gives a presentation in Barcelona's city hall, in a chandelier-lit reception room built in the fourteenth century. In 2016, the guest was Claudio Magris, one of Italy's best-known authors.

Yet—in an indication of the way sentiments have changed in recent years—Bel Olid, the president of the Catalan language writers' association, told journalists that she was upset that Barcelona's guest of honour was not a Catalan writer. Her association, she said, would lodge a complaint to ensure that a Catalan author would get selected the following year. Her plea was heartfelt, but it also introduced an unexpected element of patriotic resentment into a day of celebration, showing just how deep emotions can run when it comes to Catalan culture.

'On a symbolic day like Sant Jordi, it's important that this space is given to Catalan literature,' Olid said. 'Catalan writers don't get a lot of exposure, so if we aren't given the public space to express ourselves, where else are we going to go?' She added: 'It's not that we don't want Magris—we love Magris—but today wasn't the day.'

Among her other complaints, Olid said she had once been shortlisted for a literature prize, alongside a nominee from Galicia, which also has its own language, and one from Madrid. The winner was the Madrid writer, and according to Olid, it boiled down to a language issue. 'The jury couldn't read our books, so we never had a chance to win,' Olid claimed. Overall, she said, writers in Catalan get 'ignored', particularly by the Cervantes Institute, a state agency charged with promoting Spanish culture worldwide.

REVIVING A LANGUAGE AFTER DICTATORSHIP

A major shot across the bows came in September 2014, when the Cervantes office in the Dutch city of Utrecht cancelled the presentation of *Victus*, a novel by Albert Sánchez Piñol that talks about the siege of Barcelona in 1714. The book had been a bestseller in Catalonia, but the writer's Dutch publisher said that Spain's embassy in the Netherlands had decided it was politically 'too sensitive'. Catalans were infuriated.[1]

According to Eduard Voltas, a magazine publisher, the bias of the Cervantes Institute, which was created in 1991, is implicit in the institute's choice of logo ('Ñ'). The logo highlights the tilde—a special feature of Castilian Spanish grammar that is used in the actual word for Spanish, *español*. Catalan does not have the equivalent—to produce the same sound requires adding a letter, *espanyol*. 'The Spanish state simply doesn't consider the Catalan language and culture to be something worth showcasing,' said Voltas. From Madrid's perspective, Catalan is 'either a disturbance or an anomaly,' he claimed.

At the time of writing, Íñigo Méndez de Vigo, Spain's Culture Minister, had told the Spanish Senate that the Cervantes Institute would in future aim to give better representation to Spain's different languages. But the malaise over how institutional Spain handles Catalan culture has not been confined to literature.

'Any state should create connections between its languages and cultures, not use them to divide,' said Joan Matabosch, the Catalan musical director of the Teatro Real, Madrid's opera house. He highlighted the benefits of co-producing between the opera houses in Madrid and Barcelona. The reopening of the Teatro Real in 1997, after almost seven years of refurbishment, was 'one of the best things that happened to the Liceu,' Barcelona's opera house, Matabosch recalled. 'It led to a spectacular surge in national enthusiasm for opera that helped us both.'

Matabosch ran the Liceu before switching to the Teatro Real in 2013, joining several other Catalan arts directors in moving to Madrid. The Catalan presence in Spain's capital is such that 'I'm not sure if the people who seem to have so many problems with Catalan are even aware of how much Catalan is actually spoken in Madrid,' he said.

It is equally true, however, that Catalans continue to read mostly in Castilian, so only about a quarter of the books sold in Catalonia are written in Catalan, according to the journalist Aragay. This does not stop a hard core of publishers selling books in Catalan, like Quim Torra, who claims to lack the resources to diversify into Castilian. Even for Torra, though, the classic paradox is that he feels more comfortable writing in Castilian than Catalan. 'That's the dreadful reality for those who were taught at school in Castilian and then had to teach themselves Catalan literature,' later on as adults, he told me. As far as he was concerned, Franco's clampdown on Catalonia was 'an attempted cultural genocide'.

Franco fought against cultural diversity, as part of his authoritarian control over Spain. But academics disagree over how far his cultural censorship stretched, particularly after the 1950s, once Franco began reducing Spain's diplomatic isolation. For instance, a Catalan publisher, Edicions 62, was launched while he was in power, on the day of Sant Jordi in1962. Its first book was a work by Joan Fuster in Catalan about the history and culture of the people of Valencia.

'When I hear people say that everything to do with Catalan was forbidden until Franco's death, that didn't happen in the Catalonia that I lived in,' said Josep Cuní, a television presenter. Born in 1953, Cuní was an altar boy in a church where he could speak Catalan and he spoke both Spanish and Catalan with his primary school teacher. He performed in amateur theatre in Catalan and danced the sardana, the Catalan folk dance, while growing up in Tiana, which is near Barcelona. In 1972, he joined a small radio station in Terrassa, which had broadcast programmes devoted to the sardana since the 1950s. 'The director of the station was pro-Franco but he was fine with us broadcasting sardanas,' Cuní explained. 'We have now reached a situation where everything is presented in Manichaean terms—where if you don't say one thing, you're clearly saying the opposite, but our past and our present are much too complex for that.'

REVIVING A LANGUAGE AFTER DICTATORSHIP

After Franco's death, Spain could have given full recognition to Catalan, Basque and Galician as minority languages. Instead, lawmakers in the Spanish Congress continue to debate only in Castilian. Similarly, when Spain joined the European Union in 1986, the then Socialist government did not try to add Spain's minority languages to the tower of Babel that is Brussels, home to twenty-four official European languages.

'The Spanish Congress is the only European parliament that has four official languages at its disposal but has decided only one of them can be used,' said Narcís Serra, a former mayor of Barcelona and former Spanish Minister of Defence. 'It is probably impossible to get a Swiss person to understand this.'

In stark contrast, Santi Vila, a lawmaker, recounted a debate in the Catalan regional parliament with Mireia Boya, a lawmaker who spoke Aranese, a variant of the Occitan language used in the Vall d'Aran, a valley close to France. 'We understand each other more or less,' Vila said. Other Spanish politicians, he argued, have 'never seen an asset in such diversity.'

As a former member of the European Parliament, Raül Romeva recounted how he and his Catalan colleagues had tried to introduce their language into the European assembly and had even offered for the Catalan authorities to pay for the related costs. But the idea went nowhere because it was blocked by Madrid. This left Romeva feeling that he would remain 'a second-rate citizen of Europe' as long Catalonia stayed within Spain, he said.

The Catalan language has also received scant attention in Spain's education system. One astonishing fact is that while only eleven Spanish universities outside Catalonia offer courses in Catalan, twenty-seven German universities provide the opportunity for students to study the Catalan language and culture.[2] This came to particular public attention through Julian Brock, a German student who had gone on a university exchange programme in Lleida. Brock enjoyed fleeting celebrity in Catalonia in October 2016 when he won a spelling competition organized by Catalan television.

It is perhaps this sense of cultural persecution that makes some Catalans so aware of their place in European literature. Xavi Bes i Martí, a wine distributor, rattled off to me a list of European authors who have mentioned Catalonia in their works, from Dante to Thomas Mann. 'We have always been present in European literature,' he told me. 'I don't feel that I have to justify my Catalan language and identity to anybody.'

While Castilian Spain has the Cervantes Institute, Catalan writers have been supported by Catalonia's own cultural agency, the Ramon Llull Institute. Ramon Llull was a thirteenth century monk, philosopher and logician. Around 1283, he wrote *Blanquerna*, a work considered by many to be the first major work of Catalan literature. In 2007, the institute founded in his name helped organise a Catalan exhibition at the Frankfurt Book Fair. Its €12 million budget was one of the largest regional investments at the fair, and drew criticism at the time, not least from certain Catalan authors. One of them, Sergi Pàmies, turned down his invitation to Frankfurt, while *Der Spiegel*, the German magazine, challenged Catalonia for its 'closed-minded policy of not including the many Catalans who write in Spanish in its definition of Catalan literature.'[3] However, despite such controversy, Pàmies has subsequently changed his mind. When we talked, he said that he now realised that Catalonia had got a good return on its Frankfurt investment, since it had given important international exposure to several Catalan authors.

Ancient origins

The Catalan language is derived from the Latin spoken by the Roman soldiers who disembarked at Empúries in 218 BC, a Mediterranean port that had already served as a Greek colony. However the oldest texts preserved in Catalan are far more recent, dating back to the twelfth century. Torra, the publisher, told me that the oldest known document in Catalan was a feudal oath made by Radulf Oriol to Raymond IV, the count of Pallars Jussà, written between 1028 and 1047. The first printed version of Catalan is from 1474, *Les trobes en lahors de la Verge Maria*, a work of poetry about the Virgin Mary that was published in Valencia and was also the first book printed in Spain.

After the surrender of Barcelona in 1714, Spain's Bourbon monarchy banned the official usage of Catalan. It was not revived until the nineteenth century, when a Romantic movement of Catalan poets and patriotic authors pushed for a *Renaixença*, or a rebirth of Catalan culture. As well as promoting art, theatre and literature, the movement sought to re-establish the rules for a Catalan language. In the early twentieth century, Catalan became standardised in dictionary form. Typically, there was nothing simple about this process, which turned into a struggle for authority between two sources—the Pompeu Fabra dictionary and the extensive Alcover-Moll compendium.

Pompeu Fabra i Poch trained as an engineer but also developed a passion for linguistics. In 1912, he published a book of Catalan grammar, followed two decades later by the dictionary that Catalans simply call 'the Fabra'. The Alcover-Moll, on the other hand, was a collaboration between writers from the island of Mallorca, where Catalan is spoken. Antoni Maria Alcover, a writer and monk, and Francesc de Borja Moll, a historian and publisher, wanted to compile every word used in every Catalan-speaking region, from France to the islands of the Mediterranean. Their work, covering both old and new forms of Catalan dialects, is arguably the most ambitious project of lexicography undertaken for any Romance language.

In the end, the more concise Fabra dictionary eclipsed the more complicated Alcover-Moll dictionary, which was split into ten volumes. But the Fabra also prevailed because it was 'closer to those in power' in Catalonia, Pompeu Fabra being part of the patriotic establishment, according to Albert Boadella, a leading playwright who has also become an outspoken opponent of secessionism. Compared to the Alcover-Moll dictionary, the Fabra 'seems to me an impoverishment of the language,' he complained.

The Cat that walks by itself

After Franco's dictatorship, Catalans played catch-up in terms of publishing books in Catalan. But they were some of the quickest to understand the potential offered by the internet. Started in 2005, the internet domain name '.cat' received the first approval worldwide for a domain dedicated to a language. One of its promoters was Amadeu Abril i Abril, who left his law firm in 1995, after its founder died. He then took up a part-time job as a university professor, while spending the rest of his time studying the development of the internet.

With some help from Jonathan Poster, one of the American gurus of the internet, Abril i Abril started an association to register '.cat', based on language criteria rather than territorial identity. Catalonia had previously failed to register '.ct' as a territorial domain, because Catalonia did not fulfill the rules of the internet's international agency. These stated that contiguous territories could only have their own domains if they operated as separate economies, with their own taxes or currencies. The alternative approach amounted to 'swapping the passport for the dictionary,' he said. The Catalan government provided about €200,000 in funding, while the project was also helped by the arrival of a new Socialist government in Madrid, whose Industry Minister was a Catalan, José Montilla.

Somewhat amusingly, some American web experts accused the Catalans of wanting to register '.cat' surreptitiously, as a commercial venture for cats. 'Americans know as much about geography as I know about Saturn,' Abril i Abril said. 'Some said we were cheating by promoting a language spoken by nobody when what we wanted is to sell things for cats, which represent a valuable market.' However, the absurd took on its own form of reality when Catalonia took legal action against a dozen cat-linked websites for usurping its domain. One of them used a mock page of *The New York Times* to promote news about cats.

'We had to generate a new concept to get Catalonia on the web, but we ended up really believing it was the right approach,'

Abril i Abril said. 'The languages that didn't manage to get good access to television then faded—and the same will happen to languages that aren't on the internet.'

Following Catalonia's lead, two other regions of Spain have registered their languages as domain names, Galicia and the Basque Country. At the time of writing, 104,000 websites were registered as '.cat', representing an above-average annual growth rate of 18 per cent, according to Santi Ribera, the director of the foundation that manages the '.cat' domain. The domain, he argued, 'has clearly been helping normalise the presence of Catalan online.'

Catalonia has also worked hard to assert its identity in film, adopting a cinema law in 2010 that obliged foreign film distributors to provide their films in both Castilian and Catalan if released in Catalonia. However, the Hollywood juggernaut was not going to let language sensitivities get in its way. The Hollywood studios warned they would no longer release movies in Catalonia if the law was enforced. The studios 'declared war' because they feared Catalonia would set a costly precedent for dubbing into other minority languages, according to Eduard Voltas, who was working as a Catalan culture official at the time.

Hollywood prevailed when the issue was taken to a European court. Voltas said the experience helped convince him that Catalonia should become a state to help win such arguments in the future. 'To legislate in favor of Catalan is not a hobby or an obsession, but an important response to 300 years of mistreatment,' he said. The issue of movie dubbing has not gone away. In November 2016, a large group of Catalan artists and journalists signed a manifesto to denounce the fact that only one eighth of movies shown that month had been dubbed.[4] The dispute might seem a trivial sideshow to some, but it highlights just how far the struggle over Catalan identity can stretch.

Classroom fights

So is Catalan fighting for its survival? Statistics would appear to prove not. In late 2016, the Catalan government presented a study showing that 94 per cent of residents understood Catalan while 80 per cent could speak the language. This was from a population among which 35 per cent had been born outside Catalonia. 'The Catalan language isn't at risk of extinction,' said Oriol Soler, who runs a Catalan publisher called Som. But he argued that Catalan still needs state protection 'because ultimately you need to have public policies in favor of a culture and language.'

On the other hand, unionists protest that separatists are imposing 'Catalan cultural hegemony'. Emilio Lamo de Espinosa, a sociologist who is the president of the Real Instituto Elcano (a political research group in Madrid) told me that, 'The problem is not so much Catalonia's place in Spain as that of Spain in Catalonia. The goal now seems to be to expel anything with a whiff of Spanish, starting with our language.'

The usage of Catalan varies significantly between rural and urban Catalonia, as well as within cosmopolitan Barcelona. Olid talked about how it upset her whenever her request in Barcelona's cafés for *café amb llet*, or coffee with milk, reached her table instead as iced coffee, or *café amb gel*, as waiters mixed up the two Catalan phrases. 'If I can't ask for coffee in Catalan in my own place, where should I go?' she asked.

The most potent battleground for the Catalan language, however, is the classroom. The debate dates back to the redistribution of powers after Franco, when Spain's regions took charge of education. Spain's regions chose different ways to resurrect the languages banned by Franco. The Basques introduced an education model in which parents can decide whether or not to send their children to a state school in which Basque is the main language. The Catalans, however, made their language compulsory in state schools, with Castilian taught as a second language.

Meritxell Ruiz, the Catalan regional Minister for Education, gave different reasons for why Catalans and Basques had made these decisions. First, by the time Franco died in 1975, almost nobody spoke Basque, she said, while Catalans kept their language alive, particularly at home. Second, the Basques were willing to adopt a system 'in which ethnic Basques should learn their language but not necessarily outsiders,' she said. In Catalonia, on the other hand, integrating migrants was a major concern. 'If we created two schools, migrants would go to Spanish schools and Catalans to Catalan ones,' she declared. Third, Catalan children will pick up Castilian outside the classroom as both languages come from Latin—unlike Basque, which has a peculiar grammar. 'The school makes up for the social usage of Spanish outside school, which is higher,' Ruiz argued. 'My child uses Spanish as the playground language.'

Another crucial difference is that Catalonia's elite was reinvigorating a language that had already had widespread use a century earlier. In contrast, Euskera, the Basque language, never took hold among the financiers and industrialists of Bilbao and other Basque cities. Jaime Mayor Oreja, a former right-wing politician, recalled how his great-grandfather, who was a doctor in the Basque village of Ibarjangerua, forbade the use of Basque in the family because it would stop anybody from getting a good city job. Speaking Euskera, Mayor Oreja said, was 'a barrier to social and professional progress'. In such circumstances, Basque separatists prefer nowadays to describe Euskera as a striking example of the survival of Europe's oldest living language, maintained by about 600,000 speakers.

There have been opponents of the Catalan approach within Catalonia itself. Some parents have complained to Madrid that their children could not learn Castilian while being educated in Catalonia. However, Ruiz said that such parents were falsely 'spreading the idea that Spanish isn't being taught.' In fact, she said, Catalan schoolchildren have been scoring as highly in Castilian language tests as children from other regions. Yet though she had a slew of statistics to back her claim, she also acknowledged that it was a problem that education and politics had become so entangled in Catalonia. 'This has switched from a pedagogic subject to a political topic,' she said. 'I can understand why it's creating discomfort.'

Under Franco, Catalans had to use the Castilian version of their names in their official papers. In no small irony, the first person to get an exemption was a Dutch football star, Johann Cruyff, who named his son Jordi after Catalonia's patron saint, when he was born in 1974 during Cruyff's stint for FC Barcelona. Even after Spain's return to democracy, the Catalans were made to realise that old habits died hard. In the early 1980s, Joan Majó, a Catalan electronics entrepreneur, became Spain's Industry Minister. Upon arriving in Madrid, he realised that the letterhead that was being prepared for him carried the Castilian name of Juan rather than Joan. His first instruction was for them to change it. 'I was coming to work for Spain, but I was still a Catalan,' he recounted.

Of course some Catalans worry nowadays about the political emphasis on the Catalan language. 'We have this epic and proud story of defending our language against Franco's regime, but it doesn't mean we should impose it on anybody now,' said Bru Rovira, a Catalan journalist. 'I want Catalonia to be led by politicians who respect Catalonia's diversity.' As a child during Franco's dictatorship, Rovira insisted upon using his Catalan name. But after Spain returned to democracy, he didn't bother to change his official papers to Bru from Bruno, the Castilian version of his name. 'When I was younger I couldn't stand being told who I was and what to call myself. But later on it became less of an issue,' he said.

I could identify with Rovira's change of attitude. Growing up, I fiercely defended what I felt was the special part of my name, Raphaël, namely the umlaut used in French. Once I started working in English, however, I dropped the fight for the umlaut. Instead my focus switched to making sure people wrote the rest of my name correctly.

Daniela Ortiz, a Peruvian artist who lives in Barcelona, said to me that Catalonia had been discriminating against non-European migrants since 2014, when compulsory language tuition was added to the requirements for getting access to basic social services. Catalonia should either abolish the test, she argued, or extend it to every foreigner. 'If the Catalan authorities really want to defend their language as an instrument of social cohesion, then they should require everybody speak it, not just those who are desperate for residency papers, as if they were savages who needed to be civilised,' she said.

Some famous Catalans complain that they have experienced discrimination because of their opposition to independence. Isabel Coixet, an award-winning film director, said her anti-secessionism meant she was no longer invited to join culture programmes on Catalonia's public television. In April 2016, Coixet went to Paris to receive a French cultural knighthood. Official congratulations came from Madrid, but there was not so much as a text message from the Catalan authorities.

'I've done enough in my life not to care that much, but that's not perhaps the case for younger directors who need all the visibility they can get,' she said. As a result, Coixet suggested that some artists have probably been coerced into supporting separatism, because not to do so might hurt their career prospects.

Beyond Catalonia

Defending the Catalan language and culture also provokes debate in the regions outside Catalonia. In the Pyrénées-Orientales, along the French border with Catalonia, Catalan is taught in about twenty-five bilingual state schools, as well as some private schools. The region's most famous Catalan school is the Bressola, which welcomed 1,040 students in 2017, compared with seven when it opened in 1976. The waiting list is more than three times capacity, according to the Bressola's director, Eva Bertrana. 'With a much stronger Catalonia now next door to us, Catalan is no longer seen as a backward language, spoken just by peasants and grandparents,' she said.

In 1981, a group of teachers from the Bressola created their own Catalan school, Arrels, which means 'roots' in Catalan. Arrels chose a different bilingual model to give Catalan a head start, with children taught only in Catalan until the age of seven, after which French is introduced. One of the first teachers at Arrels was Pere Manzanares, a thin man with a trimmed white beard, whose parents both migrated to France. His father left Murcia, in southern Spain, while his mother fled Catalonia after the civil war. Manzanares, who is fifty-seven, changed his name when he turned eighteen, from Pierre to the Catalan version, Pere.

Manzanares is no longer a teacher, but he still contributes to a local Catalan radio station. We met in his orange-painted recording studio to talk about France's handling of minority languages.

In Manzanares' opinion, the revival of Catalan in France has been even more of an uphill struggle than it has been in Spain. The teaching of French was reinforced in the late nineteenth century, when the French statesman Jules Ferry introduced compulsory state education. Another turning point was the First World War, according to Manzanares, during which a disproportionate number of Catalans were killed. Joseph Joffre, France's commander-in-chief, was born in Rivesaltes, a Catalan town. He valued the courage of men from his home region and therefore probably selected more Catalans for the frontline.

These wartime losses significantly eroded the Catalan language. A generation of Catalan men left for the frontline speaking Catalan, 'with only vague notions of French. But when they died, their families were left essentially with the memory of relatives who had sacrificed their life for France,' said Manzanares. After the war, he observed, 'the Catalan inhabitants of these villages would all have been able to see their family names on the monuments put up to the glory of those who died for France. The war's dead acted as a factory to make more Frenchmen around here.'

France's carrot-and-stick approach toward Catalans is particularly in evidence in two small villages at the foot of the Pyrenees. Every November 11, on Armistice Day, the French army sends a general for the commemoration in Oreilla, the French village that proportionally lost the most soldiers during the First World War—eighteen out of a population of 130 residents. Oreilla's monument honouring the dead bears Catalan names, including Botet and Grau. But a more hostile message is in evidence in Aiguatebia, another village, where an abandoned school still carries the inscription: 'Parlez français, soyez propres,' or 'Speak French, be clean.'

According to Catalan separatists, the Spanish politician José Ignacio Wert, formerly education minister, is the individual who most embodies hostility to Catalan culture within Spain itself. During a parliamentary session in 2012, Wert said that 'our interest is in making Catalan schoolchildren more Spanish, so that they feel as proud to be Spanish as they are proud to be Catalans.' Wert also lamented the teaching of 'history' in Catalan schools, rather than 'the history of Spain,' as the course had previously been labelled on the syllabus. His call to make schoolchildren more Spanish, or '*españolizar*', drew comparisons in Catalonia with Franco's authoritarianism. Raising tensions further, Wert then drafted an education law that increased Madrid's control over the syllabus.

A bilingual society

I have found that nothing gives Catalans a stronger sense of identity than having their own language. But I haven't felt excluded by Catalan speakers. On the contrary, I have attended several meetings and dinners during which Catalans immediately switched to Castilian Spanish because I was the non-Catalan speaker at the table (to my own embarrassment). Their switching brought back memories of my first journalism experience in Zurich, when I used *Hochdeutsch*, or standard German, in a city whose inhabitants clearly prefer to speak Swiss German.

However, other Catalans take the defence of their language to extremes. As secessionism has gathered pace, so too have the calls to make Catalan the only official language of Catalonia. Certain separatists have shown a complete disregard for the benefits of a multilingual upbringing and society. This peaked in March 2016, when a group of 170 Catalan writers, academics and language experts presented a manifesto that demanded the abolition of Catalonia's bilingualism. Among its signatories were five winners of a major Catalan literary award.[5]

The irony, of course, is that part of the wealth of Catalonia's literary tradition lies in its ability both to attract and interact with other cultures. Take Najat el Hachmi, who was born in Nador in Morocco, and moved as a child to Vic, in the heartland of Catalonia. Nowadays she writes in Catalan and also speaks the language to her children, rather than her Berber mother tongue. Growing up in Vic, el Hachmi became enthralled by Catalan literature, particularly books written by Catalan women. In the works of Catarina Albert or Mercè Rodoreda, 'I found all these themes that were already familiar to me, coming from a traditional and patriarchal society' in Morocco, she said. Many of the stories concerned Catalan women facing social prejudice and forced into marriage. El Hachmi argued that the richness of these books made it seem 'very strange that Catalan literature is not being promoted in Spain. Catalan, Basque and Galician are somehow treated as not belonging within Spanish culture and literature.' Her own books have been translated into Castilian as well as several other languages, mostly with the help of Catalan public subsidies. Such subsidies should not be essential, she said, but in practice 'they really encourage foreign publishers to bet on Catalan books.'

Catalonia's bilingual authors make critical choices about the language they use. Many of the best contemporary authors born in Barcelona—like Eduardo Mendoza and Juan Marsé—write in Castilian. Some grew up with another language, like the writer Sergi Pàmies, who was born in Paris and first spoke Castilian and French. Pàmies learnt Catalan when he was eleven, after moving with his family to Barcelona. He now writes all his novels in Catalan, which he described to me as his language for intimacy, the language in which he wrote his first love letters. For his journalism columns, however, he switches between Catalan and Castilian, depending on the publication. He also does his own translations, normally starting from Catalan. 'I don't think there are many writers who have the privilege of writing in two languages,' he told me. 'I don't see it as a problem but as an opportunity.'

Catalan, Pàmies argued, 'is not threatened, even if a lot of people might think that it is.' On the contrary, Catalan is special in that residents of Catalonia only need to understand rather than speak Catalan, since Castilian is also understood everywhere. Such flexibility contributes to the 'greatness' of Catalonia and its language, he declared.

Laura Freixas, who was born in Barcelona and kept a diary in both Spanish and Catalan, also sees the benefits of the bilingual approach. When she was about nineteen and opted to become a writer, she decided that 'Castilian felt a lot richer.' At the time, Freixas was also interested in living outside Catalonia, which influenced her choice. But the main reason for her decision, she said, was the philological challenge of Catalan. 'There is a colloquial Catalan that is spoken in the cities and is very impure, filled with Castilian words, or a purer one from the Catalan villages, which is more beautiful but is really the language spoken a century ago rather than now,' she said. Among the weaknesses of the modern Catalan language, she cited a shortage of proverbs, as well as a more limited technical and legal vocabulary.

Boadella, the playwright, grew up in a bilingual family where 'language was not an issue.' To me, his story sounded like that of a regrettable loss in cultural openness. His parents were both journalists for *La Publicitat*, a Catalan newspaper that was initially printed in Spanish but then switched to Catalan. Boadella's grandfather spoke Spanish to his wife while his wife spoke Catalan to her husband. 'This was pretty common at the time,' Boadella said. 'We grew up with an open attitude to Catalonia and also Spain—even if Spain felt a bit distant, almost like an economically underdeveloped territory compared to Catalonia.'

In 1962, Boadella was a co-founder of a theatre company with a Catalan name, Els Joglars, because 'I wanted to normalise what I then understood to be Catalan culture.' He became famous, eventually joining the ranks of Catalan directors in charge of major cultural institutions in Madrid. By the time we met, Boadella had just completed a term as director of the Canal theatre centre, which opened in 2009 as a flagship cultural project.

However, Boadella has refused to produce any play in Catalonia since 2006, after experiencing attacks that he believes were connected with his promotion of Ciudadans, or Citizens, an anti-secessionist party that has become one of the main political forces in Spain. Summing up his relationship with Catalonia, Boadella called himself 'a director exiled within his own nation.' Up till that point in our conversation he had been smiling. But as he said these words, the smile vanished from his face and was replaced by a cold glitter in his blue eyes.

To be or not to be

Against this fraught backdrop, some Catalan politicians are looking for ways to tap into their language to underline their separatist claims. Catalan is different to Castilian, they claim, just as their Catalan nation should be. In one interview I carried out, Oriol Junqueras, the leader of the main left-wing separatist party, Esquerra Republicana, turned the tables on me when he unexpectedly asked whether I really understood the tricky usage of the verb 'to be'. As I hesitated to give an answer, Junqueras, who is also a university professor, explained that the verb has two main forms in both Castilian and Catalan, but they are not precisely the same. An apple, for instance, is said to be good in Castilian using the phrase '*está buena*'—denoting its temporary condition of well-being, as it will eventually rot, he said. In Catalan, however, the apple can be described as '*és bona*'—it is just good to eat, full stop, without worrying about whether it will then rot.

This subtle linguistic twist takes on an even greater force in a political context. The Catalan question becomes a matter not just of words, but of nuance of tense. 'We, the Catalans who want independence,' Junqueras said, '*estamos independistas*,' since that condition will stop once Catalonia finally breaks away from Spain. On the other hand, he concluded, '*somos europeos*'—Catalans who are now and forever part of Europe.

6

CATALONIA'S GREAT MELTING POT

In October 1940, Hitler's right-hand man Heinrich Himler visited Montserrat, the spectacular Benedictine retreat nestled in the Catalan mountains. His chief interest was not the stunning scenery of jagged rocks but the Holy Grail. Nazis believed it was once located in the area and Himmler intended to search the monastery archives in his attempt to track it down.

The visit was part of Himmler's strange attempt to infuse the Nazi cult of the Aryan race with both mysticism and medieval mythology. He thought his SS could become a modern breed of Teutonic knights, and also created a unit of academics to back his racist beliefs about Aryan supremacy. On top of this he funded expensive expeditions to find the Grail—which was believed to confer eternal life—sending people to Italy and even as far afield as Iceland. These expeditions were initially led by a medievalist scholar, Otto Rahn, who had searched in the early 1930s for the Holy Grail on the French side of the Pyrenees, around Montségur, the last fortress held by the Cathar religious movement.

Rahn's theory was that the Cathars managed to hide the Grail before they were massacred as heretics during a crusade ordered by the Vatican. But he ran into his own problems when the Nazis outed him as a homosexual. He was sidelined and then forced to join the guards at the Dachau concentration camp. He ended up committing suicide in the Austrian Alps in 1939.

After his death, Himmler and other academics continued searching for the Grail. Some thought that Rahn had confused Montségur with Montserrat. Others believed that the mountain of Monsalvat—central to Wagner's opera *Parsifal*—was in fact Montserrat. Goethe's assertion that 'nowhere but in his own Montserrat will a man find happiness and peace', seemed further to point some transcendent truth contained there.

To Himmler's disappointment, however, the monastery had few historic documents to verify any of this. Another rampaging foreign force had got there first. In 1812, Napoleon's troops had destroyed much of the monastery and its archives during the Peninsular War.

The frustrated SS chief decided he would console himself by visiting Montserrat's museum. Inside, he became extremely excited when he saw the skeleton of a very tall man whose body had been discovered in a nearby mountain cave. 'Definitely Aryan!' Himmler allegedly shouted out, after examining the bones. But a Catalan monk, who had been assigned to guide Himmler because he spoke German, bravely contradicted the SS leader. 'Catalans are not Aryans, they are not of any race,' the monk told Himmler.

Hilari Raguer, a Catalan monk and historian of Montserrat, explained this story to me further. Unlike Basque identity, 'there has never been anything ethnic about the Catalan concept of identity,' he said. 'I think we could be considered to be a bit like the United States, a welcoming land where people arrive from everywhere, but then develop a national consciousness and strong sense of patriotism.'

Praying in Badalona

Clearly a strong sense of national consciousness has fuelled Catalonia's drive for independence. Yet Raguer's words fail to convey the extent to which it has been a struggle to incorporate Catalonia's migrants into the secessionist movement. Catalonia's welcome has not so far translated into the political representation of residents born overseas.

In the autumn of 2012, Artur Mas, Catalonia's then leader, called a snap early election. He sought a vote of confidence over his decision to launch a separatist challenge against Madrid. Shortly before the election, I asked Mas how foreign residents fitted into his plans for Catalonia and whether they would get to vote in an independence referendum. His response was strikingly evasive. He argued that specific voting rights and rules could only be decided once he was in a position to call a referendum.

As a result of our conversation, I decided to visit Badalona, a city of 220,000 inhabitants just north of Barcelona. Badalona had grown considerably in the previous decade thanks to the arrival of an eclectic population from places like Morocco, China, Pakistan and Bangladesh. Most had originally been lured to Spain by a construction boom that had come to an abrupt end with the financial crisis of 2008. In the previous decade, Catalonia had welcomed about 1.5 million overseas migrants, equivalent to one fifth of its population. While most acquired legal residence, far fewer gained citizenship. This left them excluded from voting in regional as well as national elections.

In an industrial zone on the outskirts of Badalona, I walked down a block of streets lined with warehouses. Inside, Chinese workers stored crates of cheap consumer goods ranging from alarm clocks to garden furniture. Spain was struggling with a recession and record unemployment, but these warehouses showed no signs of a slowdown. On the contrary, Chinese entrepreneurs said that business was improving, as Spain's financially-squeezed consumers downgraded to cheaper purchases.

I talked to Enrique Shen, a wholesaler of Catalan flags. Shen was one of the few people in the area not run off his feet. He explained to me with a huge smile that he had sold his entire stock ahead of a giant street rally scheduled for Catalonia's national day. Ten thousand flags had been purchased in one week. 'It's a special time for Catalan flags,' he said happily. Yet for Shen, the enthusiasm for the Catalan flag was purely commercial. He told me how he had emigrated twenty years earlier from Shanghai, and still believed that the size of a country mattered, particularly in terms of economic strength. 'It's always best to be part of a larger country, just like having a bigger family to help you,' Shen said.

Despite the clear benefits of its immigrant population, the city hall in Badalona was at the time clamping down on migrants. In 2011, Badalona elected a hardline conservative mayor, Xavier García Albiol, who had a towering physical presence and clear-cut views on the need to restrict migration in his city. García Albiol was also one of the few politicians from Spain's governing Popular Party to win office in Catalonia. According to a United States Department of State human rights report, his election was 'in part due to his polemical views linking immigrants from Romania and other countries to crime and promising a tougher stance on illegal immigration.'[1]

As mayor, the six-foot-six García Albiol quickly made his presence felt. Early on, he faced a lawsuit for inciting racist hate against the local Roma population. I found him surprisingly happy to discuss and defend his tough approach to migrants. 'One reason I got elected is because people could see that I was ready to identify a problem and take action to resolve it,' García Albiol told me. The problem, he argued, was that 'a large number of the migrants came here to work, but a small number also arrived with the sole intention of becoming delinquents, stealing and making life generally impossible for all their neighbours.' For this minority, he concluded, 'the only solution is police pressure, efficient judicial action and if possible to send them back to their countries.'

Earlier that year, García Albiol had blocked the opening of a mosque in Badalona. By that point, Catalonia had the highest concentration of Muslims in Spain, but it had no formal mosque. Muslims were allowed instead to worship in any of Catalonia's 200 prayer centres. García Albiol, however, announced that the Muslim community would be banned from using public spaces to pray on Fridays and during the month of Ramadan, after 2,500 Muslims had prayed in a city square during the previous Ramadan. Instead, García Albiol wanted Muslims to pray in the courtyard of a shuttered school, which they could use at a cost of €31 per hour, in addition to an initial deposit of €6,000.

The mayor's religious policies were 'a bad joke,' according to Abdelkrim Latifi I Boussalem, who had left his native Casablanca twenty-two years earlier and was then helping run Amics, an association providing Islamic teaching and Arab language classes. Even before García Albiol's arrival, he said, Badalona's city hall had been reluctant to integrate the Moroccans and Pakistanis who dominated its Muslim community. 'All the major political parties display some fear of Islam,' he said. 'It's never been easy, but at least other politicians used to talk to us and didn't just call us a problem.' He argued that migrants should definitely be involved in the decision of whether Catalonia became independent. 'We're not here to dilute Catalan identity and we're ready to work hard to understand the place in which we live, especially since Catalonia has always been a land of welcome and refuge,' he said.

Salvador Cardús, a professor of sociology at the Autonomous University of Barcelona, gave me statistics that backed Raguer's argument that Catalonia, like the US, had been shaped by waves of migration. However, the data also highlighted a crucial difference, which was that most of the migrants came from other parts of Spain. During Catalonia's modern history, Cardús explained, immigrants accounted for about half its population growth. In the seventeenth century, for instance, about 30 per cent of Catalonia's population came from Occitania, a vast region covering southern France and beyond. (See Chapter 3)

In the first four decades of the twentieth century, Catalonia's population swelled from 1.9 million to 2.9 million people. Between the civil war and the 1990s, the population reached 6 million, as farmers abandoned the poorest parts of Spain during Franco's dictatorship. Indeed, García Albiol's own father was a migrant, who left southern Andalusia for Badalona in the 1960s, and got a job driving a street-cleaning truck. It is unlikely that he could have imagined that his son would ascend the political ladder and become the regional leader of Spain's governing party.

'There are very few people in Catalonia who can say that one of their grandparents didn't come from somewhere else,' said Professor Cardús. The pro-independence movement needs 'to add as many different profiles as possible and open its doors to diversity, in order to avoid contradicting itself,' he said. 'This debate is about civic nationalism, and is in no way based on race or ethnicity.'

The Punjab of Spain?

Catalonia's migrant population became far more diverse in the 1990s, when Spain opened its doors to overseas workers to sustain its construction boom. The construction bubble burst in 2008, however, and overseas workers were often among the first to lose their jobs. In the following five years, many headed home, but others scrambled to find alternative employment in Spain.

Fatima Ahmed is the former spokesperson for Ibn Batuta, a Barcelona-based association that offers legal and social services to immigrants. 'Most of the immigrants we help are preoccupied with finding a job, making sure their papers are in order and meeting basic needs,' she said. 'These issues are entirely separate from a political debate in which they don't even have the right to vote.'

Yet some of the migrants in Badalona have adapted quickly to Catalonia and its shifting politics. Gagandeep Singh Khalsa, a spokesman for the Sikh community, told me that he felt such 'harmony' with Catalans that he preferred to speak their language. He went as far as to say that Catalan secessionism reminded him of the Sikhs' own struggles. 'We have been facing the same problems with India over the Punjab as they have with Spain,' he said.

Four years after our first conversation, Khalsa sounded even more optimistic about the role of Sikhs in Catalonia. With some pride, he recounted how Carme Forcadell—the president of the Catalan Parliament—had joined the Sikh festivities of Baisakhi in Badalona in April 2016. She invited Sikhs to help build 'a new country' in Catalonia and 'she even took off her shoes to join us. So that certainly felt like an important moment,' he said.

About 21,000 Sikhs moved to Spain after 2000, of whom some 13,000 settled in Catalonia. But during the financial crisis, some left, mostly for Canada, Khalsa said. Canada has one of the largest Sikh communities in the Western world. Justin Trudeau, Canada's prime minister, even put Canada's defence in the hands of a Sikh minister, Harjit Singh Sajjan. 'With a bit more time and a better economy here, I'm sure we can reach the same level of integration and representation in Catalonia as Sikhs have achieved in Canada,' Khalsa forecast.

When talking to Khalsa, it is difficult not to be swept up by his enthusiasm and confidence that his goals will be realised. His assertions are a powerful reminder of how migrants can see their new homeland not only in terms of economic progress but also with the eyes and passion of people who are making a fresh start in life. However, the sad reality is that overseas migrants barely feature in Spanish politics. This is true even in the cities of Catalonia that most stridently promote their history of social integration.

One such city is L'Hospitalet de Llobregat, another centre for migration. South of Barcelona, it has been a bastion of Socialism since Spain's return to democracy. In 1900 it was a rural town of only 5,000. But migration transformed it into the second-largest city in Catalonia, with 267,000 inhabitants.

When Spain stayed out of the First World War—which ravaged neighbouring France—textiles and metals factories flourished in places like L'Hospitalet. Workers arrived from southern

Spain. They filled the factories and also built Barcelona's Metro system. They then added the infrastructure for Barcelona's 1929 International Exposition. In the 1950s, Franco's regime set up a Spanish car company, known by the acronym SEAT, and started car production near L'Hospitalet. During the 1960s, the population of L'Hospitalet doubled. Industrial workers piled into new neighbourhoods like La Florida, which still ranks among the most densely populated districts in Europe.

In 2016, a quarter of L'Hospitalet's registered population had been born overseas. But this was not reflected in the city council—not one of the twenty-seven members had been born outside Spain.

Getting overseas migrants to hold political office 'is a work in progress,' said Núria Marín, the Socialist mayor, who welcomed me into the city hall that had been built in 1895, before L'Hospitalet became a magnet for migrants. Zero political representation, she argued, did not reflect a lack of social integration. 'This is a diverse society in which we don't look much at colour or ways of dressing,' she said. Still, some historians believe migration has put a cap on Catalan secessionism. Joaquim Nadal, a historian and former Socialist politician, told me that in terms of pro-independence voters, 'the huge migration phenomenon puts the upper limit at around 50 per cent.'

Yet the case of the Sikhs shows that it is risky to make broadbrush conclusions. Another complex situation involves the Moroccans, who—according to 2016 statistics—form Catalonia's biggest overseas migrant community, accounting for one fifth of foreign passport holders. The Moroccan-born writer Najat el Hachmi noted that many Moroccans in Catalonia came from the Berber minority, which faced its own difficulties in Morocco. This meant they could probably relate to Catalan arguments about an oppressive Spain.

El Hachmi described to me how when she was was eight, she and her family had migrated to the city of Vic. At the time, few migrants lived in La Calla, their working class neighbourhood, so that Islam sparked curiosity rather than hostility and concerns about terrorism. 'You had to explain where you came from, because people were curious, but you didn't get the questions that you now get, which are based on fear, if not actual rejection,' she said.

El Hachmi's own integration was eased by Catalan school-teachers who acted 'almost as a replacement' for the large family entourage of uncles, aunts and other relatives whom she had left behind in Morocco. Nowadays, she said, La Calla 'is very much a Moroccan neighbourhood' in a city that has become both cosmopolitan and firmly committed to separatism. Secessionist flags flutter all around the sand-covered main square of Vic. But even while Vic is happy to display its secessionist tendencies, most migrants have stayed 'on the margins of the debate' over independence. 'I think there is now a fair bit of segregation in Vic,' she told me.

The issue of segregation came to the fore in Vic in 2010, when the municipal authorities refused to register migrants who did not have all their administrative papers in order. This was even though Spanish law obliged each municipality to keep a record of all residents, irrespective of their nationality or administrative situation. Under considerable pressure, Vic's city hall was eventually forced to drop its veto.

El Hachmi said she was both 'sceptical about independence' and a strong defender of Catalan culture. 'I defend the right of each person to make herself Catalan in her own way because, apart from the language, there is nothing else that defines what it is to be Catalan,' she said.

Some experts do not believe that there is any meaningful integration of overseas migrants at all—whether in Catalan politics or in the rest of Spain. 'Whatever some might want to think, the new migrants are not being politically taken into account in any way,' said Marina Subirats, a sociologist. 'Their profile is normally more conservative and religious. But overall I would say that the presence of these new migrants from outside Spain has had a minimal impact on the political debate.'

THE STRUGGLE FOR CATALONIA

From the basketball court to parliament

Ana Surra is one of the exceptions. She is also one of the very few Catalan politicians born overseas to have reached the top of Spanish politics, as a lawmaker in the Spanish parliament. Surra was born in Uruguay and calls herself a Marxist. She has been leading efforts to involve migrants in the Catalan separatist movement with the same determination that she showed with everything else she tried to achieve in the earlier chapters of her life.

As a child, Surra fell in love with basketball. She eventually qualified as a referee, and then successfully threatened Uruguay's basketball federation with a gender discrimination lawsuit for not having any women refereeing men's matches. The federation wanted to avoid a courtroom scandal, but 'they then assigned me to the worst games in the toughest neighbourhoods, in the hope that I would give up,' Surra said. Despite insults and abuse, 'the machismo made me even more determined,' she said. Eventually, Surra made her mark. Some clubs even asked for her to referee their matches, because of her reputation for toughness and impartiality. 'It became clear to everybody that I would only blow the whistle based on what I saw,' she said.

Surra did not just want to overhaul basketball in Uruguay, but also its politics. There, however, she ran into even more serious problems. She joined a revolutionary student movement in 1968, before enrolling in Uruguay's National Liberation Movement, also known as Tupamaros, which launched urban guerrilla warfare against the regime. Eventually she was forced into hiding. Fearing for her life, Surra fled to Chile. In September 1973, however, when Chile's left-wing government was overthrown in a military coup led by General Augusto Pinochet, Surra sought refuge in the embassy of Panama. From there she was granted political asylum in France.

In 2005, Surra moved to Barcelona to join her son there, after he had his first child. 'My son didn't get to see his grandparents for eleven years because of the dictatorship in Uruguay and I didn't want that kind of situation to happen again with my own grandson,' she said.

Despite her background as a political militant, Surra initially steered clear of Catalan politics. In July 2010, protesters took to the streets of Barcelona after Spain's constitutional court ruled against a Catalan statute of autonomy. Surra stayed at home, preparing to celebrate her birthday while watching Uruguay play football in the World Cup on TV.

As the financial crisis deepened, however, Surra became involved with a local association of Uruguayans. Many of her countrymen were out of work and struggling to claim unemployment money or other Spanish social benefits.

'I realised that nobody understood or cared about what could happen to migrants in a crisis and that we needed better representation', Surra said to me, as she played distractedly with the large beads of her necklace. For a migrant, she added, 'it's difficult to settle down anyway in a new country. But it can often become much harder to claim anything if there is a crisis and things go wrong.'

Surra and a few others decided to approach Súmate, a Catalan organisation set up in 2013 to represent residents of Catalonia whose family arrived from other parts of Spain. But she was encouraged to create her own organisation, working for the Latin Americans of Catalonia. She called the association 'Si, con nosotros', or 'Yes, with us,' taking the letter 'S' as its multicoloured logo, with an arrow pointing towards a Catalan flag.

Soon the association was pushing for the creation of a Catalan state that could give every resident better and more equal living conditions. In December 2015, Surra was elected to the Spanish parliament, as an independent representative of the Esquerra Republicana party. 'In the last 100 years, all countries that gained independence then gave their new nationality to those living within their borders,' she said. 'Catalonia needs to go down the same route, turning itself into a nation in which all who live here are Catalans from the word 'go'.'

A new Catalan state, Surra suggested, should also have higher standards of tolerance and fairness toward migrants than those set by Spain's legal system. 'It cannot be that somebody driving recklessly without a license will not go to prison in Spain, while somebody without legal residency documents will end up in a detention centre that is worse than a prison,' she said.

Avoiding xenophobia

It is worth considering, however, that overall ethnic integration has been a success story in Spain, particularly when contrasted with some other countries in Europe, where far-right politicians have fuelled xenophobia and sometimes even condoned racial crimes. At the time of writing, Catalonia, home to the largest Muslim population in Spain, has been spared major acts of violence related to radical Islam. Even at the height of the economic crisis, I never heard anybody embrace the kind of controversial 'America first' protectionism that helped Donald Trump become president. In Spain, nobody is campaigning for jobs to be earmarked for domestic rather than foreign workers amid high unemployment.

Christophe Bostyn, a Belgian consultant working in Barcelona, recalled how difficult it had been for him to get his head around how different Catalan nationalism was from other forms of nationalism. He said that during his first stay in Catalonia, as a university exchange student, he spotted a banner on campus put up by students that read 'Catalonia is not Spain'. Coming from Belgium, where the far-right Flemish nationalist party was at the time making strong political gains, 'I thought not here as well!,' Bostyn said. Yet as he settled down, he came to appreciate that 'nationalism here wasn't right-wing and excluding, but instead one of the most integrating and open forms of nationalism I have seen.' Bostyn is nowadays convinced that Catalonia would fare better as an independent state. 'Catalonia has done everything possible to change Spain and it is hopeless,' he said.

However, despite its many positive aspects in Catalonia, social integration is obviously never entirely straightforward. This is the case even among people of the same ethnicity, as is shown by the pejorative usage of the term *charnego*. The word is thought to originate from the name of a dog breed, to describe the economic migrants who reached Catalonia from poorer parts of Spain. In the sixteenth century, it was first used to describe Catalans who had a parent born on the French side of the Pyrenees. But during the Franco regime, its use developed to describe those who had migrated to Catalonia from other parts of Spain, as well as their children.

In 1988, Jordi Pujol, then leader of Catalonia, visited Santa Coloma de Gramenet to inaugurate a new hiking path. Santa Coloma had developed as one of the dormitory towns of Barcelona and was filled with migrant workers who lived in basic housing. These residents viewed the path's inauguration as an affront, given the shortage of more essential infrastructure. As a result they welcomed Pujol with protest banners and insults. Some threw stones as the official cars of his cortege drove past.

However, Pujol braved the hostile crowd and challenged one of the protesters, who was wearing a bright-red jersey. In front of journalists, Pujol started lecturing the protester, in Castilian, and at one point told him to shut up. Pujol's intervention was subsequently shown on television as an example of his strong leadership, rather than the public humiliation of a *charnego*. The protester refused to have his family names published by the media and therefore became known only as Gabriel, or 'the man in red'.

In an interview with newspaper *El País*, Gabriel later said that he felt ashamed, but also saddened by the way in which Pujol and other officials dealt with legitimate complaints from local residents. He admitted that he had thrown a lump of earth at an official car after it had driven over his foot. He said that what had hurt him most about Pujol's attitude was that 'he made us shut up and then left without listening to us.'[2]

Since that incident, Santa Coloma has had a major image change, as has the status of the *charnego*. This pejorative term is very rarely heard nowadays, but it has somehow featured in the political debate over Catalan independence.

In 2016, another Gabriel—Gabriel Rufían, a self-appointed *charnego* from Santa Coloma—rose to prominence as a lawmaker in Spain's parliament by delivering several provocative speeches attacking Spain's political establishment. Rufian was born in 1982 to a working class family originally from southern Andalusia. As a leftwing activist, Rufian became one the main protagonists in Súmate, the political movement formed to rally Castilian-speaking Catalans behind the independence cause. After being elected to the Spanish Parliament, he took the *charnego* issue to Madrid.

'I am what you call a *charnego* and I am pro-independence,' Rufián told Spanish lawmakers in March 2016. Recalling his family's humble origins, he compared the development of the migrant neighbourhoods of Catalonia with the building of a new Catalan state, a project considered to be a chimera by the Spanish establishment. He questioned the idea that holding an independence vote in Catalonia could be considered impossible, when much more complicated things had previously been achieved in Catalonia. During the overhaul of his home town of Santa Coloma, he said, people had added 'a roof, light and water where there had been absolutely nothing, only mud.'

Later Rufián said that he had essentially picked the term *charnego* to elicit an identity debate in Spain's parliament, and not because it seriously bothered him. In a modern society, 'it really doesn't matter where you are born, what is important is where you live,' he argued. But he acknowledged that Catalans born outside Spain still had a long way to go in terms of gaining adequate political representation. 'That is something that will get better with time,' he forecast. Rufián may well be proved right, but for now it seems that Catalonia's more recent economic migrants will mostly remain bystanders in this political debate no matter how much it impacts on their lives.

CATALONIA'S GREAT MELTING POT

Cuba's rum and wealth

Catalonia has of course sent its own migrants out into the world, looking for better living conditions elsewhere. In one notable example in 1830, a fifteen-year-old boy left the family groceries store in his native Sitges on a ship bound for Cuba, a Spanish colony where his brothers already lived. The boy, Facundo Bacardí i Massó, made rapid progress in Santiago de Cuba. After first working in a goods store that sold food as well as rum imported from Jamaica, he set up his own venture. But in 1852 an earthquake struck Santiago, ruining his business. Unable to collect unpaid accounts, he filed for bankruptcy.

However, Bacardí managed to pick himself up, focusing this time exclusively on rum, which was popular but normally sold as a rough and fiery drink. In 1855, Bacardí started to experiment at home with sugar cane molasses, which he believed would produce better rum than the sugar cane juice used at the time. Using a small distillery, he started making this higher quality rum, turning it into one of the leading brands. In 1888, his success was marked by a license to supply rum to the Spanish royal household, followed by a warrant to use the Spanish royal coat of arms on the Bacardí label.

These documents are now kept in a Bacardí museum in Sitges, in a building that used to be the food market. Meanwhile, the Miami-headquartered company that bears Bacardí's name sells more than 200 million bottles a year, not only of rum but also of other spirits including whisky and vodka.

Bacardí only returned once to Sitges, to get his family to safety after the Santiago earthquake, according to Juan Bergaz Pessino, the company's archivist and a sixth-generation member of the Bacardí family. But this did not stop him from using Catalan superstitions to attract good fortune. One of these involved the bats that lived in neighbouring banana trees, and were strongly attracted to the molasses used in his rum. Since bats are 'an important Catalan symbol of good luck' according to Bergaz Pessino, '[Bacardí] really welcomed their presence.' The bat famously went on to become Bacardí's company logo.

THE STRUGGLE FOR CATALONIA

The seaside promenade of Sitges is dotted with mansions and small palaces built by the so-called *Indianos*, people like Bacardí who left Spain to become rich in its overseas colonies. Some returned to make a significant contribution to Spain's industrial revolution. The construction of the first railway line in the Iberian peninsula, for instance, was spearheaded by a man who previously worked in Cuba, Miguel Biada Buñol. The line opened in 1848 between Barcelona and Mataró.

For many Catalans, Cuba represented a chance to make money overseas, after missing out on the rewards of Spain's earlier conquests in Latin America. Some also thrived in the Philippines, as is showcased by the arts museum of Sitges, which opened thanks to the donation of the artwork collection of Jesús Pérez-Rosales, the son of the last Spanish mayor of Manila.

Spain would finally lose Cuba, Puerto Rico and the Philippines in 1898, a date that has become etched in Spanish history under the sombre label of *'el Desastre'* or the Disaster. The end of the Spanish colonial empire had significant consequences for the political relationship between Madrid and Barcelona. Cuba's independence demonstrated for many Catalans that 'autonomy and independence were not chimeras,' according to Jordi Canal, a historian.[3] At the same time, many Catalan entrepreneurs lost the belief that Spain was essential to their economic welfare.

In fact, several Catalan historians have argued that Cuba marked Catalonia's main opportunity to make up for what they believe to have been their unfair sidelining from Spanish colonial trade in the sixteenth century. 'The discovery of America was a Castilian adventure and the Catalans were excluded from it,' said Joan Boadas, a Catalan archivist. This Catalan perspective, however, is regularly contested by Madrid historians. Some foreign historians also offer a more nuanced reading. In a lecture delivered in 2016 in Madrid, John Elliott, a British historian who has written extensively about Spain's American empire, rejected the Catalan complaint about 'being excluded from the lucrative American business,' since 'there was no prohibition for Catalan merchants to go to the Americas.' The main restriction on the Atlantic trade, he said, was that it should be done through the port of Seville, which made sense for the monarchs at the time. In any case, Elliott noted, 'quite a few Catalan merchants' simply moved to Seville and established themselves there.

'You cannot explain the relative economic weakness of Catalonia in the sixteenth and seventeenth century in terms of the supposed legal exclusion from the trade with the Americas,' he continued. 'What it is possible to say is that Catalans stayed mostly on the sidelines of the greater empire business, partly because of their own lack of interest but also because Castilians kept non-Castilians from the top jobs.'

Ironically, some Catalans are now leading efforts to reclaim Spanish assets from Cuba, in the face of likely changes in both American and Cuban politics, following the election of Donald Trump as American president and the death of Fidel Castro. Jordi Cabarrocas is the director of the 1898 Company, a Barcelona-based investment fund that represents about 300 Spanish families who had property in Cuba. He estimates that the farms, factories and other assets seized from his clients are worth $2.2 billion nowadays. Overall, he said, Spanish claims in Cuba could amount to about $20 billion. Cuba, however, is showing no inclination to discuss compensation claims. This is in part because Spain and Cuba signed an agreement in 1986 in which Cuba agreed to pay about $40 million in compensation for seized assets over a 15-year period, partly in cash and partly in goods including tobacco.

Cabarrocas was partly inspired to start the investment fund for personal reasons. His own family left the Catalan village of Sant Feliu de Guíxols around 1850 and made a fortune in the construction sector of Cuba. Félix Cabarrocas was then one of the architects of the grandiose National Capitol building that opened in 1929 in Havana. After prospering in Cuba, the Cabarrocas family paid for running water to be installed in their home village in Catalonia.

Cabarrocas himself remembered that when he was a teen-ager and Franco died, 'nobody knew exactly what would happen next in Spain, just as nobody can now predict what happens next in Cuba or Catalonia.' However, he argued, what is all too clear is that 'when emotions are very involved, it is harder to find any rational solution—and small problems generally become bigger ones.'

7

A CONSERVATIVE DIVORCE

In April 1996, a group of conservative politicians from Madrid met with their counterparts from Catalonia's governing party in the five-star Majestic hotel on Passeig de Gràcia, Barcelona's famous shopping avenue.

The Madrid delegation was led by José María Aznar, the leader of the conservative Popular Party. Aznar had just won the most votes in Spain's general election, but had fallen short of a parliamentary majority. This meant that he needed Jordi Pujol to persuade the lawmakers of his Convergence and Union party to use their votes in the Spanish parliament so that his Popular Party could govern Spain for the first time.

Pujol arrived at the hotel with a track record of deal-making with politicians in Madrid. During the previous parliamentary legislature, his Catalan party had helped keep Felipe González, the Socialist prime minister, in office. Now the inconclusive election of 1996 had thrust him again into the role of king-maker. Yet this time the stakes were very different. He had the choice of either preserving the status quo—by giving González his party's votes—or ending fourteen years of Socialist rule by helping appoint Aznar instead.

The final round of talks between Aznar and Pujol took place over dinner in the Barcelona hotel. The resulting deal became known as the Majestic Pact. A famous group photo captures the deal makers at that moment in time. A beaming Aznar stands in the centre. He is flanked by Pujol and six other negotiators, including Rodrigo Rato and Mariano Rajoy (who both became key ministers in Aznar's government). While all have secured their immediate future, none can foresee that two decades later, Rajoy will be the only participant in the hotel dinner to remain in politics, as prime minister of Spain.

Most political observers define the Majestic Pact as a key moment in the relationship between Madrid and Barcelona. In his autobiography, published in 2011, Rajoy celebrated the fact that he had taken part in a negotiation that opened 'one of the most brilliant periods in the recent history of contemporary Spain.'[1] Yet there is also profound disagreement about what exactly was achieved in the Majestic hotel. The pact is seen by some as an outstanding example of entente between the conservative politicians of Madrid and Barcelona, as portrayed by Rajoy. Others view it as the beginning of an irreversible political divorce.

According to many separatists, Pujol drank during that dinner from a poisoned chalice. Far from playing his cards well as kingmaker, Pujol sacrificed Catalonia's longer term interests in order to strengthen his control over his own party and over Catalonia.

The Majestic Pact 'is proof that Convergence had zero interest in anything beyond keeping itself in power for as long as possible and maintaining its grip on Catalonia,' declared Josep Fontana, a Catalan left-wing historian. 'Pujol thought that he could count on a party like the Popular Party to continue developing Catalonia as an autonomous region, but that proved a massive mistake.'

Predictably, those in the Convergence party see it differently. Francesc Homs, the Convergence leader in the Spanish Parliament, argued that the party was caught between a rock and a hard place in 1996. On the one hand, he said, Pujol considered González to be a great statesman, the Socialist premier who had led Spain into the European Union in 1986. On the other hand, González was by then presiding over a fraudulent administration, which was engulfed in major scandals, including its secret support of a paramilitary unit to kill terrorists from ETA, the Basque separatist group.

As González had become enmeshed in greater and greater difficulties, Pujol and his party had initially helped protect him, notably by blocking a parliamentary investigation into the paramilitary killings. However, as more evidence of Socialist fraud and illegal party financing emerged, Pujol finally pressured González into calling an early general election.

The inconclusive vote led to an unattractive choice. According to Homs, it boiled down to backing 'either González, a man steeped in corruption, or Aznar, a character viewed by most Catalans as hostile.' Aznar's election could also show that politics had come full circle, Homs said, since it would mean that a conservative party rooted in Franco's legacy would be governing democratic Spain. Aznar's Popular Party had emerged from what was the Popular Alliance, a party founded by Manuel Fraga, one of Franco's ministers.

Yet perhaps most tellingly, Pujol said it was González himself who helped him make up his mind. In one of their meetings, González had acknowledged that 'he couldn't really form a viable government.'

The Majestic Pact ushered in important changes—which at first seemed to be to the benefit of Catalonia. While Aznar started his premiership by abolishing Spain's compulsory military service, he also gave the Catalan police, the Mossos d'Esquadra, greater responsibilities. Catalonia also received more taxation powers, as part of a new regional financing scheme. This honeymoon period between Aznar and Pujol even led Aznar to wax lyrical about the Catalan language during a television interview, claiming that he himself enjoyed speaking Catalan in private circles—a claim that was derided by his opponents in Madrid.[2]

Some academics take a favourable view of Pujol for the bargain he struck with Aznar. They recognise that Pujol gained concessions without ruffling feathers in other parts of Spain and without forcing Aznar to make similar concessions elsewhere. Josep Maria Castellà Andreu, a professor of constitutional law at the University of Barcelona, told me that Pujol understood that 'you achieve more step-by-step than if you ask for a formal change, which sets the alarm bells ringing.'

Three years later, the bargain still seemed to be holding good when Aznar returned the favour to Pujol. After his Convergence party won a Catalan regional election without a parliamentary majority, Catalan lawmakers from the Popular Party provided the votes to allow Pujol to stay in office.

The tipping point in the relationship came in 2002, according to Aznar, when he offered Pujol the opportunity to appoint more Catalan ministers in his Madrid government. The offer was 'a historic bet on integration' and a chance to align politicians in Madrid and Barcelona, Aznar told me when we met in 2016.

As we sat together at the headquarters of a conservative think tank—known by its acronym Faes—over which Aznar presides, he recalled the point at which Pujol rejected the deal. Instead of a rapprochement, it became the moment 'when Pujol and Convergence started their path toward radicalisation,' he declared. Raising his glass of Coca-Cola, Aznar said that Pujol had shown that he was no longer interested in filling the glass and getting 'involved in the development of Spain.' Instead, 'what he wanted was to break the glass and take another one.'

In response, Aznar made another attempt to lure the Catalan conservatives into his government by inviting Artur Mas, Pujol's then deputy party leader, to meet one of his most senior ministers, Rajoy, in the Spanish government's vacation retreat. The setting—in the national park of Doñana, a pristine stretch of land on the estuary of the river Guadalquivir—was peaceful, but the meeting turned out to be less serene. Aznar and his party 'seemed to be attempting to make a hostile takeover of Convergence and Union,' Mas told me when I interviewed him. 'Our aim was not to represent the Popular Party's brand in Catalonia, but to have our own party, a party built on Catalan loyalty that was also involved in the governance of Spain.'

A CONSERVATIVE DIVORCE

Josep Piqué, a Catalan economist who became one of Aznar's ministers, suggests that both Aznar and Pujol should share the blame for a divorce that was accelerated by Aznar's crushing general election victory in 2000. In this election, his Popular Party managed to win one quarter of the votes in Catalonia. Encouraged by his electoral triumph, Aznar 'fell into the trap of governing only for his own party,' Piqué said, since he no longer needed his erstwhile Catalan ally to have a parliamentary majority. Pujol himself told some of his own party colleagues that he was sceptical that Catalonia would benefit from a greater presence within Aznar's government.

'If you believe that you will be eclipsed just by having ministers in the national government, it shows you have very little trust in your own strength,' Piqué told me.

As ever, in politics, there are several sides to the story. Just as Catalan separatists nowadays talk about Aznar's treachery, conservatives in Madrid believe Pujol did not respect his side of the Majestic Pact. Aznar transferred more powers to Catalonia 'in return for more loyalty, but the result in fact was disloyalty,' said Emilio Lamo de Espinosa, the president of the Real Instituto Elcano, a political research group in Madrid. 'It became clear that the Catalan political project was essentially about hegemony over a territory by a certain group of people.'

Twenty years after the meeting in the Majestic, Aznar was still adamant. If Catalan politicians felt short-changed by the outcome of the Majestic Pact, he told me, 'they should recognise that this was either because they didn't negotiate well or because we were more clever than them.'

A Socialist revival

The irony was that the falling out between Aznar and Pujol opened the door to precisely the kind of left-wing coalition in Catalonia that both politicians had sought to oppose.

In November 2003, Convergence lost power in Catalonia after twenty-three years in office under Pujol's leadership. Mas, who replaced Pujol as party leader, won the Catalan elections, but without enough votes to prevent three opposition parties from forming their own coalition government, led by the Socialists.

So it was Pasqual Maragall who became the new leader of Catalonia—the former mayor of Barcelona and one of the main architects of the 1992 Olympic Games.

The government switch felt almost like a 'fin de siècle moment,' said Josep Ramoneda, a political columnist. It was the end of 'Pujolism', or Pujol's particular way of managing politics. Rather than seeking to crush his rivals, Pujol had believed in the strategy of 'the perfect power-share'. According to Ramoneda, this meant that his Convergence party could dominate in Catalonia, while its main competitor, the Socialist party, could control big Catalan cities as well as the government in Madrid.

It didn't matter how powerful Pujol became—the biggest city, Barcelona, always remained beyond his reach. In 1995, Pujol's main deputy, Miquel Roca, failed in his bid to replace Maragall as mayor of Barcelona. It was not until sixteen years later, in 2011, that Barcelona finally elected a conservative mayor, Xavier Trias, from the Convergence party.

Barcelona's city hall building and the headquarters of the Catalan government are on opposite sides of the square of Sant Jaume, which was already the forum of the city in Roman times. So Maragall's new job was just a few steps away from his old one. Politically, however, the journey was much more arduous and tricky. Maragall was taking charge of a left-wing coalition that had none of the political stability that he had enjoyed as Barcelona's mayor.

Shortly after taking office, Maragall drafted a new Catalan statute of autonomy with his coalition partners. This aimed to increase Catalonia's powers in a wide range of areas, including the judiciary, as well as guaranteeing minimum levels of state investment from Madrid. For many, Maragall was an unlikely flag bearer for this greater Catalan sovereignty.

A CONSERVATIVE DIVORCE

'It seems ironic that Maragall, who had defended Barcelona as a very open and diverse capital—a world away from the conservative nationalism of Pujol—then launched this statute,' said Ramoneda. 'In Madrid, people like to present the Catalan problem as black-and-white, but it is at the very least a multicoloured one.' Francisco Longo, a professor of public management who previously worked in Maragall's city hall administration, went further. Maragall is 'an outstanding person who had his great moment as mayor, but then made plenty of mistakes that I still cannot explain,' he said.

According to Longo, Maragall saw in the statute an opportunity to strengthen his grip over his coalition. The statute was probably not 'a fight about Catalan identity but one about how to hold the reins—deep down it was a power struggle,' he said.

Four months after Maragall's election, the Socialists unexpectedly took office in Madrid, after terrorists bombed trains heading into Madrid's Atocha station in March 2004, just days before the general election. The Atocha bombings were the most deadly terrorist strike on European soil. They would go on to change the course of Spanish politics. After the bombings, Spain's conservative government tried to pin the blame on ETA, despite mounting evidence that Islamic and not Basque terrorists had planted the bombs. Spain's Interior Minister, Ángel Acebes, even held a news conference in which he called anybody who doubted ETA's responsibility 'wretched'.

Shocked by the government's response, citizens took to the streets and then took their outrage to the ballot boxes. As a result of this protest, the relatively inexperienced Socialist leader, José Luis Rodríguez Zapatero, became Spain's new prime minister.

For many, the assumption was that with the Socialists now in office both in Madrid and Barcelona, the stars were in alignment for the Catalan statute of autonomy promoted by Maragall. But in fact it proved to be the start of a tortuous path that would lead to major controversy six years later, when Spain's constitutional court struck down part of the statute. This was despite the fact that the text had already been approved by Spanish lawmakers.

On top of this, the debate over the Catalan statute helped the Popular Party to recover from its stinging election defeat in 2004. Rajoy's party appealed against the statute both in court and on the streets, sending volunteers to collect signatures against it.

Joan Matabosch, the Catalan artistic director of Madrid's opera house, recalled being stopped on Calle Serrano, one of the main shopping streets in Madrid, by an elegantly-dressed old lady. In an indication of how all-pervasive the debate had proved, rather than seeking directions she stunned him by asking for his signature on a petition against the Catalan statute. 'Using a territorial conflict to gain votes is the opposite of what politicians should do, which is to create consensus,' said Matabosch. 'It has created a monster that today frightens the very people who created it.'

The Popular Party also managed to use the Catalan statute as a means to pressurise Zapatero, who had promised to defend it from the onset. In 2008, during his re-election campaign, Zapatero told a packed concert hall in Barcelona that 'nobody owns the intellectual property over the future of Spain.'[3] But as the Popular Party stepped up its attacks and Zapatero's popularity started falling because of the financial crisis, he lost his nerve and stopped prioritising the statute, according to Homs. 'The Socialist party presented itself as the victim of the statute, but we knew it was trickery and it destroyed whatever faith we had in the Spanish system,' Homs said.

In one of his books, Pujol harshly condemned Zapatero's failure to defend the Catalan statute more strongly. The only doubt, Pujol wrote, is whether Zapatero acted out of 'cynicism, bad faith or simply out of necessity.'[4]

The unhappy fallout from the statute not only helped convince many Catalans that the Spanish political and judicial system was flawed, it also left a strong feeling of betrayal by a Socialist party that had counted on its voters in Catalonia to win office in Madrid. Six years later, at the time of writing, I continue to hear Catalans dismiss out of hand any Socialist initiative as a pile of empty words. It has created a situation in which neither of the two main parties of Spain is seen as a reliable partner in Catalonia.

Despite his success in the rest of Spain, Aznar never won an election outright in Catalonia but, as he himself noted, he still received 23 per cent of Catalan votes in 2000. Since leading the opposition to the statute, however, Spain's Popular Party has pretty much been sidelined from Catalan politics, and now focuses instead on building up its support in other regions. Under Rajoy, the Popular Party 'decided to stop doing politics in Catalonia,' Aznar claimed. 'That has been a catastrophic and disastrous tactic.'

Yet this Catalan disaster has not prevented Rajoy from starting a second term as Spain's prime minister in late 2016. If anything, Rajoy actively won his re-election by promising to quash any Catalan attempt to break Spain's unity. In the June 2016 general election, the Popular Party won the most votes across Spain. This was despite the fact that in Catalonia, Rajoy's party won only 460,000 votes, a share of 13 per cent.

Joan Tapia, a political columnist, reflected on how different the situation was under Aznar. Even if he was never a champion of Catalonia, he 'at least made an effort' to meet influential Catalans, he said. By contrast, he declared, Rajoy's idea of a perfect evening in Barcelona was dining with officials from his own party.

At the time of writing, in 2017, Rajoy was trying to revive the dialogue with Catalan politicians, in an effort led by his deputy, Soraya Sáenz de Santamaría. But there was no question of discussing an independence referendum in Catalonia, as promised by the Catalan government. Even if Aznar and Rajoy no longer see eye-to-eye, they remain united in their belief that Madrid should not yield any ground to the separatists in Barcelona.

'Do you think Abraham Lincoln would have been successful if he had offered something to the secessionists?' Aznar asked me. 'His success was built upon maintaining the unity of his country and pushing to abolish slavery.'

The journalist from Girona

Since January 2016, Catalonia's independence drive has been led by Carles Puigdemont. He emerged as a compromise candidate to break the deadlock between separatist parties over whether or not Mas should be replaced. Puigdemont, a former mayor of Girona, comes from the same party as Mas, but has stronger separatist credentials. While Mas was a late convert to secession-ism, Puigdemont has always pushed for independence.

Over a dinner in the medieval headquarters of the Catalan government in Barcelona, he repeatedly told me that his one and only reason for wanting to occupy such sumptuous sur-roundings was to help secure Catalonia's independence. As soon as that goal could be reached, he would want to bid fare-well to Barcelona and the turmoil of national politics. As if to underline that point, Puigdemont then headed off in his official car back to Girona, where he has kept his home and family, rather than staying over in Barcelona.

Puigdemont came into office after a smaller left-wing party—the Popular Unity Candidacy, or CUP—forced the removal of Mas. The CUP held Mas responsible for deep spending cuts, as well as for the alleged corruption within his Convergence party.

Puigdemont never formed part of the inner circle of Pujol and his party. David Madí, the former chief of Mas's cabinet, told me that his appointment was 'almost an accident'. While Mas needed three elections to become leader of Catalonia, it took Puigdemont 'just one day' to get propelled to Catalonia's top political job, he noted. 'There are some people who are lucky and others less so.'

Puigdemont started out as a journalist in Girona. He himself acknowledged that he felt that he had left the comfort of Girona for 'the electric chair' of presiding over Catalonia. 'I don't have a vocation for political leadership at this level,' Puigdemont told me. 'I like to work and serve my country but that can be done while holding other responsibilities.'

He can, however, trace his separatism to his youth. During our dinner, he recounted having his photo taken during a thinly-attended pro-independence rally in Barcelona in 1981. 'My country is Catalonia—and not any other,' he said.

'Puigdemont is not seeking power—he took this job with a single idea in mind, to lead Catalonia to independence,' said José Antich, a newspaper editor. 'His top priorities are independence, independence and independence—it's not about also improving education or creating a better government.' Josep Puigbert, a Catalan official who worked with Puigdemont in the early 1990s, when both were journalists, said that Puigdemont stood out even among separatist newsroom colleagues. 'Twenty-five years ago, some of his views sounded surprising, but they were actually similar to those expressed now by many' pushing for independence, Puigbert said.

On paper, Rajoy should have had more in common with Mas than with Puigdemont. Rajoy and Mas knew each other from the time of the 1996 Majestic Pact, and then followed similar trajectories. Both were understudies to powerful party bosses, respectively Aznar and Pujol, who eventually selected them as successors. Once in charge, both Rajoy and Mas led their parties into bitter election setbacks, each losing twice before finally getting elected.

In 2012, however, after Mas failed to get fiscal concessions for Catalonia during a brief and tense meeting with Rajoy in Madrid, their political relationship broke down. Mas's enthusiasm for the secessionist drive deepened divisions within his own political movement that ended up splitting it apart. Following that split, Mas pushed for the renaming of Convergence as the Catalan Democratic Party—a rebranding also designed to draw a line under past corruption scandals.

For many political observers, Mas is the great and late convert to Catalan politics, the politician who took his party from almost neutral to fifth gear on the road towards independence, even at the risk of fracturing his own party. Mas, however, protested to me that such a portrayal was 'a caricature'. He also argued that his case was far from unique. During the twentieth century, no major Catalan party had truly set independence as its goal, he said. Instead, they sought more Catalan autonomy while backing successive governments in Madrid.

In the 1980s, 'Puigdemont was among the few who defended the independence of Catalonia. He was in a total minority,' Mas said.

Mas was placed in a difficult position when he came into office in late 2010, in the depths of the financial crisis. From the start, he was under pressure from Madrid and financial markets to make deep spending cuts, in part because of the unsustainable debt accumulated by Catalonia's previous Socialist-led coalition administration. It was a challenge that Pujol had not faced up to during his years in office.

Pujol's view had been that 'if Spain stays relatively weak and Catalonia stays relatively strong, we can build together, but if Spain is too strong, it will destroy us,' said Madí. 'Pujol was a pragmatic politician capable of all sorts of pirouettes, but who would never have gone as far as Mas.'

Pujol himself would eventually endorse secessionism. But he insists that he made the switch 'after many years spent dissuading those who were opting for independence.'[5]

At the time of writing, Rajoy and Puigdemont were at loggerheads on the main issues, but seemed to have a better personal rapport. In April 2016, Puigdemont visited Rajoy in his Moncloa government compound. The meeting produced little of substance. But the two politicians exchanged a few niceties and Puigdemont received a gift from Rajoy—a facsimile of the first edition of the part of *Don Quixote* in which the knight-errant travels to Barcelona.

Shortly after that Moncloa meeting, I asked Rajoy what the main difference was between Puigdemont and Mas. 'Sometimes it's not just about politics but also personalities,' he replied. 'There are some people with whom things are just easier than with others.'

Basic goodwill, however, will not be enough to solve the Catalan dispute. While neither side has any incentive to declare open warfare, the arithmetics of Spain's politics and electorate are also no longer stacked in favour of finding a solution, particularly since both Rajoy and Puigdemont maintain a fragile grip on office.

It's an almost impossible situation. Puigdemont and his party have pinned their colours to a separatist coalition that risks implosion if there are any U-turns on secessionism. Yet according to the columnist Ramoneda, whatever concession Rajoy might now offer to the separatists, the Popular Party could probably hope to gain only a few 'tens of thousands more votes' in Catalonia. By contrast, a major concession to Catalonia could cost him 'one or two million votes' in the rest of Spain. It would also destroy his claim to be the flag bearer of Spanish unity.

In that sense, at least, the divorce between the two main conservative forces in Madrid and Barcelona has perhaps reached a point of no return.

8

THE SHARED DISEASE OF CORRUPTION

On 25 July 2014 Jordi Pujol published a confession that stunned Catalans. In his confession, the founder of the Convergence party and longtime former leader of Catalonia admitted tax evasion. His family, Pujol explained, kept money offshore that had been inherited from his father, Florenci Pujol. He had died in 1980, five months after Pujol was elected as president of Catalonia's regional government.

'I am the only person responsible for the facts described and for all their consequences,' Pujol declared. His statement, however, only disclosed some of the facts. He did not say how much money had been inherited, how much was owed in back taxes and how much overall his family had kept offshore. Only later did he reveal that he had inherited 140 million pesetas from his father—the equivalent of about €840,000.

Unsurprisingly, political opponents jumped on Pujol's confession like dogs on a bone. 'You have lied to all Catalans,' Alicia Sánchez-Camacho, the then leader of the Catalan branch of the Popular Party, told Pujol during a parliamentary hearing held two months after his confession.

Opposition lawmakers demanded a full investigation into Pujol's assets, to establish whether any family money beyond this had originated from kickbacks received while Pujol had led Catalonia. As a result, within weeks of the confession, fraud investigations had been extended to several other members of his family. Journalists also took it upon themselves to re-examine old cases, including the 1984 collapse of Banca Catalana, a bank set up by Pujol's father.

'It was a great blow for Catalan society to discover that the person who wanted to be our moral compass and our great reformer was a person with concealed funds,' Màrius Carol, the editor of newspaper *La Vanguardia*, told me. Carol argued that the scandal had permanently ruined the reputation of a politician who 'had been obsessed with how history would treat him.'

Even though rumours of fraud had swirled around Pujol and his family for some time, the confession itself came as a bombshell. The fallout also threatened to discredit the Convergence party that Pujol had founded and run for over two decades, even if 'the Catalan bourgeoisie had always seen him as an outsider,' said Carol.

Ponç Feliu Llansa, a former judge, declared—in an opinion piece written shortly after Pujol's confession—that Pujol 'will go down in history not just as a tax evader but as a traitor to Catalonia.'[1] Some have gone even further. According to Luis Bassets, a leading political columnist, the impact of Pujol's confession on Catalonia could—somewhat extraordinarily—be compared to the effect that Nikita Khrushchev had on Soviet Communism, when he acknowledged the extent of Stalin's crimes in 1956. In the book that he published shortly after Pujol's confession, Bassets argued that Pujol was transformed from an icon to a person infected with the plague.[2]

Bassets, of course, was not trying to compare tax fraud to Stalin's mass-murders. But he did think that Pujol's confession had discredited everything he stood for, and gave two strong reasons to consider why. First, he said, the confession punctured Pujol's squeaky clean image, carefully constructed to make him contrast favourably with Madrid's lower ethical standards. The confession had been made by 'a politician with Catholic roots, obsessed with principles and values, who had personally taken on the cavalier attitudes of nouveaux riches Spaniards facing the crisis,' Bassets wrote.

THE SHARED DISEASE OF CORRUPTION

Second, Pujol only made his confession after three of his seven children had separately become enmeshed in serious legal problems. In 2012, the newspaper *El Mundo* was already claiming that Pujol's family had €137 million hidden in a Geneva bank. Pujol tried to sue the newspaper for libel, but his lawsuit was rejected by a judge, in part because the newspaper had accessed a draft police report. In 2014, Pujol claimed there had never been 'an opportune moment' to declare his father's offshore inheritance. But by the time Pujol confessed, suspicions of wrongdoing already swirled around his family. As Bassets neatly summarised it, 'everybody knew it, but everybody was surprised.'

Following Pujol's confession, Artur Mas, Pujol's successor as party leader, tried to draw a line under the scandal. Mas said there was 'no relationship' between his party and 'a private family matter'. Yet if the Stalin comparisons seemed over-dramatic, it did not feel so inappropriate to compare the impact of Pujol's downfall to that of Helmut Kohl in Germany. This was the parallel drawn by José Antich, a newspaper editor, who had earlier written a biography of Pujol. In 1999, Kohl was caught up in a party financing scandal only a year after leaving office. The German Christian Democratic Party, or CDU, 'turned its back on the great chancellor who had managed to unify Germany', Antich recalled. 'Something similar happened to Pujol, the man who had been in prison under the dictatorship and then managed to stay in office for twenty-three years.'

In an interview I did with him in August 2016, Pujol asked not to discuss his finances. However, he did present himself as the victim of a political witch-hunt by opponents determined to erase his past achievements. 'I have lost everything, except for my hope, my sense of pain, and my profound sense of being linked to my country and its people,' he said.

Pujol's confession revived interest in his early life. He had studied medicine, then joined his father's bank and finally switched to politics. The transition, however, wasn't clean cut. Pujol managed to keep a foot in both business and politics. He remained a shareholder in Banca Catalana, his father's bank, even after being elected as leader of Catalonia in 1980.

Over the ensuing four years, Banca Catalana accumulated such major losses that it needed state intervention and rescuing by a consortium of other Spanish banks. Other banks collapsed during that period, but Banca Catalana was the most politicised case. In 1984, the Spanish state prosecutor indicted Pujol and other directors of the bank for allegedly falsifying documents and other fraudulent practices.

However, Pujol was eventually exonerated from any wrong-doing. Some would even argue that the case increased Pujol's influence over Catalonia, as he deftly presented the accusations as persecution orchestrated from Madrid by political opponents of Catalonia.

'The government has made an unfair attack,' Pujol said in a speech delivered from the balcony of the Catalan government building. 'From now on, we will speak ourselves about ethics, morality and fair play.' By seizing the rhetorical upper hand in this way, Pujol managed to win another Catalan election in 1984, right in the middle of the Banca Catalana scandal. This turned him into a poster boy for Madrid's conservative politicians, who were themselves still struggling to make the transition from Franco's dictatorship.

In late 1984, *ABC*, one of Madrid's main conservative news-papers, made Pujol its Spaniard of the year. In its editorial, *ABC* explained that Pujol had 'contributed considerably to ensuring the viability of the constitution and the monarchical democracy that restored liberties in Spain.' The newspaper also argued that Pujol's election victory in Catalonia should set an example for conservative politicians in Madrid in terms of beating the Socialists, ahead of a national election scheduled for 1986. In its assessment of Pujol, *ABC* ignored the Banca Cantalana scandal.

In defiance of *ABC's* hopes, the Socialists—led by Felipe González—went on to win the 1986 national election. Pujol was one of those who gave them parliamentary support. *ABC's* response—and that of the conservative establishment in Madrid—was to vilify Pujol, who became a magnet for insults from supporters of the conservative Popular Party. The list of insults was so long that Carol, *La Vanguardia*'s editor, said he kept a compilation.

In the early 1980s, 'when I travelled to Madrid, taxi drivers would ask if I was Catalan and immediately congratulate me for having a leader like Pujol. But a few years later, these same Madrid drivers would just ask me about the dwarf,' said José Martí Gómez, a veteran Catalan journalist. 'How did Pujol switch from being a role model to being a dwarf?'

Russians on the beach

At the time of writing, the investigation into the finances of the Pujol family was ongoing. As a correspondent, I only reported on the political dimension of the case. Nor did I investigate the other major corruption scandals in Catalonia, like the kickbacks allegedly paid during the overhaul of the Palau de la Música, Barcelona's most emblematic concert hall. At the time of writing, a former party treasurer of Convergence, Daniel Osàcar, was among the defendants on trial for allegedly facilitating bribes during the concert hall's renovation.

But in 2012, I tried to dig into a smaller corruption story, in the seaside resort of Lloret de Mar. It had an unexpected international dimension, since it allegedly involved Russian bribes. A century ago, Lloret was the playground of the Barcelona bourgeoisie. But during the Spanish construction boom that started in the late 1990s, Lloret became one of the most heavily built-up stretches of the Catalan coast. It attracted foreign tourists, including a steady contingent of Russian visitors.

In 2013, Lloret's conservative mayor, Xavier Crespo, was indicted. He was accused of using Russian money to keep his cash-strapped town afloat, while allowing Russians to launder their money in property investments around Lloret. The investigation was one of dozens taking place across Spain at the time, most of them related to suspect real estate transactions that came to light after the bursting of Spain's property bubble in 2008. But the Lloret case was among the few that allegedly involved a foreign criminal network that had entered Spain to fill the financing void left by struggling domestic banks.

The reporting trip to Lloret was relatively successful. The mayor, who represented the Convergence party that then governed Catalonia, denied wrongdoing. But he answered most of my questions, including one about a paid trip that he had taken to Russia. I also visited some of the suspect real estate projects, including a sports stadium financed with Russian money. One of the Russian sponsors of Lloret, Andrey Petrov, was then under arrest in Spain.

I collaborated on the story with Samuel Aranda, an award-winning Catalan photographer who has long worked for *The New York Times*. Aranda lives in a village near Lloret, so he decided to return on another day, to take more photos. He later called to say that he had spotted one of the activists who had blown the whistle on the mayor's property deals. The activist was driving a new Porsche sports car that was completely out of tune with the image he had given during our previous interview, of an ordinary citizen who felt defrauded by Lloret's corrupt officialdom. This luxury car brought into question its owner's credibility as a witness and also suggested that, beyond the mayor's suspect dealings, there was still a labyrinthine process to establish the complete truth about property fraud in Lloret. In short, I was left with the nagging feeling that too much money had been earned too fast by too many people around this town.

In November 2015, Crespo, Lloret's former mayor, was sentenced and forced to quit politics for nine-and-a-half years. He avoided prison, but he received a fine of €4,500 and had to reimburse the cost of the trip to Russia we had talked about, as well as the luxury watch he had received there.

When taking Catalonia's corruption cases into consideration, I have often asked Catalans whether they believe that their own politicians can be better trusted to handle their tax money than those in Madrid. Some have argued that the scale of fraud is smaller in Catalonia than in other regions like Valencia or Madrid, where conservative politicians from the Popular Party have faced trial for taking bribes in return for public infrastructure contracts during the property boom. In the southern region of Andalusia, which has one of Spain's highest unemployment rates, prosecutors have been investigating a scheme allegedly run by Socialist politicians to embezzle funds earmarked as severance payments for laid-off workers. But such comparisons are hard to make. They also do not help exonerate a Catalan political establishment whose financing methods were publicly questioned long before the corruption scandals that emerged from Spain's financial crisis.

In February 2005, the leaders of the Convergence and Socialist parties confronted each other during a fierce debate in the Catalan parliament. Pasqual Maragall, the Socialist leader, told Artur Mas that his Convergence party had 'a problem—and that problem is called 3 per cent,' a reference to the bribe level that the Convergence party had allegedly demanded in return for awarding public contracts.

Oriol Soler, a political campaign strategist, told me that Spanish politics was built on 'medieval systems' of corruption, relying more on bribes than influence-peddling to sustain political parties. 'The difference is that Catalan society ended up rejecting Convergence, while Spanish society hasn't even considered the idea of removing the Popular Party' of Mariano Rajoy, he said. Rajoy started a second mandate as prime minister in October 2016.

At the time of writing, however, Convergence remains at the helm of Catalonia's governing coalition, although with less influence than during Pujol's years in power. In 2016, the Convergence party changed its name to the Catalan European Democratic Party. But a name change doesn't reshape a party. Part of the problem with the Convergence party, Soler told me, is that it switched to secessionism without accepting the need to change its ways as a party in a coalition government. The case of the Palau concert hall 'clearly demonstrates their sense of entitlement,' Soler said. He also said that he had once unsuccessfully tried to convince Mas, the then party leader, to make a public apology for past corruption, similar to the way in which Pope Francis 'asked for forgiveness' for paedophilia among Catholic priests.

During the economic boom, politicians from all parties were awarding projects to construction companies that were often financed by banks controlled by the same politicians. A decade after Spain's construction bubble burst in 2008, the country remains saddled with oversized, unaffordable and sometimes half-built properties and infrastructure.

'I suspect that the main problem is having the same party in power for too long, rather than its ideological orientation,' said Ángel de la Fuente, the director of a Madrid-based economics think tank, known by its acronym of Fedea. 'Pujol's nationalists were in power for over twenty years and set up a sophisticated and widespread system for extracting commissions and kickbacks from public contracts,' he claimed. 'But they are not alone. The same has happened in Andalusia under the Socialists and in Valencia under the Popular Party.'

From the IMF to the courtroom

Corruption has been most rampant at regional level, but some of the former stars of Spanish politics have also become mired in scandal. These include Rodrigo Rato, who was Spain's finance minister during the property boom years. From this governmental post, Rato went on to become managing director of the International Monetary Fund.

The problems began in 2010, after his return from Washington. Rato took charge of a bank, Caja Madrid, whose board was dominated by people linked to his conservative Popular Party. He merged Caja Madrid with smaller banks to create Bankia, a giant institution that then revealed the largest loss in

Spanish corporate history and forced Spain to negotiate a European banking bailout in 2012.

In November 2013, Rato, who was by then entangled in several lawsuits, appeared before a committee of the Catalan Parliament that was investigating Bankia's demise. David Fernàndez, a Catalan lawmaker from the radical left CUP party, launched into a diatribe in which he took off a sandal and raised it menacingly. 'Are you scared?' Fernàndez asked Rato. 'Scared of you?' an incredulous Rato responded. 'No, of losing everything in one day, like millions of people have done,' Fernàndez replied.

In February 2017, Rato was sentenced to four and a half years in jail for overseeing a corporate credit card scheme that allowed him and sixty-four other directors and executives to make unlawful personal purchases. All of them were found guilty of misusing their cards to spend a combined €12.5 million over a decade. At the time of writing, Rato was awaiting a verdict in another fraud case relating to mismanagement of Bankia.

Fernàndez is of the opinion that independence could help clean Catalan politics. 'Corruption in Spain and in Catalonia were the same, coming from the same model of crony capitalism set up around 1978,' when Spain returned to democracy, he said. 'Corruption has no flag, it only shares a wallet.' But Catalonia's independence could be used 'as a shredder for corruption,' he continued. 'I'm not saying that corruption will just vanish, that the new Catalonia will be like Arcadia, but at least we should have the opportunity to try to shape a better future, in which there will no longer be impunity. If corruption is not rooted out, there is a risk that we will convert the Catalan state into a banana republic.'

Separatists argue that independence would help control corruption because it is easier to punish one's own politicians, dependent on Catalan votes, than those who distribute public money from hundreds of miles away in Madrid. They also want to rebuild an anti-fraud police and judicial apparatus that, in its Spanish version, has allegedly become too politicised.

Leading Catalan politicians like Mas and Xavier Trias, the former mayor of Barcelona, have been linked to secret Swiss banks by the Spanish media, based on leaked police reports. But such allegations have neither resulted in any sentencing nor even led to conclusive evidence of wrongdoing at the time of writing.

They have, however, had political repercussions. In November 2012, as Mas campaigned for re-election, *El Mundo*, the Madrid conservative newspaper, accused Mas of hiding money in Switzerland. The newspaper cited a police report. Mas denied wrongdoing, but his political opponents pounced on the claim. A few days later, Mas and his party unexpectedly lost seats in the Catalan election. However, in March 2013, Lombard Odier, the Swiss private bank in which Mas allegedly kept money, formally denied any relationship with the Catalan leader.

In October 2015, after Spanish police raided the Barcelona headquarters of his party, Mas condemned the police intervention as politically motivated. 'Convergence and I are targets for big game hunters,' Mas said. In response, Spain's Minister of Justice, Rafael Catalá, said that politicians like Mas should not question the independence of Spain's judiciary. This kind of investigation 'happens every day', the minister said.

Spain's judiciary has been overwhelmed by the caseload, handling over 200 investigations into political corruption since Spain's property market collapse in 2008. But it seems the system has also been undermined by the almost incestuous relationship between institutions that should operate as separate powers.

This was highlighted in June 2016, when *Público*, a left-wing Spanish online newspaper, released a leaked recording of Jorge Fernández Díaz, Spain's then interior minister, trying to incriminate Catalan political opponents during a private conversation with the director of the anti-fraud office in Catalonia. The Spanish government condemned the leak, without denying its content, and Prime Minister Rajoy rejected calls from opposition leaders to force his minister's resignation. Rajoy later removed Fernández Díaz—in a government reshuffle when he started a second term—but without any acknowledgement of wrongdoing. That in itself has helped to significantly intensify the Catalan sense of distrust towards the authorities in Madrid.

'The Spanish government has every right to pressurise Catalonia using legal methods, but not illegal ones,' said Antich, the Catalan editor. 'No normal state can be expected to accept the disintegration of its state without any reaction, but it isn't part of a normal democracy to interfere with justice or form a special police corps to fight independence.'

9

A DIPLOMATIC BATTLE ACROSS EUROPE

Belloy-en-Santerre, a village in northeastern France, was devastated during the First World War's Battle of the Somme. Yet a special connection with Catalonia arose out of the destruction of war. Visitors can see evidence of this in the names of the two main streets running the length of the village. One bears the label Rue de Barcelone, the other Rue de Catalogne.

On 4 July 1916, the French Foreign Legion—alongside regular French soldiers—tried to recapture Belloy from the Germans. The attackers only had to cover a short distance, but they advanced across open terrain, in full view of German machine gunners. Within minutes of launching their disastrously-planned offensive, about 900 of the 2,000 members of the Foreign Legion were killed.

Fifty Catalans died that day. Overall 900 Catalans had volunteered for the Foreign Legion. Many joined because they admired the values of the French Revolution. Some—including Camil Campanyà, a Catalan political activist who died in Belloy—believed that a French victory would reshape Europe in a way that would benefit Catalonia. They weren't the only ones. The Legion had also attracted Czechs, Slovaks and volunteers from the Balkans. All looked to this world war to redraw Europe's map and break up the Habsburg empire to which they belonged.

After the war, the Catalan authorities wanted to showcase the values of their Mancomunitat and held up Belloy as an important example. Launched in 1914, the Mancomunitat was a political project designed to restore the level of political autonomy and unity that Catalonia had enjoyed before 1833, when it was carved up into new provinces by a Spanish administrative reform. It translates, essentially, as a Commonwealth, which unified the Catalan provincial councils into a more powerful federation. The Mancomunitat's promoter and first president, Enric Prat de la Riba, wanted the project to modernise Catalonia and give each town better infrastructure, from new schools to telephone and road networks.

After Prat de la Riba died in 1917, his successor, Josep Puig i Cadafalch, decided to pay for the reconstruction of Belloy. This was a gesture of solidarity, but also a significant assertion of the Mancomunitat's influence and diplomatic reach. Yet, in an ironic twist, it came not long before the Spanish dictator Miguel Primo de Rivera took charge and stripped the Mancomunitat of all its powers. Even though Catalan conservatives had facilitated his political ascent, Primo de Rivera abolished the Mancomunitat in 1925.

Despite this patchy history, the Mancomunitat's rebuilding of Belloy was commemorated exactly a century after the battle, on 4 July 2016. Raül Romeva, Catalonia's foreign policy chief, went to France for the ceremony. In his speech, Romeva declared that Catalonia's role in Belloy was a reminder that 'as a people, we have always looked up to Europe and the world… We have involved ourselves as much as circumstances have allowed for, in fair fights but especially in the search for a solution to conflicts.'

In 2004, Romeva was elected to the European Parliament and moved to Brussels as a lawmaker representing ICV, a small Catalan party of environmentalists. He returned to Catalonia a decade later with a chic new look—shaved head, yellow-framed glasses, designer jacket and open shirt—to match his sharper political objectives. After leaving the green party, he instead spearheaded the main separatist coalition in the Catalan elections of 2015.

A DIPLOMATIC BATTLE ACROSS EUROPE

Since his appointment in January 2016, the charismatic Romeva has been striving for greater European involvement, running a de facto foreign office into which Catalonia's government has poured significant money and efforts, despite Madrid's opposition. From 2011 to 2014, Catalonia had already spent €18.5 million on its network of 25 representative offices abroad.[1] But though Romeva was allowed to take centre stage in Belloy, he has found it much harder to gain admittance to the French foreign office headquarters at Paris's Quai d'Orsay, or indeed to any other European ministry. In fact, no European leader agreed to hold an official meeting with Romeva in his first year in office. In March 2016, Romeva met Matteo Renzi, Italy's then prime minister—but because of a tragedy rather than politics. In the aftermath of a bus crash in southern Catalonia, the two men visited the wounded and the relatives of students who died on the bus, including seven young Italians.

The European Union was built as 'a club of states, so obviously it is the states that are allies,' Romeva told me. 'We are not aiming to get the official support of states but we do want the right to speak to everybody.'

Romeva believes Catalonia's diplomatic influence will gradually increase. He noted that Catalonia's position had been discussed in parliamentary sessions in smaller countries like Switzerland, Estonia and Uruguay. Behind closed doors, he said, foreign officials were showing sympathy towards Catalonia, particularly those from nations that once struggled themselves to gain independence. 'There are a lot of countries that have lived through something similar,' he said.

From Kosovo to Gibraltar

The government in Madrid significantly changed its attitude towards Catalonia's diplomatic projects as the Catalan independence drive gained momentum. Mariano Rajoy, as prime minister, switched from insisting that no foreigner should meddle in a domestic issue to welcoming any comment from a European leader that could be interpreted as a warning against secessionism. Rajoy's government also took legal action to prevent Catalonia from setting up a full-fledged foreign ministry and other institutions. 'If Catalonia's diplomacy is toothless,' Romeva said, 'then why does Madrid bother deploying Spain's considerable diplomatic arsenal to counter it?'

When David Cameron, the then British prime minister, visited Madrid in September 2015, he said during a joint news conference with Rajoy that 'if one part of a state secedes from that state, it is no longer part of the European Union and it has to take its place at the back of the queue, behind those other countries that are applying to become members.' Angela Merkel, the German chancellor, also reassured Rajoy at a joint press conference. European treaties must be respected, she said, and those treaties 'guarantee the sovereignty and territorial integrity of each state.'

The Madrid government has fought hard to make sure that the break-up of another European state could not set a precedent for Catalonia. After the British voted in June 2016 to leave the European Union, Rajoy tried to dash any hope among Scots that they could somehow remain within the EU. Scotland's first minister, Nicola Sturgeon, had rushed to Brussels to claim the right to hold her own negotiations on behalf of Scotland. Yet Rajoy told a news conference in Brussels, 'Scotland has no competences to negotiate with the EU. The Spanish government rejects any negotiation with anyone other than the United Kingdom.'

Kosovo has also established a worrying precedent in Madrid's eyes. During the Yugoslavia war of the 1990s, Spain took part in NATO air bombings on Serbia and later joined the international military force deployed in Kosovo. But in February 2008, when the Republic of Kosovo declared independence from Serbia, Spain did not join the United States and others in recognising it. This was even after George W. Bush, then president of the United States, said that an independent Kosovo would 'bring peace to a region scarred by war.'

Spain's rejection of Kosovo was not initially motivated by Catalan separatism alone. But for Francisco de Borja Lasheras, a Spanish expert on the Balkans, it is a key factor. 'Catalonia makes it hard to imagine Spain ever recognising Kosovo,' he said. 'Spain has a direct interest in putting a brake on any internationalisation of the Catalan problem.'

While fighting secessionism on all fronts, the conservative government in Madrid has rekindled Spain's own territorial claims over Gibraltar, a British territory at the southern tip of Spain that Spain ceded to Britain in the 1713 Treaty of Utrecht. José Manuel García-Margallo was Spain's foreign minister from 2012 to 2016. At times, he seemed to draw his inspiration from the imperialistic warmongering of his great-grandfather, Juan García y Margallo. Garcia y Margallo was a general who gave his name to a nineteenth-century war against Moroccan insurgents, allegedly started after the general ordered the construction of a fortress over a holy tomb.

García-Margallo had already presented Catalan secessionism as a modern insurrection. 'We are facing an uprising, an institutional coup d'état,' Margallo said in November 2015, during a presentation of his own book, *All the skies lead to Spain*. In the same week that Rajoy was pouring cold water on Scotland's European ambitions in Brussels, García-Margallo sought to use Britain's planned exit from the EU to claim co-sovereignty over Gibraltar and replant the Spanish flag on Gibraltar's rock. The response from Fabian Picardo, Gibraltar's Chief Minister, was as terse as it was memorable. 'No way, José.'

At the time of writing, García-Margallo's successor, Alfonso Dastis Quecedo, a career diplomat who previously represented Spain in Brussels, appeared to be taking a less provocative approach. But the tensions over Gibraltar remained, in part fuelled by warmongering reports in the British tabloid press.

Ambassadors of 'ham and flamenco'

Many Catalans believe Spain's foreign ministry has lost any interest in also representing Catalonia. Ignasi Guardans, a former member of the foreign affairs committee of the European Parliament, said he had seen Spanish diplomats behave mostly as promoters of 'bullfights, ham and flamenco'. He added: 'There are way too many diplomats and other Spanish officials who present Spain as a monocultural state.'

Some Spanish diplomats, however, base their fight against secessionism on their intimate understanding of Catalonia. Spain's consul in Perpignan, Gauden Villas, is a career diplomat who grew up in Barcelona, with the Estelada flag pinned on his bedroom wall. By the time he started university in Barcelona, however, Villas had removed his separatist flag, along with the Catalan patriotic fervour that he picked up at school. 'We were told that it was great to be Catalan, while being Spanish was marginalised,' he remembered. In Perpignan, Villas instead came to appreciate how a centralised government in Paris could unify citizens, even in regions where a minority language like Catalan is also spoken.

'The best aspect of France is its centralisation. It is a model of a state that has worked for them,' he said admiringly. He argued that Spain should basically treat Catalan separatists like rowdy children. 'Imagine you have kids who want to assault Fort Knox with wooden swords and spears,' he said. 'You have two possibilities: either let them try it, or call the police and tell them to stop causing a nuisance and recognise that this is actually Fort Knox.'

Romeva and García-Margallo once sat in the same European Parliament. Romeva told me that he couldn't understand why García-Margallo, his former colleague, would no longer meet with him.

Yet García-Margallo, as foreign minister, wanted to show that independence would only bring 'isolation and poverty' to Catalonia, including rejection by international institutions. 'It is absolutely unimaginable that a unilateral declaration of independence would be recognised within the Security Council' of the United Nations, García-Margallo told a party conference in September 2016.

But what is unimaginable now may not be in the future as the world changes fast and unpredictably. Whether García-

Margallo likes it or not, international arrangements are not set in stone. Sixty years after its creation, the European Union has often been showing more signs of fragmentation and fragility than unity. Its most ambitious project to date—the European single currency—was seriously strained during the financial crisis. And other Europeans are also trying to redraw borders, most notably in Scotland.

In May 2011, the Scottish National Party won a majority of the seats in the Scottish Parliament. Three years later, Scotland held an independence referendum in 2014, with the approval of the British government in London. Scottish voters rejected independence and this prompted the resignation of Scotland's leader, Alex Salmond. But the referendum did not undermine his nationalist party. On the contrary—it consolidated its position considerably in the British general election of May 2015, when Scottish Nationalists took over most of the seats previously held by the Labour Party in Scotland.

Under Sturgeon, Scotland has again raised the issue of independence, this time using the argument that Scottish voters rejected independence in the referendum of 2014 partly because they believed that Britain would remain committed to EU membership. Sturgeon has also argued that Scotland could do 'a reverse Greenland', in a reference to the peculiar status of Greenland, a Danish territory that forms part of the Kingdom of Denmark, but not part of the European Union. Some separatist politicians have proposed joining forces with Northern Ireland to leave Britain together. Whatever the conclusion of such debates, Sturgeon insists that Scotland should not be forced out of the European Union, since its own voters rejected the Brexit proposal.[2]

In March 2017, Sturgeon set out a timetable to hold a second independence referendum—between the autumn of 2018 and the spring of 2019. To turn this goal into a reality, Sturgeon must still overcome several hurdles. At the time of writing, however, Sturgeon had put her plan for a second referendum on hold after her party lost seats in another British general election, in June 2017. Scotland's path therefore remains an uncertain one. But any revival of Scotland's quest for independence is certain to blow wind into the sails of Catalan secessionism.

Some Catalan separatists have framed Scotland as a classic example of how smaller nations can contribute more to the EU than larger nations. In the British referendum of June 2016, British voters overall decided to exit the EU, but 62 per cent of voters in Scotland voted instead to remain. That result showed a small nation like Scotland had a deeper commitment to Europe than England, contrary to the idea that large nations form the pillars of the EU, according to Eduard Voltas, a Catalan magazine publisher. 'The will to build Europe cannot be measured in square metres,' he said. 'A puzzle need not be weaker if it is made up of one thousand pieces rather than five hundred pieces.'

A more pessimistic view is that, if Britain's exit marks the prelude to the unravelling of the European Union project, then the issue of EU membership will also plummet in Catalonia's list of political priorities. After Britain's vote, 'the fear of being an outsider is no longer what it was,' said Romeva.

Romeva and other separatist politicians like to highlight U-turns performed by European leaders once smaller countries have pushed in earnest for independence. In 1991, Germany's then chancellor, Helmut Kohl, recognised the outcome of independence referenda held in the Baltic republics of the Soviet Union, after initially voicing concerns over the validity of such votes. In 1992, France held back from recognising Slovenia and Croatia as states, as part of the break-up of Yugoslavia, but eventually joined Germany in sending them ambassadors.

The diplomatic agency of Catalonia, known as Diplocat, has been promoting not only independence but also Catalonia's credentials as a reliable and committed European partner. It has invited foreign officials and journalists to visit Catalonia. It has also sent delegations to political gatherings in countries like Denmark and Sweden, as well as dispatching observers to monitor elections, like those in Macedonia in December 2016.

A DIPLOMATIC BATTLE ACROSS EUROPE

Yet despite such efforts, Catalonia is arguably finding it harder to gain diplomatic recognition than in the days when Catalonia's main politicians gave their parliamentary votes to whichever Spanish party was in office in Madrid. In October 1996, Jordi Pujol was warmly welcomed in Bonn by Chancellor Kohl, one week before Kohl was due to meet José María Aznar, Spain's then prime minister. As a daily reader of some of the main European newspapers, Pujol displayed language skills and an understanding of European current affairs that Aznar probably lacked. It was just one of many instances when he was treated almost as 'a head of state,' according to journalist Lluis Bassets.[3]

The Scottish example

Fast forward two decades and 'the European response to the Catalan claim has been zero, not even one gram of understanding' for independence, said Josep Piqué, a former foreign minister of Spain. 'Not even the Scottish nationalists have wanted to get mixed up in it. They always insist that Scotland and Catalonia are in different situations.'

Indeed, the Scottish National Party has kept both Catalan and Basque separatist politicians at arm's length. This is not least for fear that any rapprochement with secessionists in Spain would further antagonise Madrid toward Scotland's own independence project, according to David McCrone, a co-founder of the Institute of Governance of the University of Edinburgh. 'Why would the Scots be interested in stirring things up within the Iberian peninsula and then getting accused of making mischief?' he asked. 'If Scotland was located where Portugal is, then its realpolitik would perhaps be very different. Then you could talk about a shared peninsular issue.'

However, Scotland and Catalonia do have similarities. In both, separatist parties are challenging ruling conservative parties. In both, though the conservative parties dominate the country as a whole, they only have marginal representation in the regions that want to break away. (In the 2015 general election, the British conservative party only won one seat in Scotland, even as it secured a British parliamentary majority.) But the differences are also striking, not least the contrast between a Scottish independence movement dominated by a single nationalist party and the tensions between Catalan separatist parties that have radically opposed economic and social agendas.

English and Spanish nationalism have also offered very different responses to secessionism. 'Things have just been blocked in Spain in a way that they never were in Britain, because there is an essential sense of insecurity that sees any concession to Catalonia as a blow to Spain. In Britain the attitude has been much more relaxed,' said Michael Keating, a politics professor at the University of Aberdeen.

Keating noted that, even amid significant political tensions within Britain, there was never any question in England that Scotland is a nation with its own culture. In fact, English nationalism is steeped in the belief that, within Britain, 'the periphery is almost dispensable,' he argued. For Spanish nationalists, however, 'there is no equivalent to the view of a strong England, on which the people of the south can fall back.'

In sum, as Scotland has attempted to progress towards independence, its nationalist politicians have not seen any benefit in banding together with an independence movement that faces greater obstacles in Catalonia. 'Nationalist movements that do quite well tend to dissociate themselves from the others,' Keating said. The Scots, Catalans, Flemish and others have shared a sense of disenchantment that smaller regions have been sidelined within the overall structure of Europe, he continued, citing the toothlessness of the Committee of the Regions in Brussels. But, their disillusionment has clearly never gone as far as rejecting the European Union.

When I talked to Pujol, he acknowledged that separatists needed to adjust their international expectations, particularly within a European Union whose legitimacy rests upon the support of member states rather than regions. In 1991, 'Estonia, Latvia and Lithuania gained independence because they wanted it, but above all because the Soviet empire was exploding,' he said. 'Catalonia is like Lithuania, but Spain is not the Soviet Union.' For Pujol, Catalans must show resilience and be ready to hit more bumps on the road towards independence. 'A lot will depend on what capacity Catalonia has for maintaining the pressure over a long period, democratically and peacefully,' he said.

10

BARCELONA, A CITY BEFORE A NATION

Alfons Cànovas walks with difficulty, clutching a cane. His infirmity makes it hard for him to visit his swimming club as often as he used to. But he still manages to get there occasionally, even if he swims widths rather than lengths. 'It now feels more like taking a dip rather than really swimming,' he said.

At almost ninety-nine years of age Cànovas remains deeply enamoured of a club that he calls 'my second son'. As a young man he played water-polo in one of Spain's best teams. For thirty years, he was also the president of Atlètic-Barceloneta, a club that he helped transform into one of Barcelona's most important swimming centres, with about 11,000 registered members.

His neighbourhood, the Barceloneta, is 'the cradle of swimming, not just for Catalonia but for the whole of Spain,' he told me. It was once simply a working class district, inhabited by humble people with 'one major asset, which was to live next to the sea.'

The Barceloneta's relationship with the sea has changed dramatically over the past century. A district that once housed fishermen, as well as factory and dockworkers, has now become a tourism hub and the gateway to Barcelona's city beach. During the summer, tourists in swimming gear and flip-flops fill the Barceloneta, looking for a café to have lunch, or just seeking a break from a day spent lying in the sun. Amid the tourism boom, rental prices have soared, which in turn has created tensions.

In 2014, the neighbourhood associations of the Barceloneta started protesting against the higher cost of living and the illegal subletting of apartments to tourists. They also complained about tourists' drinking and partying, which all too often led to acts of debauchery or vandalism. One protest took place after the media published photos of a group of Italian tourists partying nude in the Barceloneta in broad daylight.

'The Barceloneta has completely lost its distinctive atmosphere as a fishermen's district,' Cànovas said. 'We used to treat the beach not only as a place to have fun but to work—to put out, dry and repair nets.'

Cànovas knows his neighbourhood like the back of his hand. He started working there as a teenage apprentice jeweller and eventually set up his own jewellery workshop. He was also once the president of an association of local businessmen. He often switched homes within the Barceloneta and reeled off his former addresses to me with impressive precision: Carrer Salamanca 45, Carrer de la Maquinista number 18, Carrer de Berenguer Mallol 5, Carrer de Balluard 6, Maquinista 18 (but on the fifth floor, after he got married,) another apartment on Maquinista 18 (on the fourth floor, after he returned from fighting in the civil war) and Paseo de Juan de Borbón number 2, his most recent residence.

Yet Cànovas was not born in the Barceloneta, but in the village of Guadalupe, in the southern Spanish region of Murcia, a place then so isolated that 'it didn't even have a school,' he said. When he was three years old, his father abandoned Guadalupe and his precarious farming life and went with his family to Barcelona to find factory work. They settled in the Barceloneta district because many other migrants from Murcia already lived there.

Initially, however, his father could not find a steady job. So he travelled alone to the United States, where he found work in factories and road maintenance in New Jersey. Eventually, he got an offer of work in a warehouse in the Barceloneta, which allowed him to rejoin his family there.

Then came Spain's civil war. The Barceloneta was bombed, mostly by Italian aircraft that took off from Mallorca, where Franco's Fascist ally, Benito Mussolini, had set up an air base. On 19 January 1938, in what was then the largest air raid on Barcelona, Cànovas father was killed by a bomb. He was working in a small orchard right next to the warehouse, where he grew potatoes, onions and other vegetables to help feed his family. The bomb fell shortly after noon, 'probably only about a quarter of an hour after he had finished his normal work shift,' Cànovas said. 'It was very unlucky timing.'

By a strange twist of fate, the bombing coincided with the only day during the civil war when Cànovas was reunited with two of his brothers who, like him, were among the Republican troops fighting against Franco. Their different regiments had crossed paths in a village in Teruel, a region that witnessed some of the fiercest fighting of the war. During their joyful reunion, none of them was aware that tragedy had struck at home. It was some days later that Cànovas received a letter telling him the bad news.

After the war, Cànovas returned to making jewellery and swimming. He helped rebuild the swimming club, since it had been destroyed in the war. 'We really had no money, but we had plenty of electricians, painters and other people who could volunteer and do great work for free,' Cànovas said.

The bombing had damaged several other buildings, including a far more impressive structure that had housed a casino and a pool. Ahead of the 1992 Barcelona Olympic Games, Cànovas lobbied the city hall to turn the disused casino into a new swimming centre that could house both his club and another one, Atlètic. His campaign was successful, and the city hall agreed to pay for the construction works. In 1995 the new structure was inaugurated as the Club Natació Atlètic-Barceloneta.

Cànovas is still the club's honorary president. In the upstairs offices, he used his cane to point out black-and-white photographs of former swimming champions shaking hands with Francesc Macià, the Catalan leader from the early 1930s. He spoke nostalgically about what it had been like then. Before showers were installed along Barcelona's main beach, he said, 'the last part of the swim was always the race back to the street corners that had public fountains, to rub off some of the salt.'

When asked about the surge in tourism, Cànovas replied that he was not among local residents opposed to it. But he did draw a line on the issue of Catalan independence and questioned whether it could benefit his cherished Barceloneta district. 'There is no need for independence for us to live well together,' he said.

Local initiatives like his swimming club, he suggested, brought more benefits to residents than a grand statehood project. 'I consider myself to be from the Barceloneta, then from Barcelona, then from Catalonia and then from Spain—in that order,' he said. 'If things go well for the Barceloneta, that is good for Barcelona, which is good for Catalonia and good for Spain.'

A metropolitan area

Cànovas's story is special but not unique. Barcelona is full of people committed to improving their city without necessarily wanting Catalonia's independence. The irony is that the independence movement has relied heavily on the size and importance of Barcelona to argue that Catalonia would be a sustainable state. Yet according to Manel Manchón, the editor of online publication *Economía Digital*, it has not been able to conquer the hearts and minds of many of Barcelona's citizens.

Separatist parties, he argued, have fallen well short of their electoral goals in the former dormitory towns surrounding Barcelona. Collectively this is known as the 'metropolitan area' of Barcelona. That area is 'the missing part of the puzzle' in Catalonia's independence drive, he said.

According to Francisco Longo, professor of public management at Esade—a Barcelona-based university—the political relationship between Barcelona and its surroundings was purposely complicated by Franco after the civil war. Franco wanted to stop Barcelona from competing head-on with Madrid. In the 1940s, Madrid absorbed neighbouring towns like Carabanchel and expanded significantly as the capital city. But 'in Barcelona this didn't occur because Franco didn't want Barcelona to grow at the same scale as Madrid,' argued Longo, who previously worked as a senior administrator in Barcelona's city hall.

Instead, Barcelona's political management structure was set up according to a model that endures today. The mayor is in charge of the city itself, but doesn't control a metropolitan area that stretches across 250 square miles and is run by separate city halls.

'The importance of the metropolitan area of Barcelona can only be understood if we think about how Madrid would have been governed without absorbing its dormitory towns,' Longo said. Franco's divide-and-rule policy in Catalonia explains some infrastructure problems to this day, including the construction of a metro line between Barcelona and its airport in El Prat. The line opened in 2016, after major administrative delays. 'The development of infrastructure gets very difficult when there is no central authority,' Longo said.

Rivalries within Barcelona's metropolitan area also led to 'a battle of symbols and identity' that the Catalan regional government sometimes used to weaken Barcelona's city hall. Longo recalled the furious reaction of the regional government when a city hall official suggested that the metropolitan area should have its own flag. The proposal was dropped, but 'this was used to criminalise the metropolitan area, for planning something that went against the national identity of Catalonia,' he said.

Despite these restrictions on its expansion, Barcelona's population has reached 1.6 million and dwarfs any other Catalan city. In terms of size, the next two cities are Barcelona's neighbours, L'Hospitalet de Llobregat and Badalona, which developed as dormitory cities. Each has fewer than 300,000 inhabitants. Overall, Barcelona's metropolitan area has 3.2 million people, or two-fifths of Catalonia's population.

The historical perspective

It's worth noting that historically neither Barcelona nor Madrid was initially the seat of power. In 218 BC, Roman troops disembarked in Empúries—on what is nowadays Catalonia's Costa Brava—during their second Punic war against Carthage, in order to attack the rearguard of Hannibal's army.[1] The main Roman city then became Tarraco, or modern day Tarragona, where a forum and circus were built and the Emperor Augustus settled in 26 B.C. Barcino, or Barcelona, was a later Roman addition. Madrid, for its part, only gained importance in the sixteenth century, when Philip II's royal court moved there from Toledo.

Joan Tarrida, owner of the publishing house Galaxia Gutenberg, said to me, 'If Barcelona only had 400,000 inhabitants nowadays, the Catalan issue wouldn't exist. What power would Catalonia have as a separate nation without such an important city?' On the other hand, he argued, Barcelona is 'probably the most important city of Europe without a state.' As such, it is sufficiently strong to develop whether it is within a Spanish or Catalan state.

Barcelona's own residents have not always appreciated the remarkable features of a city that was overhauled using an innovative model of grid blocks after 1858. This was the moment when the authorities lifted a prohibition on building outside Barcelona's original defensive walls. The expansion made Barcelona the playground for some brilliant architects, headed by Antoni Gaudí, who developed a Modernist style characterised by its stained-glass windows, ceramics and wrought ironwork. Gaudí was a devout Catholic but also a fervent Catalan patriot, who believed that Catalonia, as the cradle of the Roman civilisation in the Iberian peninsula, was 'the concrete' and authentic part of Spain while the rest was more 'abstract'.[2] His passion for the region led him to decorate his works extensively with emblems of Catalonia.

Tragically Gaudí was run over by a tram in 1926. His funeral was a major event, with some 10,000 mourners following his coffin to the crypt of his own Sagrada Família. But in 1936, as Spain was entering civil war, anarchists ransacked and burned down the crypt, as well as Gaudí's workshop. For the next decade and a half his legacy was ignored.

Foreign architects led the rediscovery of Gaudí in the 1950s. Many were fascinated by Gaudí's design technique, including his inverted scale models made with weighted strings or chains. Daniel Giralt-Miracle, an art critic and exhibition curator, talked to me about the impact of his innovations, saying, 'Gaudí did not have a computer, but he was also not ready to stick to the pencil-and-paper approach to architecture of his time.'

Even after he had been rediscovered, it would take decades for his buildings to become valuable tourism magnets, including La Pedrera, which now welcomes about 1.2 million paying visitors a year. In 1986, Caixa Catalunya, a savings bank, bought La Pedrera from a group of families for 900 million pesetas, equivalent to €6 million. Until the bank made an offer, 'nobody really wanted La Pedrera,' said Josep Ramoneda, who previously headed one of Barcelona's main cultural centres. 'The recognition really came very late.'

These days there is no danger of Gaudí being undervalued. In October 2016, Christie's auctioned a church bench designed by Gaudí for £347,000. Giralt-Miracle bemoaned the situation to me, saying, 'There is a point when things can start to get out of control. Anybody who has anything linked to Gaudí now tries to get some kind of commercial benefit from it.'

Olympic triumph

Yet in terms of recent history, the real moment of transformation for Barcelona was brought about by sports rather than culture. In 1992 it hosted the Summer Olympics.

The city had been encouraged to take this on by Juan Antonio Samaranch, the Catalan who was then president of the International Olympic Committee. Initially this created political tensions with Madrid, which had never hosted the Olympics, as well as within Catalonia, then led by Jordi Pujol and his right-leaning Convergence party. However, Barcelona's mayor was the Socialist Pasqual Maragall. According to Eduard Voltas, who publishes the *Time Out* magazine in Barcelona, he was determined to modernise his city and 'save Barcelona from mediocrity.'

I talked to Pujol both about the Olympics, and about the way he views the relationship between Barcelona and the rest of Catalonia. His latest office is still situated in the city—the pictures on the walls comprise an oil painting of Barcelona itself and a photo of Queralbs, the mountain village where his wife has a house.

'A city as large as Barcelona could consume Catalonia,' he told me. 'Catalonia must resist that, but without hurting Barcelona's development.' It should be remembered, he continued, that after the surrender of Barcelona to the Bourbon troops in 1714, Catalonia's economic recovery started in the countryside rather than in Barcelona. 'Catalonia without Barcelona is half of what it is, but Barcelona without Catalonia isn't the same either,' he said.

Pujol said he had always opposed developing Barcelona according to the 'Hanseatic concept'—in which it would become a port city with its own economy cut off from the rest of Catalonia. But he insisted that he had given '100 per cent support' to its hosting of the Olympics, even if some in his Convergence party did not share his enthusiasm.'I told the people of my party that this was a unique opportunity and we had a very important ally in Samaranch,' he said.

Inevitably some of Barcelona's citizens used the event to try to air other issues and grievances. Longo recalled seeing Catalan protesters hoisting signs warning that 'Catalonia is not Spain' in 1992, in reaction to the Olympics. He also remembered a failed attempt by supporters of Pujol to disrupt the opening ceremony, among them Pujol's youngest son.

When asked about the discontent at the time, Pujol said that he could not control his sons, nor people who wanted to promote Catalan nationalism rather than Barcelona. In fact, he himself pushed for Catalan to be one of the official languages of the Barcelona Olympics. 'Over the course of a few days, the eyes of the world were on Barcelona. It made sense to remind people that there was also something here called Catalonia, which wanted its freedom,' he said.

Juan Antonio Samaranch, vice-president of the International Olympic Committee and the son of its former president, used the rowing boat—in which Pujol, Maragall and other leading politicians sat together during the games—as a metaphor. 'Ultimately you need all the institutions to row together, in the same direction, otherwise the games could not have happened,' Samaranch said. He contrasted the politics of the time with the current secessionist struggle. 'You can't have games if the authorities shout and bark at each other,' he concluded.

Catalonia's rival politicians lost no time in drawing personal benefits from the Olympics. Maragall, Barcelona's mayor, set in motion his bid to replace Pujol as Catalonia's leader. There were a few tensions, but 'there was no anti-Olympic party,' Enric Juliana, a columnist for newspaper *La Vanguardia*, wrote. Instead, the games united 'the old, the new and a city wanting to expand its potential.'[3]

And Barcelona did expand its potential. From being a city that welcomed fewer than one million visitors a year before the Olympics, it became the engine of Spain's tourism growth, with over eight million visitors in 2016. The Olympics also allowed it to show itself off as a centre for innovation. Its opening ceremony was staged by two directors of the Fura dels Baus, a theatre company that had been part of Spain's artistic revolution after Franco's dictatorship.

The Fura had started out as a street theatre group, formed by nine members because 'that was all we had room for' in a Mercedes minivan, according to Àlex Ollé. Ollé started his career as a puppeteer but is nowadays a leading opera stage director. Back in those days, the Fura found their audiences by touring from one Catalan town feast to the next. They developed a radical style and their show for the Olympics—directed by Ollé and Carlus Padrissa, another director of the Fura—departed from the 'Walt Disney version' of previous ceremonies. They showcased many of the tragic issues of that time, from the war in the former Yugoslavia to the AIDS epidemic. In Barcelona, 'there was a greater desire to take risks than in other cities and to project a modern image,' Ollé told me during a break from rehearsing a Wagnerian opera.

Following the Olympics, Barcelona started to host such events as the Sonar music festival, which was launched in 1994 in the city's recently opened contemporary culture centre. Sonar nowadays organises some of the world's main experimental music gatherings, with events staged from Reykjavik to Hong Kong. In 1994, 'I don't think any other Spanish city would have been willing to risk opening a new structure for this kind of project,' said Enric Palau, a musician who co-founded the Sonar festival. Barcelona's authorities, he recalled, somehow accepted 'that people would come in with a glass of beer, smoke, perhaps stain the floor, wear crazy clothing and listen to electronic music.'

Victims of success

Barcelona's development has continued apace ever since. But for many residents, it's time to recapture the spirit of the city, rather than continue to push Barcelona commercially. Several complain that in the covered market of La Boqueria, tourists rather than grocery buyers taste the olives and ham.

'Maybe it's been good for business, but we now have a tourism attraction rather than a normal market,' said Juanito Bayén, the eighty-two-year-old owner of the Pinotxo bar, one of the establishments in La Boqueria. 'You see people enter as if they were visiting the Sagrada Família.' With his colourful waistcoat and matching bow tie, Bayén is himself a tourist attraction. After serving one of his special coffees, in which he pours first milk and then the coffee, he almost invariably gets asked to pose for a selfie with a tourist.

Josep Maria Roig also feels tourism is robbing Barcelona of its authenticity. Roig is the owner of La Colmena, a pastry shop that was founded in 1872 and has wood panelling made by Cèsar Martinell i Brunet, a student of Gaudí. He talked to me about the 'criminal loss of heritage in a city that is getting drowned by big money and international brands.' He himself is the secretary of an association that is fighting to maintain historic stores. Like Bayén, he has a warm relationship with his customers. He carefully wraps up cakes, takes the money, and then reaches into a glass jar to take out a handful of colourful sweets, which he hands over to the client with a big smile, along with the change.

Roig is particularly concerned about the way in which multinational brands are acquiring more and more retail space within his Gothic quarter. In Spain, an overhaul of the rental law allowed property owners to raise rental contracts from 2015, forcing many stores out of business. But Roig holds Barcelona's city hall responsible for failing to grant special protection to historic stores like Monge, a stamp shop converted into a shopping gallery. 'Do we really want tourists to go home with no more than souvenirs from a shopping gallery that are made in China and have zero to do with Barcelona?' he asked.

Alfred Bosch, a historian and politician, said that the improvement in the streets in the Gothic quarter, where he lives, was some compensation for 'the tourism saturation that is endangering the whole downtown area.' Still, he said Barcelona was 'approaching a Venetian situation,' whereby tourists are more valued than residents. 'If somebody can get €5000 a month out of renting an apartment to tourists, why rent it for €500 a month to a family?' he asked.

His question goes to the heart of Europe's efforts to offset its dwindling manufacturing importance by becoming a hub for tourism and other services instead. It is a difficult balancing act, in which Barcelona and other historic cities risk becoming giant museums, catering more to first-time visitors than residents. While residents react against this, trying to set up new boundaries to defend their local identity, visitors are equally keen to discover places unlike those they've experienced before. In both cases, embracing multinational brands is not the way forward.

Beyond Barcelona

The debate over tourism isn't confined to large cities like Barcelona. Nor is it all that recent, as is shown by the development of the Costa Brava, the rugged and beautiful coastline that starts about fifty miles north of Barcelona and stretches all the way to the border with France. A toll highway runs along it. But the journey becomes more complicated on the final stretch to Cadaqués, a picturesque port at the bottom of a narrow and windy road.

For several days of the summer of 2016, the access road to the port was clogged by cars and coaches filled mostly with day tourists from Barcelona. Local residents were extremely upset about the tourism overflow and traffic jams.

'We will end up being victims of our own success,' said Pere Vehí, the owner of Boia, a bar founded by his family in 1946. 'We just don't have the capacity to deal with all the people arriving here in Cadaqués.' Rafael Martín, a restaurant owner, said it was 'shameful' that Spain did not have a dedicated tourism ministry that could control the flow of visitors. (Tourism is listed as the third sector that falls under the responsibility of Spain's ministry of industry and energy.) 'We absolutely don't need more tourists—what we need is a better system for filtering and selecting them,' he said.

Even before the arrival of mass tourism, Cadaqués already had a peculiar relationship with the outside world. A port with a thriving maritime trade, it was cut off from inland Catalonia. The first road between the nearby town of Figueres and Cadaqués was built in 1911. Until then, 'there were lots of people from here who had been to Havana or even New York, but never Figueres,' said Vehí.

A generation later, Cadaqués and its sheltered bay became a favourite haven for artists, led by Salvador Dalí. However, Dalí made enemies in Cadaqués, not least after he helped deprive the town of compensation subsidies for a freeze that destroyed olive trees. Dalí told the authorities that the trees had survived the cold without a glitch. But his own olive trees were planted at sea level and therefore were more protected than those in the main olive grove high above Cadaqués, which made the comparison deceptive.

Catherine Perrot—the Swiss-born widow of Captain John Peter Moore, who was Dalí's personal secretary—defended him. During his life, 'Dalí did a lot more for Cadaqués than people here have acknowledged,' she said. 'People here somehow thought that he should just be handing out dollar bills.' As for complaints about summer traffic jams, Dalí should be thanked for turning Cadaqués into a year-round cultural destination, she argued. 'Just go to Port de la Selva,' she continued, referring to the neighbouring port village, 'and you will see that it is dead in winter.'

Joan Vehí, a retired carpenter who made frames for Dalí's paintings, has turned his workshop into a shrine for the photos that he took of Dalí and Cadaqués since he got his first camera in 1945. 'I have always carried a camera and taken photos out of pure passion,' Vehí said. 'I've never used the name of Dalí, not like others who took advantage of him.'

A perfect illustration of both the positive and negative aspects of tourism was the resort inaugurated by the Club Méditerranée in 1962. It was both the Club Med's first European venture outside of France and one of Spain's most ambitious tourism projects, at a time when Franco's regime wanted to open Spain to foreigners. The French company built a holiday village of 1,000 bungalows in the wilderness around the Cape of Creus, the easternmost point in the Iberian peninsula.

The area's rocky landscape was famously a source of inspiration for Dalí. In one of his masterworks, *The Great Masturbator*, he had adapted the peculiar shape of the rocks to create the figure at the centre of his canvas. Dalí also set up a bedroom mirror in his house to reflect the cape, so that he could be the first person in Spain to see the sunrise every morning.

Not surprisingly Dalí himself was wary about the resort development. In 1961, he drew some sketches for Pelayo Martínez, the architect of the Club Med project, to caution against excessive construction work. The natural setting, Dalí wrote, was 'made more for God than for men and so should continue just as it is.'

Yet while his fame was enough to make the area a magnet for tourists, his influence was not enough to get in the way of the region making money. The resort went ahead. It wasn't till the 1990s that Dalí's wish to leave nature alone was fulfilled. Environmentalists lobbied to remove the Club Med village and create instead a nature park around the cape. The resort was closed in 2004, in return for Spain paying financial compensation to Club Med. In a final ironic twist, the Club Med village—a project that helped kickstart tourism in Catalonia—was removed, down to the last brick, just as the rest of Spain was in the midst of a massive construction boom, triggered in large part by tourism.

There is still disagreement in Cadaqués about the lessons to be drawn from the Club Med. Martín, the restaurant owner, was one of those who campaigned for its removal. But Vehí, the bar owner, noted that the French resort provided local jobs as well as tourists. 'Environmentally, it is best not to spoil such a beautiful spot,' Vehí said, but the Club Med 'did have economic advantages for Cadaqués.'

An alternative mayor

In Barcelona, residents also have mixed feelings about the city's development under a far-left mayor, Ada Colau, who was elected in 2015. Global retailers and tourists fill the Gothic quarter, but purple-and-yellow stickers can occasionally be seen on dustbins and lamp posts. The stickers have a skull and cross-bones symbol and an ominous slogan written in English: 'Tourism kills the city.'

Roig, the pastry-shop owner, was adamant that Colau's administration was 'putting on a nice show for the gallery, but not making any real changes.' His letters to her city hall, asking for stronger protection for iconic stores, had gone unanswered, he said. This came as a surprise because Colau had seemed very concerned about the conservation of historic Barcelona when I first met her in 2014, before she launched her campaign to become mayor. She told me that she and her family had actually stopped going to the Gothic quarter because it was invaded by foreign tourists and global brands.

'The main attraction of Barcelona is a certain style of living. But we're allowing this to be replaced by what I would call a fast food model,' she said at the time. 'The traditional stores are getting evicted and the big multinationals are winning.'

Back then, Colau was leading an association fighting housing evictions by banks. She had a long track record as an activist. In 2001, she joined protests ahead of a scheduled World Bank meeting in Barcelona, which was then cancelled.

Colau switched to politics and was elected mayor at the helm of a formation, Barcelona En Comú, which translates as 'Barcelona Together.' In 2015, far-left candidates also won office in other Spanish cities, including Madrid, where Manuela Carmena, a former Communist and retired judge, became mayor.

Colau's and Carmena's unexpected victories proved something of a political bombshell. Few would have predicted that female outsiders could defeat candidates from the conservative establishment and take charge of Spain's two largest cities. Both went on to put a brake on real estate projects. In Madrid, Carmena put on hold a major construction project to overhaul the district around the Chamartín train station. In Barcelona, Colau declared a freeze on hotel construction, including a plan to convert a tower occupied by Deutsche Bank into a luxury hotel. By 2017, both mayors had imposed tighter control on apartment rentals to tourists, while Colau's administration was also fighting in court Spain's largest utilities to prevent them from cutting off poor households—whether or not they were paying their bills.

The initial reaction of the Catalan business community to Colau's election was one of shock and dismay. But fast forward one year and the opposition had toned down, as Colau made her presence increasingly felt in regional politics, distancing herself from her earlier activism. It reached a point where Colau's former colleagues in the association fighting housing evictions published a letter in late 2015 saying that the association was breaking any ties with Colau. Colau responded diplomatically, saying that she understood that an association needed to act as a critical watchdog for the authorities.[4]

In the struggle over Catalonia's future, Colau has managed to use her own ambivalence towards independence to position herself between parties fiercely opposed to secession and hard-line separatists. 'I've never been pro-independence, nor a nationalist, and I'm in fact more in favor of overcoming borders,' Colau said in an interview in 2016.

She argued that it was wrong to prioritise Catalonia's independence over social issues, like income inequality. 'There is clearly a majority in Catalonia in favour of the right to decide and in favour of having a say about Catalonia's future, but there is also a majority that is asking for political change, for an end to corruption and for a reduction in economic imbalances,' she said. 'It's a mistake to create a hierarchy between all these different rights.'

On 11 September 2016, Colau took part in the pro-independence rally held in Barcelona to mark Catalonia's national day. She denounced Madrid's refusal to allow Catalans to vote over their future, but also purposely avoided standing next to the main secessionist leaders attending the rally.

BARCELONA, A CITY BEFORE A NATION

'Colau is the only politician who can claim to represent and understand the people who take to the street because she really came from the street,' said José María Martí Font, president of an association of Catalan correspondents. 'She has managed to promote the referendum without getting labelled as a Catalan nationalist because she has also put city politics ahead of the state debate.'

The brand from Argentina

Overseas, Barcelona's brand overshadows that of Catalonia. Foreign officials are sometimes more excited about meeting Barcelona's mayor than the regional president of Catalonia, said Gonzalo Rodés, the president of Barcelona Global, a business association. 'Catalonia is very unknown, but when you say that you're from Barcelona, that awakens some sort of special reaction,' he continued.

Similarly, cities around Barcelona recognise that 'internationally, the important brand is Barcelona, more than Catalonia,' according to Núria Marín, the mayor of L'Hospitalet de Llobregat. L'Hospitalet hosts the Mobile World Congress, an annual telecom event held in an exhibition centre connected directly by metro to the airport of El Prat, which means participants need not enter the city of Barcelona. Yet, very few of the Japanese or Americans who attend the mobile congress realise they are outside Barcelona, said Marín. L'Hospitalet has the space and infrastructure, she said, but 'what we have to preserve as our umbrella brand is Barcelona.'

In fact, if any brand name can challenge Barcelona, it is not Catalonia but the city's main football club, FC Barcelona. Some Barcelona residents get irritated when they hear confused foreigners talk about their visit to 'Barça', as the club is known, rather than 'Barna', the shorthand for the city.

Abroad, Catalan entrepreneurs often advertise themselves as being from Barcelona even when they come from other parts of Catalonia. Nandu Jubany, a chef who was born in the village of

Monistrol de Calders, is one of them. Jubany nowadays has restaurants worldwide, including three in Singapore, which serve sausages, cheese and other produce shipped from the Catalan countryside where Jubany lives. But his Asian marketing is all about Barcelona, either as a city or as the home of a great team with a star player, Lionel Messi, who also captains his national team, Argentina.

'I offer authentic Catalan cooking, but it is Barcelona that works and is known there,' said Jubany. In Asia, 'you say the word Barcelona and you get back at least an aaaaaaah Messi!' It is just one of the many paradoxes in this lengthy complex debate. In the end, the best ambassador for Catalonia might be a sportsman born in Argentina.

11

THE SYMBOLISM OF A TOWER AND A TREE

It took just one minute for the child to reach the top of a wobbly human tower measuring about forty times his own size. Spectators all around him packed the main square of Valls. After steadying himself, the child raised his hand in victory. Shouts and applause erupted from the crowd,

Valls is the birthplace of the elaborate human towers that were first constructed in the early nineteenth century, and are known as *castells* in Catalan. The nerve-racking balancing act—the *castells* sometimes collapse just before the hand-raising attempt—has become increasingly popular across most of Catalonia in the last forty years.

Recently their construction has also taken on political connotations. In 2014, *castells* featured in Catalan separatist events held across Europe, from Berlin to Rome. In Paris, participants symbolically built their human tower in front of the Eiffel Tower. The Valls festival of that year was particularly patriotic. Catalan flags draped the trees along the road into Valls and separatist banners hung around the main square and most streets.

Valls held the first official *castell* event in 1801. Josep Solé Tarrago, a former president of the oldest *castell* team in Valls—the *Colla Vella*—said that once a second team was created—the *Colla Joves*—it didn't take long for tournaments to spring up. He compared the competitive atmosphere to the one that exists between the university rowing teams of Oxford and Cambridge, saying that it was 'one of the most passionate amateur rivalries in the world.'

After the civil war, General Franco forced the two teams to merge because 'this wasn't the kind of rivalry that suited a totalitarian regime,' he said. But the passion for the competition collapsed this arrangement within a decade.

The popularity of *castells* surged in the late 1980s, after Catalonia's newly-created public television started to broadcast competitions. 'That made *castells* fashionable, when before they had really only been popular in a few towns and among humble people, like farmers and port workers,' Ángel Conesa told me. Conesa is one the judges of the largest *castell* tournament, which is held every two years inside the bull ring of Tarragona. Within about twenty-five years, he said, the number of *colles*, or teams, had doubled.

As many as 600 people gather to form a major *castell*. They clutch each other to form the *pinya*, or base. Then others clamber onto their shoulders and create the actual tower. As the tower grows, the participants become smaller and lighter. Only children can climb to the top. The participants then come back down, dismantling the *castell*, as soon as the child at the apex of the tower—who is known as the *enxaneta*—raises a hand.

In Valls, local politicians pressing for secession used *castell*-building as a symbol of their statehood ambitions. 'Great structures can be built if people are united in pursuit of a clear goal,' declared Jordi Agràs Estalella, a culture official. Albert Batet, the mayor of Valls, compared the values required to create a state with those necessary for a human tower. He quoted the official slogan of the *castells*: '*força, equilibri, valor i seny*' (strength, balance, courage and common sense). 'Both are proof that we can build great things if we come together,' he said.

Beating the drum

The Patum, another Catalan festival, has also become a symbol of secessionism. This takes place annually in the town of Berga.

THE SYMBOLISM OF A TOWER AND A TREE

Like the *castells*, the Patum is on the list of 'Oral and Immaterial Heritage of Mankind' drawn up by UNESCO.

The Patum probably dates to street performances of the fourteenth century, although the oldest documented reference is from 1621. It represents the struggle between good and evil, in a carefully choreographed display involving statues and costumes of angels, fire-wielding demons and dragons, and Turks fighting Christian knights. Late at night, masked demons, known as *Plens*, invade Berga's main square, spreading through the crowd before setting off firecrackers attached to their costumes that turn the place into a hellish ball of fire and smoke.

The festival's religious origins mean it is celebrated during the Catholic feast of Corpus Christi. But the Patum also has strong pagan elements and, for all its history, continues to be adjusted according to the demands of the times. In medieval days, the Patum's dancers only followed a drumbeat, whose onomatopoeic 'pa-tum' sound probably gave it its name. Later a band joined and the music became more varied. In 2016, one of the dances was even performed to music adapted from a Bruce Springsteen song.

The Patum in 2016 was also distinguished by the beat of the independence movement. As in Valls, Catalan flags fluttered all over Berga, as though a separate state of Catalonia was a *fait accompli*. People sang the Catalan anthem, a recent addition to the festival. For the first time, they draped the demons and dragons in the Estelada separatist flag.

Who had introduced these separatist elements? On this occasion, it was the far-left Popular Unity Candidacy, known by its Catalan acronym, CUP, which had been elected to Berga's town hall in 2015. Its mayor, Montserrat Venturós, watched the Patum from the town hall's balcony alongside other officials. Yet significantly she was not accompanied by any representative from the Catholic Church, nor by anyone from the Spanish military. It was the first time in the Patum's ancestral history that neither institution had been invited. That morning, Venturós was also the first mayor who did not attend the Sunday Mass that opens the day's festivities.

Her defiance extended beyond rewriting diplomatic niceties for the Patum. In April 2016, she refused to appear in court after being indicted for flying the Estelada flag on the town hall. A few months later, the police briefly detained her and took her to a courtroom to defend her flag insubordination. She described her arrest as an attack against the Catalan people and received widespread support from other separatists.

'I'm not going to stand in a politicised trial, shaped by the politicians in Madrid, when I'm helping build a new country,' Venturós told me ahead of the Mass. 'I'm here to respond to the will of my own people.'

Ramon Minoves Pujols, a town hall councillor from the right-leaning Convergence party, said the mayor should have stuck to the usual format of the Patum—including going to Mass, whatever her personal views on religion. 'It's just a lack of respect,' he said to me, readjusting his tie. Minoves Pujols and others from his party wore suits. By contrast, Venturós wore a sleeveless top and sandals, similar to the casual attire of her CUP colleagues.

The Patum is the only surviving festival of its kind in Catalonia, 'a source of pride and integration in our town,' said Pere Gendrau, a journalist who carried one of the 12-foot-high statues during the festival. Carriers used to get paid to lift the giant statues, he said, but 'people now fight for this honour.'

Rediscovering Columbus

Since 2015, Berga with its 16,000 inhabitants has become a bastion for the CUP. Despite being a small political party, the CUP has played a pivotal role within the secession drive. In early 2016, it forced the removal of Artur Mas as leader of Catalonia's coalition government.

As well as punching above its weight in Catalonia's politics, the CUP has also campaigned to remove cultural landmarks that it considers antiquated and inadequate for an independent Catalonia. It targeted the statue of Christopher Columbus, standing next to Barcelona's waterfront, with an outstretched finger pointing to the sea. Inaugurated in 1888—for Barcelona's universal exhibition and only a year before the Eiffel Tower—the statue was for a long time the tallest structure in Barcelona.[1]

In September 2016, the CUP's representatives tabled a parliamentary motion to remove Columbus because his discovery of America had kickstarted the Spanish genocide of indigenous people. The CUP argued that a monument that size should instead celebrate resistance to Spanish colonialism. The party also called for the abolition of October 12 as the national holiday on which Spain commemorates the discovery of America. Furthermore, it campaigned to remove the Barcelona statue of Antonio López, a prominent banker and merchant, who grew rich trafficking in slaves.

Daniela Ortiz, a Peruvian artist living in Barcelona, believes in drawing attention to the prominent placements of these symbols of Spanish imperialism. But she also points out that Catalans often have double standards. 'Catalans present themselves as oppressed subjects of Spain, but they also seem pretty proud of their role as colonialists. Many even claim Columbus was Catalan,' she said. 'It seems pretty perverse to me.'

Ortiz spoke particularly harshly about Jordi Bilbeny, a Catalan historian who leads an institute called Nova Història, or New History, which recognises Columbus as a Catalan admiral. Bilbeny says Columbus was really born into a wealthy Catalan family as Joan Colom i Bertran and set off in 1492 from the Catalan port of Pals and not from Palos de la Fronteras, in southern Spain. Ortiz probably overestimates the number of Catalans who back Bilbeny's efforts to rewrite the history of Columbus and America's discovery. But she did raise the significant fact that some Catalan academics have petitioned to carry out DNA testing on the remains of Columbus to establish his Catalan ancestry—without any conclusive result.

In one of her video works, Ortiz questioned public monuments in Barcelona that honoured historic Catalan figures like López, the banker, and Joan Güell i Ferrer, a leading entrepreneur. During the nineteenth century, both became wealthy 'by exploiting territories colonised by Spain, defending slave labour and extracting and bringing back wealth to Barcelona from other parts of the world,' Ortiz said. 'I don't see how anybody can present Catalonia as an exploited territory while defending this kind of shameful colonial history.'

Yet the fact is that countries normally have a morally convoluted past and traditions rarely have a linear history. Even traditions firmly anchored in a society, such as the sardana, the favorite folkloric dance of Catalonia. As with the formation of a human tower, the sardana puts no limit on the age, size or number of participants. The dancers hold hands and form a circle that enlarges when more people join. It is about dancing as a group, with no showcasing of individuals or couples.

'I love the sardana and everything it represents. But even if all Catalans seem to think of it as thousands of years old, we should acknowledge that it rose as part of a nationalistic drive,' said Narcís Serra, a former mayor of Barcelona. Despite its ancient origins, the sardana only spread from the countryside to the cities once the Romantic movement revived Catalan nationalism in the late nineteenth century. It made an awkward arrival in Barcelona. The newspaper *La Vanguardia* called it 'a strange dance' performed by some people during the city's 1892 centenary celebrations of the discovery of America. At that point, it may have been promoted as an alternative to the contrapás, a dance whose religious origins linked it to Carlism, a conservative and royalist movement.[2]

'Every country creates its mythology and symbols, the only question is whether they work and serve good or bad purposes,' said Jordi Pujol. The *castells*, for instance, work perfectly because 'it is all about building something with a lot of different people who are all treated equally,' Pujol said. 'It is something spec-

1. A record crowd filled Barcelona for the Diada of 2012 (Photo: Eduard Bayer)

2. Artur Mas salutes supporters in 2012, after defying Madrid's government (Photo: Eduard Bayer)

3. Readers check out books on sale during Sant Jordi (Photo: Albert Salamé, supplied by Diplocat)

4. Children climbing to the top of the Castell in Valls (Photo: Arnau Bach)

5. Franco's beheaded statue, splashed with paint during exhibition
   (Photo: Raphael Minder)

6. Berga's Patum festival overflows with medieval and separatist
   passions (Photo: Raphael Minder)

7. The excavated streets of the Born, the ground zero of secessionism (Photo: Wikicommons)

8. Barcelona suffered heavy bombing during the civil war, often by Italian aircraft (Photo: Wikicommons)

9. Franco's capture of Barcelona sparked a mass exodus across the Pyrenees (Photo: first published in "Le Patriote Illustré, a Belgian weekly, on 5 February 1939—Xavier Andreu, from Museu Memorial de l'Exili, in La Jonquera)

10. Dalí's theater in Figueres, Catalonia's most visited arts museum (Photo: Raphael Minder)

11. Salvador Dalí, a Surrealist painter and enigmatic Catalan (Image rights owned by the Fundació Gala-Salvador Dalí, Figueres)

12. Juanito Bayén prepares his coffee in the Boqueria market (Photo: Raphael Minder)

13. Barcelona's statue of Christopher Columbus, tall and nowadays controversial (Photo: Wikicommons)

14. Josep Maria Roig, defender of Barcelona's old stores (Photo: Raphael Minder)

15. Match day for FC Barcelona, "more than a club" for most Catalans (Photo: Raphael Minder)

16. Punt Avui's front page after Spain's 2011 national elections (Photo: Raphael Minder)

tacular that can actually be done and should be done as often as possible.'

That contrasts with Switzerland, Pujol argued, because nobody can reenact the story of William Tell, who fired an arrow and split an apple placed on his son's head. The story beautifully illustrates the courageous struggle of the oppressed against the unjust and powerful, but 'you can't repeat it, try it out and risk killing a child,' he said, with a flash of irony in his eyes.

Some symbols can fuel discord rather than unity. This is demonstrated by the history of an unusual dead pine tree, located in the middle of the Catalan countryside. The tree stands on the edge of a forest in the municipality of Castellar del Riu. Lightning once struck the tree, splitting its trunk into three. After that it became known as '*Pi de les tres branques*,' or the pine tree with three branches.

For a long time, the tree's tripart structure made it a potent religious symbol of the Catholic Holy Trinity, as it stood in the middle of mountainous countryside filled with monasteries and hermitages. Then nineteenth century Romanticism gave it a new Catalan significance. In 1888, Jacint Verdaguer, the writer who helped revive the Catalan language, published a poem that told the story of how King James I of Aragón, who ruled in the twelfth century, rested by the tree and watched its split trunk reach up to the sky. Marvelling at this sight, the king decided he should unite the three lands of Catalonia, Valencia and the Balearic Islands.

In 1901, a landowner donated the tree to Unió Catalanista, or the Catalanist Union, a separatist association that started holding annual celebrations there.

Such secessionist celebrations, however, did not please everybody. The tree bore the brunt of anti-independence anger, even after it was declared a national monument by the Catalan government in 1987. These days it is in particularly poor shape following an attack in 2014, when part of its split trunk was cut off. The base of the tree has been walled in, while metal strips were nailed into its trunk to prevent anybody from sawing it down. 'This tree was meant to be a symbol of unity but, in practice, it has been a major source of dispute,' said Toni Malé, the friend who took me to see it.

Malé, who works for the public administration in Barcelona, wants Catalonia's independence, but has no interest in flags, special trees or any other symbol. 'Symbols should be treated like Kleenex, something that can perhaps be used once but should then be thrown away,' he said. 'We all know the final goal is independence, something to look forward to, so there is no need to spend so much time looking at the past.'

Malé had another surprise waiting for me. A similar-looking tree stands in the forest. It is known as the *pi jove*, or young pine, and it has become an alternative pilgrimage for separatists. This tree, however, is alive rather than dead—an important and symbolic difference in itself.

A more anarchic approach to symbolism can be seen in the work of Albert Boadella, a playwright who often examines symbols irreverently. In 1974, he premiered a play, *Álias Serrallonga*, which included the first public performance of the Catalan anthem during Franco's dictatorship. At the end of the play, however, Serrallonga, its bandit protagonist, strips off and shows his backside covered with a Catalan flag.

'This was considered sacrilege by Catalans, but I have always wanted to target symbols and fetishes, even before realising just how misused they could become in Catalonia,' Boadella said. 'I believe part of the therapy of theatre is the destruction of the symbols and taboos that each society builds.'

Fighting bulls

Catalonia has not only protected its symbols and traditions but it has also distanced itself from some Spanish ones, particularly bullfighting. In 2010, the Catalan parliament banned bullfighting, as unjustified animal cruelty. Animal rights activists applauded the ban while the bullfighting sector countered that it was politically motivated, even in its timing. Catalonia's parliamentary vote came only one month after Spain's constitutional court controversially struck down part of a Catalan statute of autonomy.

'We are artists who try to stay completely out of politics. But now politicians, absurdly, are using us to promote Catalonia's independence,' Vicente Barrera, a bullfighter, told me at the time of the ban. 'If bullfighting had been something unique to Catalonia, I am 100 per cent sure that they would be fighting to the death to keep it.'

Some Catalan politicians acknowledged that the ban helped present Catalonia as more modern than the rest of Spain. 'When fox hunting was banned in England, was this about attacking English identity or defending more modern values?' asked Josep Rull, a Catalan lawmaker. 'In the same way, bullfighting used to be one of our traditions, but traditions should change if the values of a society change.'

The Catalan ban hit a bullfighting sector that had already suffered from cuts in public subsidies and a drop in bullfights because of the financial crisis. By the time the ban was voted in, Barcelona only had one bullring, the Monumental, down from three rings. The Monumental only attracted 400 season ticket holders compared to 19,000 in Las Ventas, the bullring in Madrid. Tourists normally purchased tickets.

'In the Catalonia that I grew up in, Barcelona was the place to go for bullfighting,' said Boadella, who was born in 1943. 'We had bull fights Thursdays, Saturdays and Sundays, with the kind of passionate following that you don't even have now in Madrid. But Catalan political indoctrination destroyed its popular appeal.'

In fact, the politics of bullfighting has shifted considerably over the last century. Catalan politicians have turned their back on the bulls, even though some of the great leaders of pre-war Catalan nationalism—like Francesc Macià and Lluís Companys—were aficionados.

Nandu Jubany, a Catalan chef, recounted how his father was 'such a fan that he would escape from military service to watch the bulls.' Jubany's own efforts to combine his support for independence with his admiration for bullfighting have been more complicated. He posts comments online about bullfighting, but then gets trolled by separatists. Before secessionism turned bullfighting into an unwanted symbol of Spain, 'the bulls were also ours,' Jubany said. 'If I, born in the cradle of Catalonia, cannot defend that, who can?'

Yet some Catalan patriots were already trying to ban Spanish culture from their children's education before the civil war. In his memoirs, Antoni Tàpies, a famous Catalan painter born in 1923, described how his parents would denounce Spanish culture. 'My parents considered the world of bull fights, flamenco (they called it maid's singing) and all the manifestations and festivals of folklore and religion that the other peoples of the peninsula were tethered to as low, vulgar, ridiculous and even savage,' Tàpies wrote. 'They inculcated those notions in us, and contrasted them with European culture.'[3]

In response to the 2010 ban, the bullfighting sector took legal action, claiming that the ban breached basic rights enshrined in the Spanish constitution. Six years later, Spain's constitutional court sided with the plaintiffs, ruling that Catalonia could not ban a practice that formed part of the cultural heritage of the Spanish state. While animal rights activists have since decried the court ruling, many have also questioned Catalonia's application of a ban that made an exception for the *correbous* summer festivities, on the grounds that the *correbous* apparently neither mistreats nor kills the bull.

Santi Vila, who is responsible for culture within the Catalan regional government, is a politician who likes to hedge his bets. On the wall of his office, he has a framed photo of Puigdemont, the Catalan leader and his current boss. On the other side of the frame, however, Vila keeps the photo of Mas, Puigdemont's predecessor. He joked that he likes to flip portraits depending on who visits, because 'it's best not to upset anybody within the party.'

THE SYMBOLISM OF A TOWER AND A TREE

He equally likes to keep an open mind on bullfighting. He told me that politicians should have allowed it to die 'a natural death' rather than fuelling controversy and introducing a political ban. 'We should be coherent,' he said, implying that it was disingenuous for Catalans to say that they wanted it out because it was Spanish culture.

The *correbous*, meaning 'bulls in the street' in Catalan is held mainly in Valencia and southern Catalonia. It is also considered cruel by animal activists. Some Catalan towns have banned it, such as Olot, following a local vote in June 2016.

However, in the southern village of La Galera, home to 830 inhabitants, the *correbous* went ahead a few weeks later without any protest, starting with an afternoon parade of the bulls around the streets. Later that evening, the villagers moved to a makeshift bullring on the outskirts of the village, made up of a semi-circle of concrete walling. The other half of the ring was formed by wooden barricades, sustained by trailers.

As darkness fell, the ring was lit up and the *correbous* began. Around the ring, parents held infants, watching the action as they munched crisps and salted sunflower seeds.

Once the first bull was released from the pen, a group of youngsters jumped into the ring and started to gesticulate, shouting and whistling to attract the bull's attention. Running at full speed, they crisscrossed the ring and clambered up the barricades whenever the animal threatened to charge. If the bull got too close, the runners sought shelter on a platform at the centre of the ring. At one point, however, one of the bulls managed to leap onto the platform, almost landing on top of a teenager who had been taunting the animal. The crowd screamed.

The final act involved a dozen men tying the animal to a large wooden box. They attached an iron structure to its horns and set the ends on fire. The projectors were dimmed. Once released, the bull paced around the ring in the darkness, like a ball of fire on the move.

'I don't really like bulls or make much time for them, but I really respect our traditions,' said Ramon Muñoz, the mayor of

179

the village, as he followed the proceedings. The *correbous*, he argued, needed to be defended as a specific local tradition, rather than in the name of Catalan culture. 'Other Catalan towns have *castells*, but we care zero about *castells*,' he said. 'Each to their own.'

In the past, the *correbous* used to be 'pretty wild', the mayor said, with spectators even throwing stones at the bulls. But the event has become tightly regulated since Catalonia's bullfighting ban came into force. The veterinarian who oversees the *correbous* is 'like a policeman now, making sure every rule gets respected,' the mayor said.

Along the barricades, signs warned that only spectators aged fourteen or older could take part in the *correbous*, under the new rules introduced since 2010. What about young children watching? 'If the animal isn't made to suffer, I don't see how this is such a bad example for children,' Muñoz replied. 'Personally, I've stopped going to football matches because I got sick of the abuse I hear there. Parents shout insults even in front of their children.'

Planting flags

As separatism has gained traction, Catalonia's officials have planted the Senyera, the official Catalan flag, all over its territory, while simultaneously removing the national flag of Spain. In some instances, officials like Berga's mayor, Venturos, have even used the Estelada.

There are also, however, residents who have resisted the replacement of the Spanish flag with a Catalan one. At the entrance to the village of Batea, there are two flags, the official Catalan one in the middle of the roundabout, and another one a few metres away, flying the coat of arms of Spain and looking in better shape.

This Spanish flag was raised in 2014 as an act of defiance by Josep María Suñe, a local wine farmer, and a few friends. They put their flag on a private plot of land, with the permission of the landowner, and spent about €200 on their project. They used their tractors to bring bags of cement to build the base and then got a crane to lift the flagpole.

Suñe showed up to talk to me in a local bar. He wasn't wearing the colours of Spain but those of FC Barcelona. The next day, he planned to travel to Barcelona to watch his favourite team play. 'I would die for Barça and also die for Spain—and there's absolutely no contradiction,' said Suñe. 'Removing a Spanish flag or booing the hymn is a serious failure of respect, but it would also bother me if somebody burnt a Catalan flag.' He described the independence movement as 'a process that is going backward' and is splitting society. It's just like in mathematics, he said, 'when you add and multiply, you always go forward to a bigger number, but when you subtract or divide, you're always going back.'

For all his concerns about Catalan independence, Suñe has many secessionist friends and always speaks Catalan. In fact, 'I normally never want to speak another language, certainly not Spanish,' he added. The one exception, he said, is 'after 3 am, when I sometimes switch to English, if there's been a lot of drinking.' And with that, Suñe finished his drink and walked off, proudly readjusting his Barcelona shirt.

A bloody brand

The Catalan flag, or Senyera, is linked to the coat of arms of one of the most iconic characters in Catalonia's medieval history, Guifré el Pilós, or Wilfred the Hairy. Wilfred was a count who established the House of Barcelona. He received his coat of arms for showing bravery in battle. Legend has it that the king found the wounded Wilfred and slid his blood-stained fingers over his shield, leaving red streaks. The finger streaks became the four red bars on a golden background that form the Senyera.

Wilfred fought gallantly in the ninth century. Yet the first record of the four bars as a coat of arms is from 1150, when seals were made showing King Ramon Berenguer IV on horseback, holding a shield with the striped bars. In the nineteenth century,

Romanticism swept Catalonia and turned Wilfred into a flag bearer for Catalan nationalism. Artists then started to spread the story of the bloodied fingers. It was even celebrated in a poem called *The bars of blood*, written by Verdaguer in 1880.[4]

The story of Wilfred is an essential part of the narrative of great acts of bravery that is taught in every Catalan school. According to Marc Lite, co-founder of Firma, a Barcelona branding consultancy, 'It's a version of Catalan history that is a bit like the history of Asterix and Obelix,' the famous French cartoon characters whose village resists the Roman empire. 'At school, we were told that we were the little guys in the Middle Ages, ready to defend our values and flag,' he said. 'When your country is explained to you like that, you store that information and then turn it into something as an adult, whether you use it to build up a company or a country.'

Lite has given branding advice to some of the world's biggest consumer goods companies, like Unilever and Pepsico. He is also passionate about surfing and has created a brand of surf clothing, so his studio has something of a Californian feel. Surf-boards are stacked in the entrance and employees skateboard between the desks. Lite himself wears a beach-style shirt, covered with drawings of female swimmers.

I visited Lite and other design and advertising experts because I was interested in the growth of nation branding as a field of both academic research and government consultancy work. Countries are no longer ranked only according to their economic output, productivity and other economic data. Rankings are also elaborated using valuations of each country's brand and soft power. Marketing and advertising executives switch from advising companies to governments and sometimes even enrol in public administration. Under President George W. Bush, Charlotte Beers became US Under Secretary for Public Administration and Public Affairs, having previously headed two of the world's largest advertising agencies. In short, she went from marketing Uncle Ben's Rice to explaining American values to Muslims after terrorists destroyed the World Trade Center.

THE SYMBOLISM OF A TOWER AND A TREE

I wanted to hear from Lite and others how they rated secessionist efforts to promote independence and whether they felt the separatist movement could benefit from hiring somebody like Beers, who could apply corporate branding methods.

In response, Lite explained that every city, state or region works nowadays on improving its branding, from Silicon Valley to the dozens of countries vying to become the next fashionable tourism destination. On a sinister level, even the Islamic State makes carefully planned marketing choices about its brand, such as its black flag and the orange outfit worn by hostages in its filmed beheadings, part of its anti-Guantánamo propaganda.

'When I discuss branding with a client, we start by finding things that form part of their DNA, their common values,' he said. 'The real difficulty is that independence is not a common value—or at best one shared by half of Catalans. So if the Catalan government pushed this independence branding too far, it would not be representative of all citizens.' Rather than focus on independence, the Catalan government should stick to making the referendum its goal, Lite suggested. 'There's more to be achieved by promoting this common and democratic value of Catalans wanting the right to decide,' he said.

This advice came from a self-declared separatist, who has a taste for modern culture and the latest consumer trends, but who is also excited by the ancient tale of Wilfred. 'The story of our flag is one of the greatest possible—it's so convincing, so personal,' he said. 'If our flag had just been drawn by some famous designer, the whole story would feel fake. But this is something from hundreds of years ago, written with blood, so it comes with this idea that we are supposed to pour our blood into everything we do.'

Lite's company has settled in the industrial district of Poblenou. The local authorities have sought to make this area the design and innovation hub of Barcelona, articulated around an oversized design museum that opened in December 2014. Poblenou's rebirth has been helped by lower rental prices than in downtown Barcelona, encouraging companies to relocate.

The day before my visit, 11 September 2016, hundreds of thousands of pro-independence demonstrators had once again taken to the streets to celebrate the Diada, Catalonia's national day. The branding and design professionals saw plenty of room for improvement.

Veronica Fuerte, the founder of Hey, a design studio located in one of Poblenou's former industrial warehouses, told me, 'From the point of view of a graphic designer, the Diada looked pretty much like chaos—it had no clear direction and was badly designed.' Participants in the Diada had bought an official t-shirt, on which there was the slogan—*A punto*, or 'Ready,—and a yellow concentric circle as the logo. The logo 'just looked like a fried egg,' said Tilman Solé, a partner in another company, called Mucho. 'It would have been far more powerful just to use the Catalan flag.'

In other words, the push for independence is more powerful when it is kept simple.

12

THE DECLINE OF CHURCH AND CROWN

In November 2010, Pope Benedict XVI travelled to Barcelona to consecrate the city's most famous edifice—the Sagrada Família—as a basilica. It was a historic milestone for the Catholics of Catalonia, where the Church has declined faster than in some other parts of Spain. The announcement of the Pope's visit led to a surge of building activity around the unfinished monument. As the deadline neared, about 300 workers scrambled to ensure that the nave and high altar would be ready for an unprecedented papal Mass held before 7,000 people.

Pope Benedict's visit was also a chance to showcase the latest architectural features of the Sagrada Família. The basilica is the most visited symbol of Christianity in Catalonia, but also a source of discord. It has remained a work in progress ever since its brilliant Catalan architect, Antoni Gaudí, died after being hit by a tram in 1926, and the continuation of his work has long been debated.

Critics believe the Sagrada Família has drifted too far from the vision of its creator. Some also insist that it has more appeal as one of the world's greatest unfinished buildings.

'We run the risk of simply creating a pastiche of the Gaudí concept,' Narcís Serra, a former mayor of Barcelona, told me. 'From the point of view of respecting his work, it would have been much better to stop at the point when we were no longer sure that this was exactly what he wanted.'

A local and veteran architect, Jordi Bonet, led the construction work ahead of the papal visit. When I met him he was eighty-five years old but still climbed the spiral staircases of the basilica as if he were a teenager. He seemed giddy with excitement about his latest additions, including an engraved lectern.

According to Bonet, Gaudí himself never imagined the Sagrada Família would be finished exactly according to his vision. 'Almost every cathedral has been the work of many people over many centuries,' Bonet said. 'Even when he was in charge, there were forty different sculptors working for Gaudí. Of course he inspired them, intervened and commented on their work—but it remained the work of several different sculptors.'

By the time Pope Benedict visited, Bonet had already been working on the Sagrada Família for more than two decades. Bonet's own father, who was also an architect, befriended Gaudí and helped him in his work. At the time of his death, Gaudi had completed less than a quarter of his own project. Work is now well beyond the halfway mark, although some challenging elements lie ahead.

Bonet followed the writings, drawings and revolutionary plaster models left by Gaudí as much as possible. He himself first came to the Sagrada Família as a seven-year-old, when he attended Communion in its crypt, and is deeply versed in the Catholic liturgy. The subsequent intervention of some artists, however, has sparked controversy, most notably in the 1980s when Josep Maria Subirachs, a Catalan sculptor, introduced his own style of work to adorn one of the Sagrada Família facades. The detractors—as Subirachs himself predicted—have been forced to swallow their outrage, not least because the Sagrada Família remains so popular that it is almost self-financed by its entrance fee receipts. It welcomes over 10,000 visitors a day, with large queues forming outside even on rainy weekdays.

In 2016, however, the Sagrada Família faced a more significant stumbling block in the form of a complaint from Ada Colau, Barcelona's far-left mayor, who had decided to take on Catalonia's religious establishment. Colau and her administration accused the board of the Sagrada Família of both working without a building permit and failing to submit plans to tear down existing residential structures in order to finish the basilica's esplanade. Barcelona's city hall also claimed the Sagrada Família had failed to pay its taxation dues.

The Sagrada Família's board denied wrongdoing. It said it had a building permit, but that dated 1885. It had been issued to Gaudí by the town of Sant Martí de Provençals, where the monument was due to be erected and which was at the time on the outskirts rather than within Barcelona. The board said it had never been asked for any new kind of permit.

Yet Colau's complaint hit a nerve in the middle of a broader debate concerning the tax exemptions of the Catholic Church. This was compounded by its surreptitious property registrations, not least that of the extraordinary mosque-cathedral of Córdoba. The dispute over the Sagrada Família seemed to illustrate how secular debates over money and tourism had encroached onto the spiritual realm.

Tourism has also turned Montserrat—the monastery visited by Himmler—into a place whose holy significance can be somewhat lost amid heards of visitors. Despite its remote mountain location, some 2.5 million people reached Montserrat in 2016 (compared to the 4.5 million who visited the Sagrada Família).

Many visitors are devout Catalans who pay homage to Montserrat's patron Virgin of Catalonia, whose dark statue (which was originally painted white) stands high above the congregation, at the back of the altar. Others, however, are tourists who spend more time hiking the mountain trails around Montserrat, catching the spectacular views of the monastery from above.

But at sunset, once the tourists, religious pilgrims and groups of schoolchildren head back down from Montserrat, the atmosphere changes starkly. On the drizzly October night that I slept there, the monastery became shrouded in fog, so that its bell tower could be heard but no longer seen. At 8.15 pm sharp, the monks started their dinner, in silence, while one of their number read aloud from a platform overlooking the refectory. The reading told the story of Eleanor of Aquitaine, who had married first Louis VII of France and then Henry II of England.

Outside such moments of reflection and prayer, the monks were very open to discussing the challenges facing Catalonia and its clergy with me. They did not pretend to have all the answers, but they had clearly given much thought to the changes in Catalan society. Several of Montserrat's monks are eminent scholars who combine their monastic life with giving lectures in universities or corporate seminars.

All are aware of how the relevance of Catholicism has declined faster in Catalonia than in other parts of Spain. According to Manel Gasch, a monk, theologian and lawyer who also serves as the administrator of the monastery, 'religion is in the doldrums.' He talked to me about the decline of religion within his own family. 'My grandparents were considered the martyrs of the war, part of the generation who gave their blood for the faith,' as religious Catalans were hounded by Franco's opponents during the civil war. 'My parents used to go to Mass daily, and all my cousins are baptised and at least partly educated in Catholic schools. But in the next generation, only half are baptised,' he said.

Gasch also contrasted the role of Catholicism in Catalonia unfavourably with that in some other parts of Europe. 'In northern Italy, which has a society similar to Catalonia's, the reality of Christian life is completely different,' he argued. He offered some historic reasons as to why Catholicism had fared worse in Catalan society. First, he said, Catalonia modernised early because of the industrial revolution, and then it embraced anarchism and other anti-religious ideas more enthusiastically than other parts of Spain.

In July 1909, this move towards secularism turned violent, during riots that became known as the 'Tragic Week' of Barcelona. The riots started because of an army conscription order, but the mood of anti-clericalism took hold, so that it was mostly churches and convents that got destroyed.

THE DECLINE OF CHURCH AND CROWN

After the civil war, Franco promoted his National Catholicism from Madrid. This too convinced many Catalans to break free of the church because it was an institution associated with a dictatorship. The fact that the Catalan church withdrew its support from the regime during Franco's final years did little to reverse the decline.

Clergymen and politicians often make uneasy bedfellows. But in Catalonia, I found that the Catholic clergy was facing a particular conundrum. On the one hand, most of its representatives did not want to get dragged into the secessionist conflict. On the other hand, some of them seemed worried that their silence could help widen the distance between the Catholic church and Catalan society.

In Berga, I met a left-wing mayor, Montserrat Venturós, who had decided to leave religion out of her town's main festival. (See Chapter 11) 'Just because things have always been done a certain way doesn't mean you shouldn't adapt to how we live and feel now, in a secular country,' she told me. 'In the twenty-first century, I see no need for the church to play the same role in this feast.'

After celebrating Sunday Mass, Marc Majà, the local priest, expressed sadness at the sidelining of the church from the town's Patum festival. But he also emphasised that he was not looking for 'a new conflict between church and state when we have so many more serious problems to deal with… The church is here to welcome and accompany its people, whatever path people decide to follow.'

Most of the Catalan church has firmly endorsed the message of greater tolerance delivered by Pope Francis since 2013. In Sitges, I met Father Josep Pausas Mas in his Baroque parish church, which overlooks the Mediterranean. Its beautiful octagonal bell tower can be seen from the far end of the seaside promenade.

Pausas Mas was reluctant to discuss the political divorce between Madrid and Barcelona. 'I don't speak about independence, because this is about my personal opinions,' he said. But when we talked about another sensitive issue—homosexuality and Catholicism—he had no such qualms. Sitges is considered one of Europe's top gay holiday destinations and its priest explained that giving the communion to gay people fitted with his understanding of the teachings of Pope Francis. The Catalan church, the priest argued, 'has always had a special social role, helping Catalonia to be a land of welcome, open to all races and traditions.'

Back at Montserrat, however, the community does not reflect this diversity. Not one of the monks was born outside Spain and only a handful come from outside Catalonia. 'If a candidate came from Mexico or Argentina, we would probably tell him to go and try monastic life in Mexico or Argentina, where it would be easier to integrate,' said Gasch.

Here, too, none of the senior monks of Montserrat wanted to be quoted on the topic of secessionism. Yet during my reporting, I discovered a notable exception to this reticent approach to politics within the Catalan church.

In 2014, Teresa Forcades was granted leave by her Benedictine convent, which is also in Montserrat. Forcades is both a nun and a doctor. She studied in the United States and received doctorates in medicine and theology. She used her leave to set up a new political movement fighting for Catalan independence that, she explained at the time, was driven by her belief that independence could fetter capitalism and reduce inequalities in Catalan society. She also questioned whether an independent Catalonia should remain within the European monetary union.

Some would argue that Forcades was mainly fighting the austerity policies of Catalonia's then conservative leader, Artur Mas. She told me Mas had launched 'an outrageous attack on our welfare society.' In the end, she decided not to stand in the 2015 Catalan elections. Her political movement still exists, but she spends much of her time outside Catalonia, lecturing on other topics, like the impact of technology or vaccines. Occasionally, she returns to her monastery and religious contemplation. She remains deeply committed to secessionism, but does not want to sing from the same hymn sheet as many separatist politicians.

Josep-Lluís Carod-Rovira, a former separatist politician, acknowledged the tensions between Catalans and the church, but argued this was symptomatic of a broader disagreement between Catalans and the Spanish. 'What a lot of foreign analysts don't seem to understand is that there are already millions of Catalans whose emotions are no longer invested in Spanish institutions,' said Carod-Rovira, who now heads the department of social diversity at Barcelona's Pompeu Fabra University. Catalan officers, for example, are a dying breed because most Catalans view the Spanish army as 'a hostile administration' based in Madrid, he claimed. 'Look for a list of Catalans in the Spanish military and you won't really find any.'

Royal disdain

It is the Spanish monarchy that is the most discredited institution of all. Most Catalans feel no more for Spain's King than they would for the Queen of England, Carod-Rovira claimed.

If that is true, it stands in stark contrast to the warm Catalan response forty years earlier when King Juan Carlos first visited Catalonia as monarch. In February 1976, three months after Franco's death and the re-establishment of the Spanish monarchy, Juan Carlos spoke some Catalan during a speech in Barcelona. He talked about 'the exceptional importance' of Catalonia and the lineage of monarchs tied to Catalonia. At that point he stood as a symbol of Spain's return to normality, after decades of dictatorship.

Thirty-six years later, in September 2012, just after the largest pro-independence street rally in Barcelona, King Juan Carlos tried to strike the same emotional chord. He called on his subjects to 'recover and strengthen the values that have stood out in the best moments of our complex history,' in an open letter published by the royal household. Without mentioning Catalan secessionism specifically, Juan Carlos warned that 'the worst that we can do is divide forces, encourage dissensions, pursue pipe dreams, deepen wounds.'

On this occasion the words of King Juan Carlos irked many Catalans. The separatist politician Francesc Homs responded with a mix of disappointment and sarcasm to the royal missive. 'We absolutely agree that we should not pursue pipe dreams, that is very far from what Catalonia is proposing,' Homs told a news conference.[1]

In June 2014, Juan Carlos abdicated in favour of his son, Felipe. He ended his long reign in physical and moral pain, as he became increasingly sidelined by injuries and discredited by scandals. Juan Carlos was born in Rome during Spain's civil war and grew up in exile, uncertain whether Franco would restore the monarchy. By contrast, Felipe received a broad education that included studying in America and learning Catalan, in the firm knowledge that he would become king.

Felipe VI is 'the first monarch who profoundly understands the ins-and-outs of Catalan life,' Xavier Vidal-Folch, a journalist, wrote in a book on Catalonia. But unfortunately Felipe failed to make the 'audacious but prudent' step of delivering his inauguration speech in Spain's different languages, as a new monarch in a country like Belgium would have done. That failure was particularly surprising since Felipe had arrived on the throne with a strong sense of the different atmosphere surrounding the monarchy. In 2012, he had to replace his ailing father at the football final of the King's Cup between Athletic Bilbao and Barcelona. The match was held in Madrid, but the fans of both teams booed the two symbols of Spain: its monarchy and its national anthem.

Shortly before becoming king, Felipe visited an international telecommunications congress held in Barcelona. As he was greeting entrepreneurs, a Catalan businessman refused to shake his hand. Felipe initially ignored the affront but then, brushing aside royal protocol, turned around and tried to convince the defiant businessman, Àlex Fenoll—to no avail. Fenoll told Felipe that 'you will be my friend when you respect me' and other Catalans, by facilitating an independence referendum.

Fenoll was an exception. Most Catalan politicians and businessmen have 'tried to avoid testing the waters with the monarchy,' Vidal-Folch told me. The Spanish royal family continues to make newspaper headlines in Catalonia, as well as filling the glossy pages of the popular press. The Princess of Girona foundation, a royal charity started in 2009, has been able to attract sponsorship from several Catalan companies, led by La Caixa.

But overall, it is common to find Catalans displaying an indifference towards the monarchy that sometimes borders on ignorance.

Speaking to a group of foreign journalists in 2016, Raül Romeva, Catalonia's foreign policy chief, got confused about how many children Felipe had. It was not a memory slip. 'I'm incapable of reciting the royal family tree to you,' Romeva said. 'I just don't know it.' But he had little difficulty remembering what he considered to be a major royal *faux-pas*, in 2001, when King Juan Carlos delivered a speech in Barcelona in which he said that 'nobody was ever forced to speak Spanish.'[2] Given Franco's ban on the Catalan language, the comment had sparked outrage.

Romeva contrasted the British monarchy with that of Spain. 'The Queen of England has worked hard also to be Queen of the Scots, but this has never happened here,' he said. Borja de Riquer, a Catalan historian, similarly talked about how Queen Victoria came to symbolise the British empire, while 'we have not had one single king in Spain who has been a symbol of a modern nation.'

Many Catalans view Spain's dynastic change at the start of the eighteenth century—from Habsburg to Bourbon—as a switch to a model of governance that sought to crush diversity in Spain. The Bourbons imported and imposed French centralism, which left no room for the recognition of the singularity of Catalonia. Perhaps this historical narrative is over-simplified, but it continues to undermine the reputation of the Bourbon monarchy in Catalonia.

As separatists have intensified their criticism of Spain's monarchy, they have been joined by left-wing politicians whose motives are not connected to breaking up Spain. Podemos, Spain's main far-left party, views the monarchy as a symbol of Spain's antiquated and unrepresentative institutional system. After becoming mayor of Barcelona, the left-wing Ada Colau removed the bust of Juan Carlos from her city hall. She then renamed the Barcelona crossroads that honoured Juan Carlos as Cinc d'Oros, the name it had before the civil war.

Gabriel Rufián, a lawmaker from Esquerra Republicana, believes the republican values of a representative democracy are incompatible with a monarchy. 'It seems very strange to me that a person who has received no votes from anybody lives in a palace and receives €8 million a year,' he said in reference to the budget of the royal household.

Where does this leave Spain's monarchy? In November 2016, I watched the awkward opening session of the Spanish Parliament. Felipe and his family were applauded by a majority of lawmakers, but not those representing Podemos and the Catalan and Basque parties. The King then delivered a very solemn speech in which he defended Spain's unity and the rule of law. He said that he held Catalonia close to his heart, but carefully avoided the secession issue and said instead that the monarch should stick to political neutrality.

It was not the kind of inspirational speech that could help break a political deadlock. Instead, it played into the hands of separatists who believe that Felipe's ascension to the throne was the last and missed chance to boost pluralism in Spain. Quim Torra, a separatist publisher and lawyer remarked to me, 'Naively, I thought there might be a new opportunity with Felipe VI, a chance to create a Spanish version of the Commonwealth. But that wasn't to be.'

13

FINANCING SPAIN'S ECONOMIC POWERHOUSE

When it was first lit up in 1864, the Buda lighthouse was the tallest metal lighthouse in the world. Standing 52 metres high and painted pearl grey, it looked almost like a precursor to the Eiffel Tower.[1] It dominated the delta of the Ebro, a vast and thinly-populated expanse at the southern tip of Catalonia, in whose waters fishermen catch eels and shrimps while farmers tender rice paddies along the shores.

The lighthouse went on to survive not just violent storms, but the ravages of the Spanish civil war. It was restored after being burnt down by Republican forces who feared a Fascist invasion from Mallorca and therefore removed distinctive structures along the coast that could have helped enemy aircraft.

The cause of its eventual destruction was not war but man's attempt to control nature. Once peace had been established, Franco's regime decided to build reservoirs along the Ebro river to increase usage of its water. The reservoirs helped irrigate more farming land upstream, but they also slowed the river's flow, which reduced the amount of sediment deposited in its delta and allowed more sea water to seep in. As a result, the delta retreated so fast that the lighthouse was left exposed to huge waves and collapsed in a storm on Christmas Eve in 1961. After the big Mequinenza reservoir was completed in 1964, near the border between the regions of Aragón and Catalonia, the delta's inland retreat continued until the Buda's replacement lighthouse was also submerged.

Nowadays, there is nothing but a platform with a warning light floating where the lighthouse once stood. The platform is about two miles offshore, only reachable by boat.

The delta continues to retreat at a pace of about four metres every year, according to environmentalists. The shortfall in sediment is being compounded by global warming, which is also facilitating the sea's advance. Right now Spain has the highest proportion of water held in reservoirs in Europe. Beyond this the Spanish government has been looking to add more dams and reservoirs along the Ebro.

Yet these projects have been delayed by political wrangling and fierce environmental opposition, not least from the European Parliament. A national hydrological plan was approved by the Spanish Parliament in 2005, then revised, and finally endorsed a decade later by the government of Mariano Rajoy, Spain's conservative prime minister. The plan is to divert and transfer more water from the Ebro to the main cities from Barcelona to Murcia, in southeastern Spain.

The Ebro was called Hiberus in Latin, which is why, presumably, the Romans named those living along the river as Iberian. But this rich history has not stopped politicians from believing that the Ebro should primarily be used to resolve the water problems of the eastern part of the Iberian peninsula. When Franco's regime built reservoirs, 'Spain was an autocracy and the national obsession was with making the country self-sufficient,' said Manolo Tomàs, 70, one of the main spokesmen of the Platform for the Defence of the Ebro. Nowadays, he argued, 'the model for territorial development is still the one established under Franco, of concentrating resources around some major urban economic poles.'

Under different Spanish governments, water management has always hinged on the concept of regional solidarity, between 'a rich Spain in the north with an abundance of water and a poor south that is presented as suffering acute thirst,' he continued. But in Tomàs's view, much of the water in the south is earmarked for its tourism and construction boom. 'In Murcia, nobody is dying of thirst, but they want to have more hotels and more tourism, which is of course very costly,' he said.

Tomàs told me this as we sat in a café in Tortosa, below an apartment that he and other militants first occupied in the 1970s, to run a clandestine radio station in the final years of the Franco regime. 'Unfortunately nobody listened to it,' he said, with a self-mocking smile. After Franco's death in 1975, Tomàs became something of a serial activist, protesting against all sorts of government decisions, including that of allowing NATO military bases on Spanish soil.

Ironically—given his current preoccupation—one of his first protests was in 1973, when he joined other students to demand that the local authorities build a petrochemical factory in Tortosa. 'We all took to the streets to get the petrochemical project because there were really no jobs around here,' he said. However, the factory ended up being built near Tarragona instead. Tomàs no longer backs the petrochemical industry and has also revised some of his other earlier views, including on whether the Ebro's delta was a Catalan asset. 'We used to talk about the water of the Ebro being ours, which was wrong, because it really belongs to all of us,' he said.

These days, the activists defending the delta sound almost as wary about plans drawn up by Catalan politicians to divert more water to Barcelona as about those presented in Madrid. They insist that such an environmental issue should transcend the secessionist conflict. Starting in northern Spain, the Ebro runs for 565 miles before reaching the Mediterranean.

'The borders of rivers must be defined by mountains and not by politicians,' said Susana Abella, another activist. 'The Spanish government has tried to present this as a problem of Spain versus Catalonia, but we are not interested in such a position, because there is a water problem whatever nation we build.' In 1993, the Socialist government in Madrid guaranteed a water quota from the Ebro for the Aragón region, which borders

Catalonia. That agreement removed political opposition within Aragón to the construction plans along the Ebro, but it pushed the issue to the top of the Catalan political agenda.

For the fact is that the management of the Ebro has also created tensions within Catalonia. In 2000, environmentalists protested against Jordi Pujol, then Catalonia's leader, for backing the latest Ebro plan concocted by José María Aznar. Pujol later acknowledged that supporting Aznar's plan was 'a political and psychological mistake', but not a technical error.[2] Such a plan could bring more water to inner Catalonia, he said, while the delta's inhabitants would get significant financial compensation.

'If any future Catalan government acts like the one in 2000, it would be such a disaster for the river that we would not care whether we had independence or not,' said Abella. Her point is borne out by the fact that protests continued even after separatist parties took charge in Catalonia. In June 2016, about 15,000 people—dressed in blue—marched in Barcelona, behind a large banner that read, 'To stem the flow of the Ebro is to kill the delta.' In Tortosa, which is crossed by the Ebro, giant blue graffiti adorn the bank of the river, with a similar message that 'the river is life'. Next to it, a red line has been drawn to show the water level needed for the Ebro to function as a waterway. The Ebro now flows across Tortosa at less than half its speed before Franco built reservoirs.

Listening to passionate environmentalists, it is easy to feel that their concerns over natural resources not only transcend borders but should also be pushed far higher on the political agenda. Amid a power struggle between Madrid and Barcelona, what efforts are being allocated to resolving such issues that may—apart from anything else—have a profound impact on the next generation?

Ferran Bel, the mayor of Tortosa, told me that environmentalists felt 'some distrust toward all politicians,' including those of Catalonia. But he argued that the chances of protecting the Ebro would increase if Catalonia gained independence because the debate over the Ebro would become 'state versus state, on an equal footing.' This has been the case in negotiations between Spain and Portugal over the management of the Tagus river, which crosses western Spain before reaching Lisbon. The Ebro dispute is currently 'a domestic conflict that could be turned into an international conflict,' Bel argued. The European Commission could no longer ignore the Ebro as a domestic issue for Spain, he continued, if Catalonia lodged a complaint as a new member state of the European Union.

Easing roadblocks

While water management has led to significant conflict, Catalans have found more common ground on other transport issues.

Catalan dissatisfaction concerns everything from having toll roads, as opposed to free state highways in most of the rest of Spain, to the shortcomings of El Prat, Barcelona's airport. The airport operates a significant European network, but fewer intercontinental flights than Barajas, the airport in Madrid.

However, it is the Catalan rail network that invariably tops the list of transport grievances. Since 1992, when a Socialist government inaugurated a high-speed train link between Madrid and Seville, Spain has remained at the vanguard of rail technology that it has also exported worldwide. Spain has the biggest high-speed railway network per capita in the world and is only second overall to China.

The 2008 financial crisis put Spain's rail frenzy on hold. But after Spain's economic growth started up again in late 2013, most work resumed, even as national rail companies accumulated significant losses from operating unprofitable routes. The surreal fallout from this is that Spain is still dotted with oversized and empty train stations located in the middle of nowhere next to giant car parks.

Some more recent additions to the railway have directly benefited Catalonia, including a high-speed connection linking Barcelona to Girona and Figueres that was inaugurated in 2013. But in southern Catalonia, there was still, at the time of writing, a stretch of rail running for about twenty-five miles on a single track along the so-called Mediterranean corridor. The Mediterranean Corridor is a major transport artery for both freight and passengers running along the Spanish coast toward France. When Spain added high-speed trains, rail transport was only able to help with about 4 per cent of the goods moved across Spain. Instead, the highways along the Mediterranean Corridor were filled with trucks, which carry two-fifths of the country's land exports.

The twenty-year delay in overhauling the single-track section of the Mediterranean Corridor is an example of 'total negligence' by the Spanish government, according to Germà Bel, a Catalan lawmaker and professor of public policy. Its origins date to the eighteenth century, he argued, when the Bourbons became Spain's royal family and imposed the French system as a role model. 'This resulted in a project to make Spain into a country like France and turn Madrid into a capital like Paris, on which everything converges,' said Bel. 'Transport policy becomes a metaphor for the building of a nation.'

This policy was also arguably developed because of concerns over how to supply Madrid, which as a landlocked capital stood at a disadvantage compared to cities like Barcelona or Valencia that also had shipping routes. In response to this problem, in 1870, Spain adopted a railways law to ensure that any major railtrack reached Madrid. That legislation, Bel argued, has continued to underpin all of Spain's rail construction.

Indeed, I have often found that travelling by train through Madrid is the fastest way across Spain, even if the map might suggest otherwise. The travel time between Barcelona and Alicante is roughly the same whether via Valencia or Madrid, although the detour via Madrid is twice the distance.

Another major problem with Spain's 1870 railways law was that it ran counter to Spain's industrial development, which was led by cities like Barcelona and Bilbao. The first railway line, opened in 1848, linked Barcelona to Mataró, but it was the private initiative of Miquel Biada, who was born in Mataró and had already helped build a railway line in Cuba.

None of these issues has stopped the Spanish government from continuing to focus European rail policy on Madrid. Spanish officials carried on promoting a central rail corridor—linking France and southern Spain via Madrid—even after the Mediterranean corridor was declared a European priority project in 2001 by Siim Kallas, then European Commissioner for transport. Now this foot-dragging over the Mediterranean corridor is affecting other coastal regions, particularly Valencia and its export industry. 'The Mediterranean corridor is a good example of something important that has been done too late,' said Ángel de la Fuente, an economist who is the director of a Madrid-based think tank, known by the acronym of Fedea. Even so, de la Fuente warned against jumping to the conclusion that an independent Catalonia would have easily completed the Mediterranean corridor. As in the case of the Ebro, relations with neighbouring regions can become tense. In fact, until 2015, the neighbouring region of Valencia was controlled by the Popular Party, which was far more inclined to follow instructions from Madrid than from Catalan separatists.

As with any infrastructure project, de la Fuente pointed out, there is 'a high demand for infrastructure in the abstract, but a strong resistance to anything that may affect one's backyard.' Separatists claim that Spain's rail deficiencies are disproportionately concentrated around Barcelona, in a below-par network of commuter trains. The metro link between El Prat and the city of Barcelona was inaugurated in 2016, while that connecting Barajas airport to central Madrid opened in 1999.

Yet even when you take these problems into consideration, a foreign visitor is still likely to be impressed by Catalonia's infrastructure, especially if compared to railways in somewhere like the United States, or indeed to how backward Spain's infrastructure once was. At the time of writing, Rajoy was promising to make amends and invest €4 billion in Catalonia's rail infrastructure, as well as to complete the Mediterranean Corridor by 2020.

The emphasis on Madrid's centrality has affected the airline industry too. In the 1970s, when Eduard Voltas was a small child, 'Barcelona's airport was a hut, a pretty ridiculous thing. My parents would take me to watch the planes from what looked like a home terrace,' he told me, 'when other cities already had very modern airports.' Voltas, a publisher, lamented the ongoing shortage of intercontinental flights from Barcelona. Catalans should be able 'to fly from Barcelona to any part of the world without a Madrid stopover,' he said.

Aznar, Spain's former prime minister, defended his record, telling me about the huge investments that he had made in Catalonia. But he also recalled that, whatever his government built, there would always be fresh demands made by Pujol. 'My question to Pujol was always the same: when are you going to feel comfortable?' Aznar said. 'The answer was never, because to be a nationalist, you have to remain uncomfortable.'

Asking for money

Whatever your perspective, the relationship between Madrid and Barcelona certainly soured under Aznar. But the debate over Catalonia's finances didn't become truly fraught till almost a decade later, under a different conservative prime minister amid an economic meltdown.

Mariano Rajoy's election victory in November 2011 meant that he took office during a recession, with record joblessness and a budget deficit that was significantly higher than the previous Socialist administration had declared it to be. By May 2012, the government also had to seize control of Bankia, Spain's largest savings bank, and oust its chairman, Rodrigo Rato, Spain's former finance minister. The near-collapse of Bankia and other banks then forced Rajoy's government to negotiate a European banking bailout.

FINANCING SPAIN'S ECONOMIC POWERHOUSE

By that point, Spain was at the epicentre of the euro debt crisis that had started with a bailout of Greece, before spreading to Ireland and Portugal. At the same time as facing a banking collapse, Spain was also struggling to finance its public debt. If Spain had needed a bigger bailout, it would have risked collapsing Europe's monetary union structure.

In such dramatic circumstances, Rajoy had priorities that went way beyond regional politics. But in the summer of 2012, his government was forced to supply emergency funding to several regions, exacting greater fiscal discipline in return from each area. Catalonia received €5 billion out of the €18 billion disbursed by the government's regional fund.

Going cap-in-hand to Madrid was a brutal reverse for Catalonia, which had outpaced most other regions during Spain's decade-long economic boom. Between 2002 and 2009, Catalonia had also outperformed other parts of Europe, including powerful regions like Lombardy in Italy and Rhône-Alpes in France that fell back in the same period.[3] To offset its mounting debt problems, the Catalan coalition government froze many investments that were already underway. It also decided to appeal to its citizens' patriotism. In October 2010, it successfully issued €2.5 billion of domestic bonds.

Catalonia had not sold this kind of domestic bonds since the mid-1980s. Shortly after the sale, Antoni Castells, Catalonia's then finance minister, looked visibly happy with the outcome when I visited him in his office. He described the sale as 'a big success' which would set an example for other regions.

Yet some leading economists did not applaud Castells. Instead, they criticised Catalonia for offering excessively generous terms for its bonds, which could set a dangerous precedent for other regions. According to Jordi Galí, an economist who runs a research centre at Barcelona's Pompeu Fabra university, the Catalan bond sale was 'a terrible deal for taxpayers'. Galí noted that Catalonia offered investors a rate far above that of the Kingdom of Spain and close to what was then the long-term financing cost of Greece, Europe's most distressed economy.

'One man's ceiling is another man's floor, so what makes the Catalan debt very attractive from the point of view of the investor makes it also very costly from a taxpayer's perspective,' Galí said at the time. He warned other regions against following Catalonia's lead.

Edward Hugh, a British economist living in Catalonia, also issued a dire warning in late 2010 about Catalonia's finances, predicting that the bond sale would only provide short-term respite. Catalonia's bond sale, however, was about political survival—significantly it was held one month before the Catalan elections. The Catalan government needed 'to show that it [was] managing the situation politically,' said the economics professor Xavier Vives at the time.

However, it proved too little, too late. On 28 November 2010, Castells and the rest of the coalition administration were ousted from office by Artur Mas and his party, Convergence and Union. (A year later, in Spain's national elections, voters similarly punished the Socialist government for economic mismanagement, electing Rajoy's conservative Popular Party instead.)

Once in office, Mas was forced to make deeply unpopular cuts. But he also began to raise the vexing issue of Catalonia's contribution to a Spanish fiscal system that redistributed tax revenues to poorer regions of Spain. Soon, Mas called on Rajoy's government to offer Catalonia a new fiscal pact, akin to that of the Basque region, which manages its own taxes.

Mas and Rajoy clearly were on a collision course. But Mas received support from other Catalan parties, as well as from citizens increasingly convinced that Catalonia had more to gain than to lose by breaking away from a crisis-hit Spain. As the recession deepened, secessionism shifted from fringe to mainstream political thinking in Catalonia.

A few days after a landmark pro-independence rally in Barcelona held on 11 September 2012, to mark Catalonia's national day, Mas visited Rajoy to seek better fiscal terms for

Catalonia. The meeting was short and tense. Mas left Madrid saying that Rajoy's response was 'a no without nuances'. He accused Rajoy of losing 'a historic opportunity' to improve relations with Catalans.

'The people and society of Catalonia are on the move, as we saw on September 11, and not willing to accept that our future will be grey when it could be more brilliant,' Mas told a news conference. 'We always thought that Spain would understand the aspirations of a people like the Catalans,' he added. 'I understand now that this is not the case.'

Displaying his usual caution, Rajoy did not publicly respond immediately. Instead, he used a speech before Spanish lawmakers to call for more Spanish unity. 'This is not the moment to generate more problems or political instability,' Rajoy told Parliament.

The escalation of the dispute between the two conservative leaders surprised many observers. 'The demands from Catalonia have developed a lot faster than anybody expected,' Jordi Alberich, director general of the Cercle d'Economia, a Barcelona-based business association, told me at the time. 'A crisis situation for Rajoy has become a lot more complex.'

Indeed, Catalonia had suddenly become Rajoy's biggest domestic headache, as he also remained under pressure from international creditors.

Mas was threatening to pull away with a region whose €200 billion economy was the same size as Portugal's and accounted for almost almost one fifth of Spain's output. The Catalan share of the regional debt burden was also disproportionately large. At the time, Catalonia had €42 billion of the €140 billion of debt owed by Spain's seventeen regions.

José Antich, who was then editor-in-chief of the newspaper *La Vanguardia*, said he had warned Rajoy during a luncheon in August 2012 against ignoring Mas's fiscal demands. However, Rajoy responded that his government did not have the financial resources to offer Catalonia a sweeter tax deal. 'Rajoy's big successes have always come from deciding not to do anything,' said Antich wrily.

Some conservative politicians in Madrid have gone for the jugular. They maintain that Mas turned the spotlight onto Madrid in order to obscure the mismanagement of his administration, as well as to divert attention away from his highly unpopular austerity cuts and Catalan corruption scandals.

'When you drive a place into bankruptcy, it isn't normally due to the fact that the system was bad but that it was badly managed,' said Aznar.

According to Joan Tapia, a newspaper columnist, by embracing independence Mas switched from getting boos in public for making spending cuts to receiving applause for confronting Madrid. 'It helped him change his image from cost cutter to protester,' he said.

For Rajoy's government, however, the financial crisis was a chance to push through an administrative recentralisation of Spain. It justified this as a means of increasing efficiency, according to Andreu Mas-Colell, who served as Catalonia's regional finance minister during the financial crisis. Mas-Colell told me the recentralisation continued after the crisis, with the help of Spain's judiciary. As an example, he cited a ruling in the spring of 2016 by Spain's constitutional court against new Catalan legislation to prevent utilities from disconnecting the gas and electricity of poverty-stricken households, particularly during the winter months. The issue turned into a social scandal later that year after an elderly woman died in an apartment fire in the Catalan city of Reus, started by a candle that she was using after her electricity was cut off because of unpaid bills.

'It seems that [ultimately] any regional regulation that creates a different situation is seen as suspect, because it can create differences among Spaniards,' Mas-Colell concluded.

From Sicily to Denmark

So what is the country model for an independent Catalonia? Since 2012, a dozen or so possible examples have been mentioned, mostly—but not always—flattering. That particular year, Mas recommended in an interview that Catalonia should aim to become 'the Massachusetts of Europe'. (Though perhaps he was simply seeking to connect with the American readership of *The New York Times*.) By contrast, Francesc de Carreras, a law professor opposed to Catalan independence, warned in a speech that an independent Catalonia would most likely resemble Sicily, 'filled with Mafias, gangsters and vendettas.'[4]

Joaquim Nadal, a historian and former politician, told me that the search for role models is nothing new. 'Catalans have always wanted to be like somebody else. This goes back as far as the seventeenth century, when we wanted to be Holland,' he said.

He spoke from experience. After Franco's dictatorship, in 1979 Nadal became the first democratically-elected mayor of Girona and quickly announced that Girona should model itself on Florence. 'Journalists made so much fun of the Florence model that I finally decided that enough was enough, we should just be ourselves,' he said. Country models have been swapped and dropped whenever circumstances have changed. 'Recently, we wanted to be Finland—until Nokia got into trouble,' he continued.

More often, however, comparisons have been drawn with countries from northern and central Europe that are similarly-sized to Catalonia. Strikingly, most do not have the debt and unemployment problems of Catalonia. In *Like Austria or Denmark*, a book published in 2014, three Catalan economists compared Catalonia to eight other European countries. Yet there were prominent exclusions, not least Portugal, one of the economies rescued during the financial crisis. 'In fact, Portugal could serve as a warning that independence is not a guarantee of prosperity,' they wrote.[5]

For all their search for foreign role models, Catalan economists could be proud that the region had played a historic part in shaping Spain's own economy. Before adopting the euro, Spain used the peseta, whose name comes from *peceta*, the Catalan word for 'small coin'. The peseta became Spain's currency in 1868, thanks to Laureà Figuerola, a Catalan economist who helped unify Spain's monetary system while he was a minister in the Madrid government.

Wilson economics

More recently, a significant number of Catalan economists have joined the secessionist frontline, facing off against colleagues who present independence as a financial shipwreck. In 2012, six Catalan academics launched the Wilson Initiative, to counter what they described as 'campaigns of misinformation that pollute the discussion about the real consequences of a hypothetical Catalan state.' The initiative took its name from Woodrow Wilson, the American president and winner of the Nobel Peace Prize, who tried to turn 'self-determination' into a fundamental principle that could help avoid another major conflict after the First World War.

A century later, scholars who admired Wilson happened also to be some of the most talented Catalans teaching overseas, in universities like Princeton, Harvard, Columbia and the London School of Economics. They were outsiders to the Spanish system, who could speak their mind. This was essentially because they 'never need to pass through Madrid or require any funding or scholarship from the Spanish goverment,' according to Guillem López Casasnovas, an economics professor who was not part of the Wilson group.

López Casasnovas, who also sat on the board of the Bank of Spain, continued that, 'Distance allowed them to stand apart from the Catalan establishment, because Catalonia is like New Delhi, a place where there are sacred cows on the road and if you meet one of them on your way, you have to stop.' In contrast, the Wilson economists 'have just been pushing aside' such cows, he declared. He added that the Wilson economists helped show that 'the idea that Catalans are provincial and navel-gazing is completely wrong. Those I know who are most pro-independence are all those who have spent time overseas.'

Yet Antón Costas, an economics professor at the University of Barcelona, offered a more provocative take on why economists outside Catalonia might want independence. From the nineteenth century onward, Costas argued, history was filled with examples of intellectuals who went overseas and then developed mixed feelings about their own country. These intellectuals were normally not planning to return to their country of origin, but still wanted to 'make radical reform proposals, often without any real political viability,' he said. 'They could make proposals about a country that is theirs but that is now far away from them, proposals that they would probably never make for the country in which they have actually chosen to live.'

Among these Wilson economists, Xavier Sala i Martín, a professor at Columbia University in New York, is the most colourful—quite literally. He owns about 350 brightly-coloured jackets, which he said was enough not to have to wear the same one more than once a year. His jacket craze started when he returned to Barcelona from a masters degree at Harvard to realise that 'fashion was slavery' in Spain, since everybody had switched the colour of their clothing in his absence (from pastel to military green, he recounted). Sala i Martín also wanted to challenge the idea that men should wear dark suits while women could innovate. When he showed up for a consultancy job at the International Monetary Fund and was advised to change outfit, Sala i Martín responded by checking the dress code regulations of the IMF to demonstrate that there was no rule about colour.

'It seems men are condemned to the mediocrity of grey and navy blue and I rebelled against that,' he said. But Sala i Martín's main rebellion is nowadays against anybody who believes independence would be disastrous for Catalonia. 'I don't know any intelligent economist who says Catalonia would not be economically viable,' he said.

Economists are divided over how to calculate Catalonia's current tax burden. But the debate has also been about Catalonia's future tax model, as well as how Spain's resources and debts would be split should Catalonia break away. Should Madrid and Barcelona fail to reach an amicable divorce, Sala i Martín suggested that Catalan politicians could use the debt negotiations to counter any Spanish threat of an economic boycott.

Spain's debt, he said, was nominally only that of the Kingdom of Spain, so the onus was on Madrid to convince Catalonia to walk away with a share of the debt burden. Rather than Catalonia facing insolvency, 'Spain will have to negotiate to avoid bankruptcy,' he said.

The price of secessionism

Another issue of contention is the cost for a new Catalan state to replace Spain's existing civilian and military administration. In a book against secessionism, the economists Josep Borrell and Joan Llorach challenged almost every hypothesis made by separatists about the cost of creating a new state. For instance, rather than the separatist estimate that a Catalan army could cost €350 million a year, Borrell and Llorach noted that the membership fee for joining the NATO military alliance is €3 billion per state.[6]

How would an independent Catalonia finance itself? Would its banks continue to receive funding from the European Central Bank? Would Catalonia's debt get downgraded by credit rating agencies, raising its borrowing costs? 'There are some good economists who stop being good economists when they speak about things with a national dimension,' said Ángel de la Fuente, a Madrid-based economist. 'In these things, they seem to lose their objectivity, for love of the country.'

Economists have also debated how to measure the return on what Catalans pay in taxes. The current Spanish tax distribution system offers room for improvement, but it does not fit the 'Spain robs Catalonia' argument of separatists, de la Fuente said. In fact, he argued, Spain's regional financing system is 'certainly not worse than many others and probably better than quite a few, including the German one.' The Catalan demands for a more favourable fiscal pact arguably presented Catalans in a bad light, as citizens no longer willing to support those in poorer regions. Catalans, however, insist they only want to set fairer limits on their generosity.

Solidarity in Spain has miscued incentives, said Joaquim Nadal, a former Socialist politician, pushing poorer regions to rely on hand-outs. 'Instead of teaching people how to fish, they have been fed fish every day, and with my money,' he said.

Corporate silence

However, such discussions have largely been confined to political and academic circles. The bosses of Catalonia's largest corporations have mostly stayed on the sidelines of the secessionist conflict. One exception is Grifols, the world's largest maker of blood plasma. The Catalan flag floats outside a 72,000-square-foot research and testing laboratory owned by Grifols in San Marcos, Texas. Three other flags stand alongside it, a blue one that has the company logo, that of Texas and that of the United States.

But there is no Spanish flag outside the lab, since Víctor Grífols, the third-generation chairman of the company, has made clear that he does not wish to represent a country to which he no longer wants to belong.

Grifols was one of the few Spanish corporations that went on an acquisition spree during the financial crisis, more than doubling its size. That expansion, in turn, helped distance Grifols further from Spain, even if it keeps about 3,000 employees in the country. In terms of income, Spain accounts for only about 5 per cent of the company's revenues.

Most Catalan companies do not enjoy Grifols' situation. Instead, many remain heavily dependent on the rest of Spain, where they either sell most of their products or have significant infrastructure investments. Corporate Catalonia cannot therefore cut itself off from the rest of Spain, said Andreu Missé, a

Catalan journalist who now heads Alternativas Económicas, a Madrid-based publication. As an example, Missé cited Caixabank, Catalonia's largest bank, which has two-thirds of its retail branches in the rest of Spain. 'The Catalan companies would not be as big as they are if they had not managed to occupy their natural market, which is Spain,' Missé said.

Under Isidro Fainé, who was president until 2016, Caixabank tiptoed around the independence debate because Fainé never wanted to risk 'bringing protestors to his front door,' said Joan Tapia, a newspaper columnist.

In 2013, even as the secessionist drive was in full swing, I realised it was almost mission impossible to find out how Catalan executives viewed independence. At major business conferences, executives made trite or bland comments, spoken in the kind of wooden language used by bureaucrats of the United Nations when discussing sensitive issues. As a reporter, I decided to grab the proverbial bull by the horns and visit the area around Sant Sadurní d'Anoia, the farming heartland of cava, the sparkling wine that is Catalonia's most emblematic produce. At that time, cava producers had already suffered from a boycott organised by Spanish consumer associations, to protest Catalonia's secessionist movement.

José Luis Bonet Ferrer, the chairman of Freixenet, the largest producer of cava, talked to me about his Catalan resistance during Franco's dictatorship. In 1966, he was suspended as a university professor because he backed a student protest that became known as the 'Capuchinada', since the protestors locked themselves up in a Capuchin convent. But his patriotism, Bonet said, did not mean he supported secession. 'Catalonia is an essential part of Spain,' Bonet said, 'and that is how it should continue.' Bonet also argued that 'businessmen have the right to worry if politicians create tensions rather than seek dialogue.'

Since then, the corporate response to independence has gathered force, albeit at a snail's pace.

In late 2014, Carlos Rivadulla helped set up an association of entrepreneurs opposed to secessionism, called Businessmen of

Catalonia. The association was created 'at least two years too late,' Rivadulla admitted. 'We delayed because it initially seemed to us that this independence proposal was so absurd that there was no need to worry,' Rivadulla said. 'It felt a bit like dealing with small children—sometimes it is best not to react the moment they get upset.'

Rivadulla is an energetic intellectual property lawyer, who also founded Ecofrego, a company that patents and manufactures cleaning products in Spain and Bangladesh. The company's flagship invention is a wash bucket that keeps clean and dirty water apart. Separating from Spain, however, would be 'an economic disaster,' said Rivadulla, not least since it would force many companies operating across Spain to take on the cost of splitting into two separate fiscal entities, taxed independently by Madrid and Barcelona. Rivadulla said his association had about 400 members, but acknowledged that it was hard to get some corporate opponents of independence to stick their heads above the parapet.

Many companies, he said, depend on the separatist politicians of Catalonia to run their businesses, from getting licenses and building permits to collecting subsidies. 'I honestly wonder how I would have acted if I was in that kind of dependent situation,' he said.

In fact, some Catalan bosses have warned their own employees against secessionism. In September 2015, shortly before a Catalan election, Jorge Gallardo, the chairman of Almirall, a pharmaceutical company, released a video addressed to his shareholders and employees. He did so because he felt 'morally obliged' to warn against Catalan independence, despite his company's 'deep Catalan roots'. Sitting in front of a shelf lined with ancient pharmacy flasks, Gallardo spoke in the stiff tones of somebody who was 'extraordinarily worried' about the impact of independence on his business.

Some Catalan entrepreneurs, however, seem ready to sacrifice short-term revenue in return for a brighter economic future in a Catalan state. Xavier Carbonell, the chief executive of

Palex, a supplier of medical devices, was among the separatist crowd that took over central Barcelona during the Diada of 2012. As a business strategy, Carbonell acknowledged that Palex faced 'some short-term risks' if Catalonia seceded unilaterally, since Palex got 90 per cent of its revenue from the rest of Spain. But, he still felt that 'a people has the right to manage its own resources and money.'

However, the secessionist idea has gained credence among companies based overseas. Cesar Molins heads Ames, a family-owned maker of car parts with factories in Spain, Hungary, the United States and China. He said he had come to embrace separatism because the government in Madrid refused to discuss with Catalans how to raise fiscal and economic efficiency. 'When you have a dispute that is so big and bitter, the best way forward is that each goes his separate way and goes home to manage his own money,' Molins said.

More executives could follow Molins' example and speak up—in favour or against—ahead of a formal Catalan independence referendum. In the run-up to the Scottish independence referendum of 2014, many energy companies, banks and others only joined the debate at the eleventh hour. For instance, Lloyds, the banking group, warned only a week before the referendum that it would move its official headquarters from Edinburgh to London if Scotland broke away. So far, the corporate restraint in Catalonia is perhaps mostly an indication that executives don't believe independence is around the corner, whatever their separatist politicians might say.

14

THE BUSINESS OF SHARING

The *Llibre del Sindicat Remença*, or peasant syndicate book, is one of Catalonia's most important historical documents. Yet it is not on display in any museum. Instead, it is kept in the backroom in the municipal archives of the city of Girona, in a plain grey cardboard box, stacked among rows of turquoise-coloured filing cabinets.

Dating from around 1448 and written in Latin, the book is a record of meetings held between serfs, known as *remences*, who were fighting against seigneurial abuses. In 2013, the book was added to UNESCO's 'Memory of the world' list of unique books and documents.

Before opening the book, Joan Boadas, the director of Girona's archives, put on a pair of white gloves and took a little time to explain its importance to me. Catalan peasants came together to fight feudal abuses, he said, including the right of a lord to sleep with any woman at his service on her wedding night. 'What I'm about to show you is extraordinary evidence of a very advanced social organisation, the kind that certainly didn't exist in Castile at that time, and probably nowhere else either,' Boadas said. The serfs selected representatives, or *syndics*, from different parts of Catalonia, to negotiate better living conditions on their behalf. In return, the serfs promised to stop any uprising against the abuses, which were collectively known as *mals usos*, or bad practices.

The book is testimony to 'the determination of men fighting for their basic rights,' Boadas said. In 1486, King Ferdinand of Aragón responded by removing some of the abusive feudal rights, in a document signed in the monastery of Guadalupe. This ushered in a period of peace and farming prosperity.

Shortly before my visit to Girona, Carles Puigdemont, the city's former mayor and current leader of Catalonia, used the peasant syndicate book as a historic example of Catalans successfully joining forces. 'I think this is the earliest evidence discovered of workers uniting to defeat servitude,' Puigdemont told me. 'It's incredible to think that this push for people to form associations in Catalonia dates back so far.'

While there's no direct line between what was happening in the fifteenth century and what happens now in Catalonia, it's striking that modern Catalan society continues to pivot around cooperative and associative projects, often born out of necessity. According to Spain's labour ministry, it is home to one fifth of the cooperatives in Spain.[1] Joseba Polanco, the director of the Confederation of Catalan Cooperatives, told me that the first cooperative founded in Spain was created in 1843 in Barcelona by about 200 textile workers. It was also Catalan workers who organised Spain's first trade union. The other region where cooperatives sprang up was the Basque Country, which also led Spain's industrial revolution. Amid tough working conditions in fast-expanding factories, 'a collective spirit' developed, Polanco explained, with 'the idea that it's better to resolve problems together than individually.'

Salvador Cardús, a sociologist, told me that in Catalonia, the cooperative movement also reflected 'the absence of state structures capable of responding to the needs of a newly industrial society. At the end of the nineteenth century, society was forced to find its own solutions for hospitals and other basic needs, because it had been abandoned by the Spanish state,' he said.

Similar problems affected the countryside. Catalan farmers were driven to create some of the first cooperatives as they struggled to replant their fields after Europe's phylloxera epidemic devastated vineyards in the late nineteenth century.

Over a century later, a very different disaster triggered an unprecedented collective response in Catalonia. The bursting of Spain's property bubble in 2008 led to a huge number of people being unable to pay their mortgages. An association of volunteers, the Plataforma d'Afectats per la Hipoteca, known as PAH, began a nationwide fight against home evictions in Barcelona and elsewhere. The PAH initially crusaded against Spanish banks that were trying to throw out tenants, arguing that many of these banks were demanding government rescue funding—in other words, Spanish taxpayers' money.

In June 2012, Spain's banking crisis forced the government in Madrid to negotiate a banking bailout with the European Union. The bailout eventually helped save the banks and lift Spain out of recession. But some of the problems of the property crisis lingered on. By 2016, the PAH was still fighting banks, but also Wall Street investment firms that bought Spanish assets on the cheap after the crisis. The PAH argued that Spanish banks should never have been allowed to sell housing to foreigners without first offering improved mortgage terms for distressed home owners.

As part of its protest, the PAH had occupied forty-seven buildings across Spain, from which about 3,000 people had been evicted. One of these apartment blocks stood near the Barcelona headquarters of the PAH—a stark example of Spain's uncontrolled property boom. The block had been built in 2007 by a Spanish company that went bankrupt before it could even put the apartments up for sale. Instead, squatters moved in.

In May 2016, I spent an afternoon listening to homeowners who were fighting eviction. Each had a different tale of hope, followed by setback and despair, but everybody highlighted the essential support received from the PAH's volunteers. The PAH 'gave me the weapons but also the will to fight back,' said Wilson Troya, who moved to Barcelona from his native Ecuador in 2002 to find work in Spain's then booming construction sector.

Four years later, he bought an apartment, together with a friend. In late 2011, however, he lost his job and started to fall behind in his mortgage payments. His request for leniency from his bank went unanswered until the PAH stepped in. 'When I went to the bank accompanied by their volunteer, it was the first time that somebody in the bank even bothered to notice my presence and actually listen,' Troya told me.

The PAH's activism won so much public attention that its main spokesperson, Ada Colau, then switched to politics and was elected as mayor of Barcelona in 2015. (See Chapter 10)

Santi Mas de Xaxàs, an official from the PAH, who has been volunteering for the association since 2013, told me, 'It makes sense that this kind of movement started in Spain, given our disastrous financial situation. And even more sense that it should be centred on Barcelona, which was the big anarchist city at the start of the last century. It's a place that has always combined very tight neighbourhood organisation with a high level of social discontent,' he said.

Like others, Mas de Xaxàs joined through word-of-mouth, after his cousin, who made videos for the PAH, invited him to attend one of the association's weekly meetings. At the time, Mas de Xaxàs was running two start-up companies, one developing phone apps and the other promoting gastronomy. 'I think it only takes one meeting to get hooked by the power of this movement and its people,' he said. 'This has just brought a lot more meaning to my life than trying to earn more money.'

Since then, Mas de Xaxàs has devoted almost two-thirds of his working time to an association whose mission can also be risky. In July 2016, he was indicted for occupying a branch of BBVA, one of Spain's largest banks, to protest against its evictions. Beside facing a lawsuit, Mas de Xaxàs acknowledged that there was also a personal cost to his volunteering work against evictions. 'It can be hard for a girlfriend to understand why you're not having dinner with her and why you're instead standing at 2 am inside an occupied bank branch,' he said. 'But

I guess each of us needs to decide what sacrifices are worth making in life.'

A big street party

The spirit of cooperation also extends to more sociable activities.

Every August, the Barcelona district of Gràcia holds a week-long celebration in which residents' associations compete to have the best-decorated street. Each association chooses its own street theme. In 2016, one street was transformed into textiles workshops from a century earlier, while another was redesigned to raise the profile of Europe's migration crisis. Other streets sought literary inspiration. On Travessia de Sant Antoni, for instance, the decorations were inspired by the travels of Jules Verne, with a replica of an air balloon and a bar shaped as the Nautilus submarine.

The Gràcia celebrations date back to 1817, when Gràcia was still separate from Barcelona. Though Gràcia was officially incorporated into Barcelona in 1897, it has kept a 'small town' atmosphere that helps attract thousands of Catalans to its fes-tivities, where they are joined by a horde of foreign summer tourists. The festivities receive some public subsidies, but what makes it special is that they are entirely managed by the neigh-bourhood associations. In return for volunteering their time and work, the members of each association share dinner on tables set up on their street.

On Verdi street, the local association chose a Californian theme for 2016. A copy of the lion emblem of the Metro-Goldwyn-Mayer studios was placed above an arch, and labelled as Metro-Goldwyn-Verdi. The ground had a version of the Hollywood Walk of Fame, studded with stars that each bore the name of a Gràcia street rather than an actor. Further down the Verdi street, Californian surf boards hung overhead. Each decoration had been produced at minimal cost. The roaring lion, for instance, was made with chicken wire and then covered in painted newspaper.

'Everybody comes to look at the street decorations, but the most important part of our feasts is what happens before, people coming together to make all these decorations,' said Dolors Martínez, a feisty member of the Verdi association who has always lived in Gràcia. 'This is all about having a relationship with a lot of people with whom I only really share one single thing, our Gràcia.'

The Verdi association's ninety members pay an annual fee of €50 each, but more volunteers and entire families join them to help during the week of celebrations. The children of Gràcia also feature prominently, like Artur Panasiouk, a ten-year-old who wore an oversized devil's head during a street parade of giant statues, or *Gegants*. At home, Panasiouk collects miniature versions of the giant statues, his mother explained. 'Some kids play video games, but Artur much prefers our giants,' she said.

In other parts of Spain, town halls rather than residents organise their feasts, said Sergi Font, the president of the Verdi association. As he observed the crowd, he said, 'It can seem a bit chaotic, but this is really the result of great neighbourhood cohesion, of many months of working hard together.'

Milking the forest

There is no such sense of urban chaos in the forest of La Fageda d'en Jordà, where Cristóbal Colón took over a farm in 1984. Three decades later, his company, La Fageda, was a leading producer of yoghurt in Catalonia and the main challenger to Danone, the French food multinational that has a yoghurt factory near Barcelona. But what makes La Fageda really special is its people. About 60 per cent of La Fageda's 300 employees have a mental disability, ranging from schizophrenia to Down's Syndrome.

Cristóbal Colón—his name translates in English as Christopher Columbus—became an entrepreneur after a lot of soul-searching. 'I first needed to save myself—and saving myself comes through saving others,' Colón said. Colón trained as a tailor, but also dabbled in Marxism, at 'a time of revolutionary upheaval across the whole of Europe.' After his military service, Colón did not return to his tailor's workshop and instead started studying psychoanalysis.

'Like any person with a minimum level of intelligence, I have long been asking myself who I am, where do I come from, and where am I going,' he said. 'To understand consciousness, I wanted to understand the subconscious, which is what led me to the asylums.'

In the final years of Franco's dictatorship, however, Spain's asylums operated in Dickensian conditions, with mentally ill patients treated almost like convicts. Shocked by such treatment, Colón got permission to start his own alternative project with a group of people who had been diagnosed as mentally ill. He visited the mayor of Olot, a town near the Fageda forest, to seek help.

'I went in with this beard of mine, which then had even more hair and was darker,' Colón said, stroking his white beard. 'I said that I had arrived from an asylum, that my name was Christopher Columbus and that I had fourteen mad people with me.' The mayor looked at him, Colón recalled, as if 'he was expecting somebody to come in after me and say that he was Napoleon Bonaparte.'

Yet Colón is highly persuasive. Once he had recovered from his surprise, Olot's mayor agreed to allow Colón to use an abandoned building for his project. Colón moved in, but then decided that this urban environment was not suitable for mentally ill people. He started hiking around the region and came across a disused farm in a forest, which he bought with a mix of public subsidies and bank loans. 'My dream was not to make yoghurt, but to have a company in a natural environment that would be enriching for these people,' he said. 'One of the big discoveries that I made is that work is fundamental for people, not just to earn enough for a living, but to realise their potential as individuals and feel useful.'

Colón's project also benefited from an overhaul of Spain's legislation for disabled people, following the 1982 election of the Socialists led by Felipe González. The new law gave subsidies and tax exemptions to companies whose staff included mostly disabled workers, Colón recalled.

In 2015, La Fageda added a new assembly line, with German machinery and a yellow robot arm that moves pots of yoghurt along a conveyor belt. In the adjacent farm, the cows are milked on a high-comfort rubber floor, while the animals and workers listen to Baroque music that is piped by loudspeakers around the farm.

Colón spends zero money on advertising, yet his company generates revenue of €17 million a year and his yoghurts sell at a premium of about 40 per cent above the average market price. Customers buy his yoghurt because it tastes good, Colón said, but also because of exceptional word-of-mouth publicity, spread by the 50,000 people who visit the farm every year. Such visitors, he argued, also help change the perception of the mentally ill. 'When they then see someone who is mentally ill, they can start to imagine that this guy could be doing the same as those they have seen working here,' he said.

La Fageda was set up as a cooperative, in which each worker is a part-owner who also has a say in the most important decisions. But Colón eventually changed the legal structure to that of a foundation, to ensure his mentally-ill employees would not be left in the lurch if he died. 'I have entered the final part of my life,' said Colón, who was sixty-seven when I met him. 'Death is the best reminder that life is the greatest thing.'

Colón was born in the neighbouring region of Aragón, but he argued that Catalan society was more receptive to his kind of project and work ethic. 'Clearly this initiative was not started by a Catalan,' he said, 'but Catalans have a unique way of understanding life, culture and social movements.'

Colón has not been alone in employing the mentally ill in Catalonia. In the 1980s, a team of psychoanalysts at a Catalan centre for autistic children began studying how the act of eating helped children raise self-awareness. Better usage of the mouth could then improve speech. Their work resulted in the launch of Cuina Justa, a food catering company that nowadays distributes about 4,000 meals every day to schools and companies, prepared by a staff that includes 130 workers with serious mental disabilities. Cuina Justa translates as 'fair cuisine' in English, but the name is also a word play on Cassià Just, a former abbot who promoted the project.

As with La Fageda, the starting point at Cuina Justa was the idea that a job could prevent a mentally ill person feeling like a second-class citizen, isolated and under publicly-funded medical supervision. 'The more money that is put into mental health, the more people with mental health issues there seem to be,' said Francesc Vilà, a psychoanalyst who helped launch Cuina Justa. 'People then become passive subjects of the health system instead of being part of society.'

Vilà said that Catalonia accounted for about 40 per cent of the jobs assigned to the mentally ill in Spain. That overrepresentation, he argued, also reflected the importance of the 'menestral', or artisan, in a Catalan society that valued wealth derived from working more than inherited money or property. Catalonia's work ethics are also tied to its location, Vilà argued, 'on the periphery of a state that hasn't cared for us.' In many other parts of Spain, he claimed, 'the tendency is to rely on the state, while Catalans believe in participating and cooperating.'

In 1976, shortly after Franco's death, a priest in the town of Tàrrega started helping five families with disabled children. The priest's work developed into another Catalan association that has half of its staff of 500 with some form of disability. The association offers services ranging from catering to dry-cleaning and gardening. It also has a biscuit maker, El Rosal, which was a family business dating to 1920, and was set to close when the association offered to take over its machinery. 'I had never made any biscuits before, but we were all able to learn how to make them in the same way they have been made for the past century,' said Núria Cendoya, who runs El Rosal.

As managing director, Cendoya earns €1100 a month. Her disabled workers get Spain's minimum salary, equivalent to €764 a month in 2016. Cendoya qualified as a physical education teacher and previously ran her own gym. 'I was of course doing well physically but I felt there was something missing inside of me,' she said. Her earnings are now lower, 'but there is a huge emotional return, because this is no longer a job but more like a life project.' Cendoya said that her biscuit sales benefited from the same feel-good factor as the yoghurt of La Fageda. 'People are willing to pay a bit more in order to feel better about what they buy,' she said.

Of course, you can create a similar emotional dynamic outside Catalonia, Cendoya acknowledged, but the working model of her association might be harder to replicate. 'Volunteering has really been incredible in Catalonia, especially since the [1992] Olympic Games,' she argued, when thousands helped organise the event. (There is nowadays a square in Barcelona dedicated to the Olympic volunteers.) In her own family, she said, three of her relatives travelled to Greece to help refugees fleeing war-torn Syria. 'They told me there were volunteers speaking Catalan all over the camps,' she said.

Helping at sea

A prime example of the Catalan contribution to Europe's refugee crisis comes in the person of Òscar Camps, a lifeguard who travelled to Lesbos, with a colleague and only their swimming fins, in October 2015. The Greek island was just starting to become overrun with refugees landing from Turkey. Within two hours of arriving in Lesbos, Camps and his colleague were throwing off their shirts and shoes to jump into the sea to save people from drowning, after watching a boat sink close to the island's rocky northern coast.

THE BUSINESS OF SHARING

Lesbos 'changed my view on almost everything,' said Camps. 'I realised that Europe's inaction was absolutely deliberate, a decision by the European Union to use the Mediterranean and the Aegean as dissuasive tools, to send the message to people that they shouldn't try to come because they would drown.'

While working in Lesbos, Camps started a crowdfunding campaign to launch his non-government organisation, Proactiva Open Arms. He himself initially invested €15,000 in buying equipment, as well as bringing two jet skis to Lesbos from Spain. Camps also reused some rickety vessels that had been abandoned by refugees on the shores of Lesbos. The crowdfunding was a success, but the big breakthrough came some months later, when Livio Lo Monaco, the Italian owner of a Spanish bed mattress company, loaned his yacht to Proactiva. The *Astral* was built in 1970 by Philip Rhodes, a top yacht designer, and had initially been owned by Cornelius Vanderstar, the owner of an aluminium company. The *Astral* was then refitted and stripped clean of its luxury elements, to become a rescue boat for refugees instead.

The *Astral*, which also uses two dinghies in its search-and-rescue missions, was designed to take about 60 refugees on board. Despite these limitations, the boat's crew managed to save about 6,000 people in a single day in 2016. 'I want the *Astral* to be the flagship of human rights on the sea, but the needs are immense,' said Camps, who got another rescue boat in 2017.

Before jumping into the waters of Lesbos, Camps had already built up a successful private company of lifeguards, as well as another business that supplies showers, watchtowers and other beach furniture. Camps decided to set up his own lifeguard company after standing among a group of helpless lifeguards who watched a teenager, Delfín López, drown off the Bogatell beach near Barcelona, in 1993. The drowning occurred in rough weather conditions, but was also in part due to sea currents that had been altered by the breakwater infrastructure added for the Olympics that Barcelona had hosted the previous summer. At the time, Camps was working for the Red Cross.

'I realised on that terrible day that sea rescue in Spain had to become a lot more professional,' Camps said. 'Spain was by then the third tourism country in the world, but we continued to believe that huge responsibilities could be handled only by volunteers.'

Camps said he brought 'the American model' of rescue services to Spain, drawing on professional advice from the Los Angeles lifeguards. But he also pointed to 'a Catalan factor' in his ongoing humanitarian project, particularly in terms of getting professionals to volunteer time and expertise. 'I think that in Catalonia we are a bit more sensitive to human rights,' he argued. 'There are a lot of people here who set up microorganisations that can give the kind of quick answers that much larger organisations cannot do.'

This passionate commitment to human rights was demonstrated in February 2017, when at least 160,000 people marched in Barcelona to demand that the Spanish government meet its pledge to welcome more refugees, mostly from war-torn Syria. Colau, the mayor, joined the demonstration, which its Catalan organisers claimed was the largest of its kind to date in Europe.

Beyond this sensitivity to human rights issues, Camps believes that there is a particular affinity between the Catalans and the refugees for reasons that can be seen in an old photo on his Twitter page. It shows civilians fleeing Catalonia during Spain's civil war, on board a British warship. Members of his own family escaped to France at the end of the war. 'Perhaps Catalans understand refugees better,' he said, 'because we all have relatives who became refugees during the civil war.'

15

THE VIOLENCE OF BASQUE SECESSIONISM

In June of 1968, Txabi Etxebarrieta and Iñaki Sarasketa were stopped by Spain's military police while driving across the Basque region. A policeman, José Antonio Pardines, asked them for their documentation and took a look at their white car. Yet what started as a routine inspection rapidly turned into a killing.

Etxebarrieta and Sarasketa were militants from ETA, the Basque separatist group whose acronym stands for Euskadi Ta Askatasuna, or Basque Homeland and Liberty. As Pardines made his way around the car to check its number plate, Etxebarrieta took out a gun and shot him dead at close range. The militants made a getaway in their car, but the military police soon caught up. They shot Etxebarrieta, who later died of his wounds in hospital. Sarasketa escaped but was later arrested. Years later, he insisted that Pardines had been the victim of 'a mistake,' calling him 'a poor lad.'[1]

Etxebarrieta, however, was transformed into the first martyr of the ETA revolution. He was idolised as a young, glasses-wearing economist who had been willing to abandon a promising career in order to defend Basque ideals. Pamphlets, poems and songs honouring him began to circulate.

Two months later, ETA carried out its first planned assassination, when it ambushed a police inspector, Melitón Manzanas, outside his home in Irún, on the French border. The murder would prove to be the start of over four decades of terrorism that left more than 800 people dead, many of them civilians, as part of ETA's brutal quest for Basque independence.

Bernardo Atxaga, an acclaimed Basque writer, comes from Asteasu, a village near the bridge over the river Ora where Pardines stopped the militants' car. Atxaga did not witness the killing, but he remembered villagers discussing their concerns over how the murder of a Spanish policeman could impact on their local community. He took me to a roundabout right next to where Pardines stopped the car. A few Basque flags had been planted, but there was no sign to commemorate the policeman's killing. Did Basque officialdom want to erase this dark chapter from the history books?

'Our generation will always have to run with that ball, it is not something that we can just pass along to the next generation,' Atxaga said. Reaching for another metaphor, he continued, 'It's really like a fuse that is almost impossible to put out once it has been set alight.'

The wave of terror, however, has at least subsided. ETA last killed on Spanish soil in 2009. In October 2011 the group declared a unilateral ceasefire. In November 2016, after the arrest in a French village of Mikel Irastorza, Spain's interior ministry said they had caught the last leader of ETA and concluded that it was 'difficult for the terrorist group to achieve any of its objectives.'

In April 2017, the group said it had completely disarmed. The gesture fell short of dissolving itself completely, and at the time of writing the government in Madrid continues to demand an unconditional surrender.

But the fact is that Basques no longer seem to worry about terrorism—or at least no more than any other Western community facing the threat of the Islamic State organisation. Tourists have flocked back to the Basque beaches and verdant hills, as well as filling the region's award-winning restaurants. Police surveillance in San Sebastián, the city where ETA carried out the most political assassinations, has been lowered to the point that I was stunned to find that a visitor can enter the city hall without passing a metal detection gate.

This is not to deny the fact that the psychological scars of ETA run deep, which may explain why Basque separatism receded just as Catalan secessionism took off. 'Catalonia has never been affected by the kind of violence that we have had here, which is a major distorting element,' Eneko Goia told me. Goia is the tall and dynamic mayor of San Sebastián, noted for his distinctive salt-and-pepper goatee beard. He was born in 1971, shortly after ETA's first killing. 'Here,' he said, 'you can't start a secessionist process without a strong and united social base and without first coming to terms with ETA and the consequences of what it has done.'

Even five years after ETA's ceasefire, Basque society could not reach consensus over just why the violence stopped, he continued. 'I'm not clear that we all agree on whether the violence was abandoned because everybody came to understand that killing was evil, or because killing didn't work out and achieve ETA's goals. These are two very different reasons.'

When I went to meet Atxaga—who used his village as the inspiration for his bestselling book about a wonderland called Obabakoak—I asked if the Romantic literary devices that shaped both Basque and Catalan nationalism had influenced his approach. 'Imaginary geography is a technique that starts with an empty box in which you can put whatever you want,' Atxaga replied. 'In Obabakoak, I didn't put the town hall at the heart of the village but instead the tailor's workshop, because that is where the pretty girls of the village always went. So that workshop came to symbolise eroticism in my childhood, a place that is obviously much more exciting than the town hall.'

To some extent, he explained, nationalism uses similar substitution methods, replacing the bland and common with the exciting and unique. 'Whether they are Basques, Catalans, Poles or whoever—every people believes it is unique, starting with its language,' he said.

ETA was officially born in 1959 and initially drew support from a wide range of Franco's opponents. The killing of Manzanas in Irún, Atxaga remembered, sparked widespread sympathy among left-leaning Spaniards, since Manzanas had been suspected of torturing Communists who resisted Franco.

Then, in 1973, ETA struck at the top of Franco's government. Luis Carrero Blanco, an admiral and Franco's prime minister, was killed in Madrid by a road bomb that sent his armoured limousine flying over a building. Carrero Blanco's assassination proved a turning point. When Franco died in November 1975, his regime had no other designated successor.

Even so, Jaime Mayor Oreja, a Basque conservative hard-liner who led the fight against ETA as Spain's interior minister in the late 1990s, argued that ETA was formed to dismantle Spain rather than end Franco's dictatorship.

'There is this misleading idea that ETA was a project against Franco, when in fact its worst years of violence started in 1980, just after Spain adopted its constitution,' he said. After the failure of previous projects of Basque nationalism, ETA 'found a way of marking itself out through violence,' he said.

Mayor Oreja's views, however, are not shared by most academics. According to Javier Elzo—a Basque sociologist who spent some years under bodyguard protection because of his writings about ETA—the organisation was inspired by other freedom fighters. These ranged from the Black Panthers in the United States to the Front de Libération Nationale in Algeria.

'It was an era when victory could be found at the end of a gun,' Elzo said. 'The ETA ideology was always to foment national and social revolution,' enshrined in the phrase *Izquierda abertzale*, or the patriotic Left.

Elzo also noted that ETA and its sympathisers continued to embrace Marxism long after the fall of the Berlin Wall. In May 2016, Arnaldo Otegi, a radical separatist leader with links to ETA, came out of prison, declaring himself a pro-independence Basque and a Marxist.

Terror on a small scale

I spent some time in the Basque region trying to understand why secessionism had triggered terrorism there, but not in Catalonia. I also wanted to look at whether separatists in different parts of Spain had done more to work together or instead undermine each other.

As Spain returned to democracy, there was some violence in Catalonia, but on a limited scale. Terra Lliure, or 'Free Land' in Catalan, was formed in 1978, as a violent separatist movement underpinned by a Marxist-Leninist ideology. Terra Lliure carried out attacks, but they were never comparable to those of ETA. In 1987, a man was killed in his bed after the roof of his home collapsed when Terra Lliure detonated a bomb in an adjacent court building. Later that year, an American sailor died in a grenade attack against American servicemen in the port of Barcelona.[2] (Confusingly, responsibility for the attack was claimed by both Terra Lliure and a rival group, the Catalan Red Liberation Army).

By the end of the 1980s, however, paramilitary separatism had largely been dismantled in Catalonia. Terra Lliure's leaders and militants were either arrested or killed, sometimes while failing to operate their own explosive devices properly. The organisation was officially dissolved in 1995.

According to Mayor Oreja, Spain's former interior minister, Terra Lliure could be considered 'a little brother of ETA', though it was badly organised and very weakly supported. ETA did tremendous harm, 'but it was easier to combat Basque nationalism when ETA was killing people than to fight groups or politicians who talk about a project of rupture,' he said. 'The usage of brutality and violence in fact gives [the authorities] political weapons for fighting back.'

José Álvarez Junco, a Spanish historian, has extensively studied the links between nationalism and violence in Spain. He pointed out that Basque nationalism had a long history of violence and intolerance, dating to the Counter-Reformation movement that spread across the Basque countryside and eventually culminated in the so-called Carlist wars of the nineteenth century.

These wars, which also engulfed Catalonia, were rooted in the succession claim of King Ferdinand VII's brother, Carlos, or Charles. The clergy and ultra-conservatives believed he would help them to stem the French liberalism that had led Spanish lawmakers to write a progressive constitution in 1812 in Cádiz. One of the Basque militants of Carlism, Sabino Arana, eventually turned his conservative thinking into a new Basque nationalist ideology, 'focused on race and not language,' according to Álvarez Junco. The ethnic dimension 'was never going to work in the liberal and multicultural society of Catalonia,' he added.

He also explained that the late nineteenth century was when nationalists came to the fore in Catalonia. But they drifted away from violence because Catalonia's economic progress quickly created 'an image of Catalan modernity based partly on the idea that those who use brutal and violent methods come from the Spanish state.' The Spanish state did plenty to help support that idea, especially under right-wing governments in Madrid prone to over-reaction. Álvarez Junco cited the attack on *Cu-Cut!*, a satirical newspaper that published a cartoon mocking the Spanish military in November 1905. In response, the Spanish military ransacked *Cu-Cut!'s* newsroom, burning or throwing out the furniture. For good measure, the military also destroyed the offices of *La Veu de Catalunya*, another Catalan publication that had played no part in the offensive cartoon.

The military reprisal against Catalan newspapers was swiftly followed by regulatory clampdown. Spain adopted a so-called Law of Jurisdictions, which stipulated that any insult against either the motherland or the military would be judged by a military rather than civilian court. After Spain's civil war, Franco revived the law to prevent criticism of his dictatorship.

At the end of our conversation, Álvarez Junco emphasised that though the reprisal against *Cu-Cut!* 'might seem absurd and trivial, it is an important episode. It explains why Catalans came to associate violence with Spain, and why Terra Lliure then did not get any following among Catalan society'.

Joan B. Culla, a Catalan historian, argues that the socio-political violence in Catalonia was mostly 'an extension of workers' protesting.' This was unlike in the Basque region, where the Carlist wars embedded the usage of violence to defend religion and politics rather than social and labour rights, he said. When the civil war started, the Basques took six months to organise a small army. In Catalonia, by contrast, 'the weapons were kept by anarchists and Communists.'

In modern times, there has equally been a difference between the ways Catalonia's borders and those of the Basque region are disputed. ETA and hardline militants believe that Euskadi, or the Basque homeland, should cover Spain's three Basque provinces, as well as the Basque region of France and the neighboring Spanish region of Navarra. Only a part of Navarra, however, embraces the Basque culture and language. Meanwhile, French Basques are proud of their Basque sports and culture, but do not seek to break away from Paris.

Elzo, the sociologist, pointed out that Paris had a strong vested interest in not allowing its Basques to flirt with separatism. 'The French Basque coast became a great resort for the rich and for the pensioners from other parts of France and Europe,' he said. 'The Belle Époque of Biarritz had no Basque identity.'

While terrorism created a huge split between Catalan and Basque separatists in the second half of the twentieth century, since 2012 the tensions have evolved into money and taxation differences. That was the year when Artur Mas, the then Catalan leader, failed to convince the government in Madrid to give Catalonia a fiscal pact like the one used in the Basque and Navarra regions, which collect their own taxes. It was a major turning point. After Madrid's refusal, Mas embraced secession.

In 2015, however, Ciudadanos, which was formed as an antisecessionist Catalan party, tried to reverse the situation. It called for the removal of the Basque and Navarra pacts agreed in 1979. These pacts, Ciudadanos argued, were an affront to the idea of having a level playing field, not least within the European Union.

'If you consider our progress towards fiscal unification in Europe, it doesn't make sense to keep privileged fiscal havens within Spain,' Albert Rivera, the leader of Ciudadanos, told me in November 2015, a month before his party won its first-ever seats in the Spanish Parliament.

Rivera managed to turn his Ciudadanos (Citizens) party into a national force but, unsurprisingly, his fiscal arguments proved unpopular in some regions of Spain. In September 2016, Ciudadanos failed to win any seat in the two regions that held elections that month, Galicia and the Basque Country. Since then, Ciudadanos has shelved its criticism of the Basque fiscal agreement.

Catalan separatists, however, have continued to demand to be put on an equal economic footing with the Basques. Yet the Basques have countered that Catalans should take issue with the political miscalculation made in 1980 by their own leader, Jordi Pujol.

At the time, Pedro Luis Uriarte, a Basque banker, was in charge of economics within the newly-created regional government. After the dictatorship, the Basques negotiated to revive fully the so-called 'foral rights' relating to regional administration. These dated back to the middle ages and granted a high degree of administrative autonomy to the Basques. Franco, however, had abolished the foral rights of two of the Basque provinces, which he declared traitors because they had backed his Republican enemy during the civil war. It was a situation worthy of a Kafka novel, Uriarte told me, since taxes were not collected uniformly across the Basque region.

Ultimately, the Basques came out stronger from Spain's transition democracy, while their historic rights were enshrined in the new constitution. In the summer of 1980, Uriarte attended a meeting in Madrid with his Catalan counterpart, Ramón Trias Fargas, and Spain's budget minister, Jaime García Añoveros. On behalf of his government, Trias Fargas rejected an offer to give Catalonia the same fiscal pact as that agreed for the Basque region, according to Uriarte, who is the only one of the three participants in the meeting still alive. Trias Fargas argued that Catalonia would negotiate economic concessions from Madrid without taking over the risk and responsibility for collecting taxes. With the benefit of hindsight, 'the Catalans realise thirty years later that it was a risk they should have taken,' said Uriarte.

The Catalans probably also deemed the ancient foral rights defended by the Basques to be 'antiquated', said Miguel Herrero y Rodríguez de Miñón, a lawyer who drafted Spain's constitution. 'Catalan nationalism is as romantic as the Basque one, with shared origins, but it has modernised a lot more,' he said. For the Catalans, he added, 'it was probably easier to receive money from a third party than to ask for that money from your own people.'

Rajoy's Popular Party, for its part, has sidestepped the issue of the Basque fiscal pact in order to avoid losing more votes there, according to Antoni Zabalza, a professor of economics and former Socialist secretary of state.

'Nobody has seriously tried to challenge the Basque tax system, because there used to be the ETA terrorist threat,' he said. Spain could also afford to make exceptions for regions that represented a small portion of overall taxes, but 'it would be a very different problem if this fiscal system was extended to regions like Catalonia and Madrid,' he added.

Galeusca and failed unity

Though they are divided by terrorism and taxation, there have been times when the separatists have tried to work together.

While Galeusca is an acronym that few Spaniards would recognise nowadays, it was used to promote cooperation between Galicia, Euskera (the Basque region) and Catalonia, the three regions that have their own languages and the strongest claims to autonomy. The name was first coined in 1923, when a political alliance was formed between the three regions. This alliance, however, rapidly fizzled out, amid tensions between the Basques and Catalans.

Another three-way alliance took shape in the midst of the Second World War, among politicians forced to flee Spain following Franco's victory in the civil war. These politicians found safety in Latin America, but this made them geographically too distant for their political project to make any genuine impact on their homeland.

The most recent relaunch of Galeusca came in the elections for the European Parliament of 2004, when politicians from five regional parties ran on a joint ticket. They all wanted to stop José María Aznar, Spain's conservative prime minister, from wiping out regional diversity in Spain. The Galeusca platform, however, won only 5 per cent of the Spanish votes in the European elections of 2004. By the time of the next European elections, the project had withered away.

The history of Galeusca shows how while regional politicians share certain objectives, many of them are programmed to behave more as rivals than allies. Galeusca 'has always been at best the sum of the parts rather than a real common movement,' said Ignasi Guardans, one of the two Galeusca lawmakers elected to the European Parliament in 2004.

In 1998, the main Basque, Galician and Catalan nationalist politicians signed a joint declaration in Barcelona calling for Spain to be recognised more clearly as a plural nation. However, the declaration was ignored by Prime Minister Aznar, who continued to negotiate with each region separately, thereby also exacerbating tensions between them. 'It was always divide-and-rule, not just from Madrid but also among ourselves,' said Guardans.

Basque and Catalan politicians have a long list of mutual recriminations. Many Basques resent Pujol for keeping even moderate Basque politicians at arm's length, particularly once ETA struck Catalonia. In June 1987, ETA exploded a bomb outside a Hipercor supermarket in Barcelona, which killed twenty-one people.

The sociologist Javier Elzo remarked, 'When ETA was operating and Pujol governed in Catalonia, Pujol had difficulties even mentioning anything to do with Basque nationalists.' Following Spain's return to democracy, the Basques strengthened their powers with a statute of autonomy that was approved in a referendum in 1979. But that did not stop them from continuing to push for more autonomy.

Their strongest political push started in 2001, when the then Basque leader, Juan José Ibarretxe, announced a plan for a new statute of autonomy, loosely based on the examples of Quebec and Puerto Rico. His plan included granting the Basque region the right to stage its own referendum. In late 2004, Ibarretxe's plan was narrowly approved by the Basque regional parliament. But when the plan reached Madrid, it was thrown out by Spanish lawmakers, who did not even allow for a full parliamentary debate over Ibarretxe's plan.

Ibarretxe and his Basque Nationalist Party (known by its acronym of PNV) tried to kill two birds with one stone, thinking that gaining more autonomy could also defuse the terrorist threat of ETA. In fact the controversial plan created fresh divisions among Basque society. When it was torpedoed in Madrid, few Basques went out to protest—in contrast to the scenes in Barcelona after Spain's constitutional court ruled against Catalonia's own statute of autonomy in 2010.

'Ibarretxe went ahead with his plan when the terrorism problem had not been resolved,' said Joxerramon Bengoetxea, a professor of jurisprudence at the University of the Basque Country. 'Unlike in Catalonia, the Basque process was led only from the top, by politicians rather than society.' Ibarretxe failed, but several of his proposals continue to form part of the Basque political debate. Mikel Burzako, an official from the PNV, said to me that Ibarretxe was probably 'a bit ahead of his time, but he was also a person who understood that the model for the Basques within Spain was exhausted.'

The Socialists managed to convert their successful campaign against Ibarretxe's plan into a Basque election win. But it proved only a brief interlude in what has been the clear dominance by the PNV over Basque politics since Spain's return to democracy. Since October 2012, the PNV has been back in office under a new leader, Iñigo Urkullu. At the time of writing,

Urkullu was watching the dispute between Madrid and Barcelona from the sidelines. The PNV has carefully avoided fanning the flames of independence, even though separatist parties have controlled over two-thirds of the seats in the Basque parliament since late 2016. This is far more than the support Ibarretxe had for his autonomy plan.

Nicolás Redondo Terreros, a former Basque Socialist politician, said to me that for the PNV, 'the preoccupation is mainly to avoid any contamination from Catalonia's chaos.' Catalan separatists, on the other hand, have ruffled feathers among the PNV by reaching out to Basque hardliners. In May 2016, a few months after leaving prison, Otegi, the radical Basque politician linked to ETA, was welcomed in Barcelona by the president of the Catalan parliament, Carme Forcadell. Otegi showered praise on the Catalan independence movement. 'I have come to learn from an exemplary process, which is democratically and peacefully unpicking the stitches put in place by the state,' Otegi said. (3)

Josep Piqué, a former Spanish foreign minister, argued that Galeusca and other plans for cooperation between separatists are doomed because separatists 'share something that by definition is different, a project of national construction. This is obviously exclusive since it is about building different nations,' he said. 'The only common ground is to stand up together against the same power, Spain, which helps short-term alliances but doesn't help in the longer term.'

There is also the fact that the three regions vary considerably in size as well as economic firepower. 'What has always worried Madrid is not Basque secessionism but Catalan secessionism, even in the times of ETA, because we number two million people while they stand at more than seven million,' Elzo said.

On top of this, the Basque and Catalan elites have not come together to coordinate their response to separatism. Since 2012, the Convergence party founded by Jordi Pujol has put itself at the forefront of the independence movement. Javier Zarzalejos, secretary general of Faes, declared, 'The PNV got off the separatist train on time. Convergence has not only failed to jump off but, it has tried to become the train driver without being able to determine the train's direction.'

A conservative bastion in Galicia

In Galicia, secessionism has been little more than a sideshow, in part because of the region's economic backwardness. In the late nineteenth century, Catalans and Basques led Spain into the Industrial Revolution, which also helped develop their separatist ambitions. Galicia's economy, on the other hand, only started to prosper following Spain's accession to the European Union in 1986, on the back of massive European subsidies to the continent's poorer regions. Galicia became a major fashion hub, led by Inditex, the world's largest clothing retailer.

Politically Galicia, the birthplace of Franco, stood out as the cradle of Spain's governing Popular Party. After Spain's return to democracy, the region was run for fifteen years by one of Franco's former ministers, Manuel Fraga Iribarne. Fraga also founded Spain's main conservative party and helped draft the country's new democratic constitution.

Mariano Rajoy, a fellow Galician, followed in Fraga's footsteps. He jumped on the political bandwagon during Galicia's regional elections in 1981, representing Fraga's Popular Alliance, which eventually morphed into the Popular Party that Rajoy led back into office in 2011. Even after he imposed unpopular austerity cuts from Madrid, his Popular Party maintained its grip on Galicia, under Alberto Núñez Feijóo, who won re-election in September 2016.

'Galician political nationalism has always been different because it has come purely from the political left,' without support from any conservative politicians, said Guardans, the former Galeusca lawmaker.

Ramón Máiz Suárez, a politics professor at the University of Santiago de Compostela, has an office overflowing with books on nationalism, from those in Spain to the struggles of the indigenous Mapuches of Patagonia and the Zapatista rebels in Mexico. He also keeps an intriguing grey cardboard box on a shelf, labelled 'emotions and politics'. That box, Máiz explained, contained material that could help explain the struggle for Catalonia.

'Passions and emotions are very important, particularly for understanding territorial politics,' he said. 'If you ask Catalans what the main reason is for them to fight for independence, they say mistreatment.' Feelings of resentment can drive politics, he said, and turn even a debate over taxes into an emotional rather than an economic issue. For many Catalans, the fiscal issue 'is not about reforming the fiscal system. The really powerful factor is emotional, the idea that Spain hates us,' Máiz argued.

Such emotions are harder to stir up in Galicia, where Máiz teaches, even if the region has its own language and culture. At its peak, in the 1990s, the Galician Nationalist Bloc, known by its Galician acronym of BNG, won 22 per cent of the votes in regional elections. In September 2016, it won 8 per cent of the votes, as the BNG also lost votes to new formations, led by En Marea, a far-left coalition. To make things more complicated, Galician nationalism has splintered since the 2008 financial crisis, as concerns over the economic slump and disparities have come to the fore.

One of the new Galician parties is Anova, also known as the Nationalist Brotherhood, which was founded in 2012, in the midst of Spain's banking crisis. Anova was created 'not for separatists, but for people who want to turn Spain into a real federal state, a bit like Germany,' said Branca Novoneyra. Novoneyra is a former ballet dancer with a degree in politics, who combined her two passions to become an Anova official within Santiago de Compostela's city hall, where she is now in charge of running cultural activities.

Galicia, she said, could never match Basque or Catalan separatism 'because we have always been too poor.' While economic migrants moved to the Basque and Catalan regions, impoverished Galicians left to find work in the Americas and wealthier parts of Europe. They left behind a society heavily reliant on farming and subsidies from Madrid, Novoneyra said. 'You cannot think about separating if you depend on the exchange of goods and services for political support, and have a semi-feudal structure,' she argued.

Santiago Lago Peñas, an economics professor at the University of Vigo, has studied how regional politicians purposely downplay their level of economic autonomy to discourage the push for separatism. Contrary to popular belief, he said, about half of his own personal income was taxed by his Galician regional government, while regional and local officials disbursed one third of the public money spent in Galicia.

Still, Lago Peñas acknowledged the link between wealth and separatism. 'The richer you are, the more incentive you have to become independent,' he said.

Hardline beliefs

In 2010, in the midst of the financial crisis, I interviewed Fraga, Franco's former minister and one of the main actors in Spain's transition from dictatorship to democracy. I wanted to hear how Fraga compared the mounting financial problems with past challenges faced by Spain.

Coincidentally, our meeting took place only days after Spain's constitutional court struck down the Catalan statute of autonomy. After Franco's death, Fraga was also one of the authors of Spain's new constitution. So this meeting offered a chance to listen to a veteran politician who participated in Spain's democratic transformation and could evaluate whether the country was on the cusp of another overhaul.

Fraga was then struggling physically. But at eighty-seven years of age, he was still an active lawmaker in the Spanish Senate. Dressed in a dark suit, with a cane by his side and with his hands kept crossed over his lap while he spoke, Fraga displayed a quick mind and an even sharper tongue. He swiftly swept aside any suggestion that an economic crisis could trigger a major shake-up in Spain.

Fraga said separatism was thankfully irrelevant in his own region of Galicia, and was exaggerated in Catalonia. He argued that the constitutional court's ruling should have been welcomed by Catalans, since the court only ruled against specific parts of the statute. 'Catalonia has always been part of Spain and a great part of its people would want to remain within Spain,' he said.

He went on to lambast José Montilla, the then leader of Catalonia, for manipulating separatism to consolidate his own fragile grip on power. His attack finished by questioning Montilla's right to represent Catalans, since he was not born in Catalonia. Montilla was raised near Córdoba, in Andalusia, and moved as a teenager to Catalonia. 'Their president is not even Catalan, he is Andalusian, so that already tells you all you need to know,' Fraga said.

It was the kind of argument that seemed to leave little room for further discussion. It also sounded highly dismissive of Catalonia and social diversity. Yet when I reflected on his words, I realised that inadvertently he had reinforced how important regional identity was in Spain through his forceful attack on Montilla. In his defence, too, of Spain's unity, Fraga had shown how much the country's richness derives from the vibrancy of the different cultures it contains.

16

CIVIL DISOBEDIENCE AND THE RULE OF LAW

Since 2012, the separatist drive in Catalonia has followed a tit-for-tat pattern. Separatist politicians announce a new way to move towards independence despite fierce opposition from Madrid, and the government in Madrid immediately denounces the move as illegal. However, contained within this cycle is another, more dangerous pattern.The strategies and threats employed by both sides—as well as the stakes—have been raised in each and every round.

In early 2017, for the first time Catalan politicians were sentenced for civil disobedience. The court banned them from office after putting them on trial for organising an illegal independence vote and ignoring the decisions of Spain's constitutional court.

Similar Spanish attempts at a legal clampdown have so far failed to deflate Catalan secessionism. On the contrary: separatists have depicted such lawsuits as evidence of a politicised Spanish judiciary and have stood in the courtroom almost as martyrs of the secessionist cause.

Yet encapsulated within this defiance is the concern that the constitutional court is the great nemesis of Catalan secessionism, a body whose interpretations have closed the door on any attempt to hold a legal referendum on independence. The pro-independence movement has cried foul at rulings by the court since 2010, when it struck down part of a Catalan statute of autonomy. Separatists were also incensed when the court overturned a Catalan ban on bullfighting in October 2016 that had been approved by Catalan lawmakers six years earlier.

This is despite the fact that the court has not always ruled against Catalonia. In the three years after its decision on the statute, the court ruled in favour of the Catalan regional government in thirty-five out of fifty-five cases, according to Xavier Vidal-Folch, a columnist for *El País*.[1]

So, in the absence of a political deal with Madrid, what legal avenues might be open to the separatists?

Most interestingly, the Catalan conflict has helped raise the question of whether the Spanish constitution—which was signed into law in December 1978, three years after the death of the dictator Franco—needs a complete overhaul.

Spain's constitution was constructed by seven legal experts, two of whom were Catalans, Miquel Roca i Junyent and Jordi Solé Tura. The seven fathers of the constitution were also selected to represent the different political forces at the time. Solé Tura, for instance, was a Catalan Communist.

The seven put together a document that underwent a thorough parliamentary review, in which more than 1,000 amendments were tabled. Intense debates took place over tiny issues, such as the impact of the constitutional text on the granting of licenses to fishermen. 'We ended up having big problems agreeing rules about the smallest things,' recounted Miguel Herrero y Rodríguez de Miñón, another of the seven fathers of the constitution. 'Anybody can understand that neither the identity of Spain nor that of Catalonia depends on what registration is given to shell fishermen, but emotions can be more powerful than reason, whether in Madrid or Barcelona.'

The final text of 169 articles was modelled in part on Germany's constitution, but it also harked back to the 1931 constitution of the ill-fated Second Republic, which was then wiped out by the civil war. Even though the 1978 constitution was meant to cement the transition from dictatorship to democracy, it was not the final word on how to share power in post-Franco Spain, particularly in terms of the territorial division of the country.

CIVIL DISOBEDIENCE AND THE RULE OF LAW

In 1981, Spain's main parties agreed to divide the country into nineteen regions, including two city enclaves in north Africa, Ceuta and Melilla. Between 1979 and 1995, each region drew up its own statute of autonomy, and almost all later made further changes.

'The constitution was seen as an instrument of transition and peace that in the first years could also create greater social linkage and economic development,' Herrero de Miñón told me. 'Other concepts were added later. The most disastrous of them was to generalise the map of the regions.'

For Herrero de Miñón, the territorial division of 1981 wrongly imposed a one-size-fits-all model on Spain's disparate regions. This territorial split was 'rooted in historical and cultural ignorance,' he argued, and driven by misplaced political objectives. 'Catalonia has a language, culture and identity that a place like La Rioja clearly does not have,' he said, referring to the small region that has become world-famous for its wine. For Spain's conservative politicians, 'there was a desire to submerge the Basque and Catalan bids for autonomy in a broader territorial expanse,' he said. Since Spain was dominated at the time by conservative politicians, the Socialists saw the strengthening of regional governments as their chance to get a foothold in power, before trying to take over national government. According to Herrero de Miñón, the Socialist strategy started in Andalusia, Spain's largest region, which has remained under Socialist control since the return of democracy.

The constitution did not explicitly recognise any right to secede. In fact, very few constitutions have granted such a right to elements within their territory. One exception is the former Soviet Union. The right to secede also still exists in the Ethiopian constitution, as well as that of Saint Kitts and Nevis, a Caribbean archipelago.

Yet Catalonia did get some special attention from Madrid. Adolfo Suárez, Spain's then conservative head of government, decided to restore the Generalitat as the regional government of Catalonia, as well as bring back Josep Tarradellas, Catalonia's veteran politician, from exile. As it turned out, the Generalitat ended up being the only institution of the Second Republic that was reinstated after Franco's dictatorship.

Tarradellas, who was by then seventy-eight years old, had belonged to different Republican governments during Spain's civil war. At the end of the conflict, he fled Spain and then spent much of Franco's dictatorship in the French town of Saint-Martin-le-Beau, leading the exiled Catalan opposition.

On 23 October 1977, he received a hero's welcome when he landed at Barcelona's El Prat airport, with supporters jumping the security fences to get closer to him.[2] After a limousine drive to the city centre, Tarradellas delivered a speech from the balcony of the freshly-reinstalled Generalitat. In the manner of a long-awaited liberator, Tarradellas started with a '*ja sóc aquí*!'— or 'here I am!'—before promising the citizens of Catalonia that 'our unity will make us the most advanced people in Spain.' His words drew wild applause, even if many in his audience were too young to remember the last time that Tarradellas had been at the forefront of Catalan politics.

Tarradellas died in 1980, after fewer than three years in charge of a Catalan government that in the event did not achieve memorable changes. Still, his return proved something of a political masterstroke, engineered by Suárez from Madrid, which helped 'assert Catalonia's place in the new constitutional architecture' of Spain, according to Josep Piqué, a former Spanish foreign minister.

Tarradellas also helped 'put a brake on the parties of the Left,' according to Francesc de Carreras, a constitutional lawyer who visited Tarradellas during his French exile. Tarradellas returned to Barcelona as a changed politician, he said, as well as an admirer of General Charles de Gaulle and his conservative concept of French unity.

In 1978, a year after Tarradellas' return, Spanish voters overwhelmingly endorsed Spain's new constitution in a referendum. The support was particularly high among the electorate of Barcelona, which voted 91 per cent in favour of the constitution.

Nowadays, however, most separatists insist that the 1978 referendum did not reflect Catalan enthusiasm for the new constitution, but rather their determination to secure democratic stability.

'When I went to vote for the constitution, nobody had asked me what kind of constitution I wanted. Nor was I asked whether I really liked a text that had been developed by a limited number of people and presented as a promise of more changes to come,' said Josep Fontana, the veteran Catalan historian. 'People really believed then that they were voting for something that marked the start of a new path, along which there would later be more changes.'

So was the 1978 constitution meant to confirm a return to democracy, or was it supposed to set up a permanent structure for democratic Spain, right down to the last detail?

In 2015, ahead of the general election, Spain's main opposition Socialist party started to campaign for constitutional reform. The Socialists were also trying to jump on the reform bandwagon because they faced a dual challenge. They hoped to unseat the conservative Popular Party. But they also hoped to resist unexpected pressure from Podemos, a far-left party that was competing for the first time in a general election and was promising radical institutional changes.

The Socialists, however, did not detail their constitutional reform project. In particular, they did not explain how it could resolve the thorny issue of Catalonia, which in turn left many of their own Socialist partisans in Catalonia frustrated.

Mariano Rajoy, the conservative prime minister, entirely sidestepped the issue of constitutional reform in his re-election campaign. He and his Popular Party feared that any level of constitutional reform could allow Podemos and others to challenge each institutional pillar of Spain—not least the monarchy—without even necessarily solving the territorial dispute with Catalonia.

Francisco Sosa Wagner, a former European Parliament lawmaker and a law professor at the University of León, declared that constitutional reform cannot be carried out in a country that lacks 'the basic elements of constitutional loyalty,' including respect for Spain's monarchy.[3] At best, 'discussing whether we are monarchists or republicans can be an entertaining way of wasting our time,' he told a conference on constitutional reform.

After two inconclusive elections and almost a year of political deadlock, Rajoy was re-elected as premier in October 2016. It was only at this point that he started to talk about possible constitutional reform—with the condition that it should touch upon a limited number of issues and should not endanger Spain's unity.

Some of the fathers of the 1978 constitution have watched the debate over the rewriting of their text with dismay. 'Politicians are discussing things they don't understand,' said Herrero de Miñón, citing the suggestions made by some politicians that Spain needs a federal system. 'Almost no Spanish politician knows the difference between a confederation and a federation,' he said.

For Herrero de Miñón, Spain's main politicians have also misrepresented the concept of sovereignty. 'There are some pseudo-juridical arguments that are now used to talk about Spain's undivided sovereignty, but such concepts serve whatever purpose one wants them to,' he said. 'Sovereignty can be delegated to Brussels, as it has been by Madrid and other capitals.'

Roca, one of the two Catalan fathers of the constitution, echoed such views. Federalism, he argued, 'is incompatible with creating specific provisions for a specific people like that of Catalonia.'

The specificity of Catalonia, he noted, was already part of its legal and administrative structures, which include a civil code that is unique to Catalonia. Separatist politicians, however, have fudged some of the legal issues by loosely invoking their 'right to decide' their statehood. 'The right to decide is technically neither a right nor is it to decide,' Enoch Albertí Rovira, a professor of constitutional law at Barcelona University, told another conference on constitutional law.[4] At best, he said, 'it is a political aspiration.'

A flawed statute

Before secessionism got into full swing, Catalans tried to get more freedom from Madrid by adopting a new statute of autonomy in 2006. Four years later, parts of the statute were struck down by Spain's constitutional court.

The court blocked far fewer articles in the Catalan statute than those that the main conservative Popular Party judged to be unconstitutional. But the fact that they were struck down still made blood boil in Catalonia. The court said that Catalonia could not be specified as a nation in the statute's preamble. It also vetoed some important changes forecast by the statute, such as giving Catalonia greater judicial independence or setting minimum levels of state expenditure in Catalonia.

Nowadays, it is hard to meet Catalans who have actually read their disputed statute of autonomy. But it is equally impossible not to have heard about how upset Catalans got when Spain's constitutional court ruled against it. Since that 2010 ruling, Spain's constitutional court has lost any of the credibility it had earned in Catalonia in the previous three decades. Catalans were also upset because the ruling seemed discriminatory, since the court blocked some changes that were deemed acceptable in a similar statute in Andalusia, including the creation of a more autonomous judiciary.

'The court waded into issues that were not legal but political,' Herrero de Miñón told me. 'The constitutional court waited four years to rule and then unfortunately failed to follow the American doctrine of self-restraint in political issues.'

The reaction to the court's ruling in 2010 was far greater than the response the statute generated when first broached. In 2006, the statute was approved by almost 74 per cent of Catalans in a referendum, but with a turnout of just under half the electorate. 'The statute didn't generate much enthusiasm but it irritated a lot people when it was rejected—which I think is a very Catalan trait,' said Gonzalo Rodés, a Catalan lawyer.

How many Catalans have since read their rejected statute of autonomy? 'Somewhere between zero and zero,' joked Meritx-ell Batet, a Catalan Socialist who is a member of the Spanish Parliament. Still, she said, it was undeniable that the constitu-tional court's ruling changed the mindset of many Catalans. 'The ruling didn't perhaps change that much in terms of legal content, but it changed everything in terms of legitimacy and in terms of polarising emotions,' she continued.

Batet gave an example from her own family. 'My mother and her husband are not pro-independence and have not studied constitutional law, but they equally could not under-stand how a court could suddenly rule against what they had voted,' she said.

The statute suffered from two major problems from the out-set. First, explained Batet, the Catalan Socialist party 'made the mistake of pushing for a statute without knowing exactly what it wanted to achieve.' Second, the statute was drafted by leftwing parties without taking any account of the Popular Party, 'a party that is not very important in Catalonia but very important in the rest of Spain.' Batet suggested that Catalonia's coalition government should have involved moderate Catalan conservatives like Josep Piqué to help widen support for the statute. Ignored inside Catalonia, Spain's conservative party then led the backlash against the statute from Madrid, once it became a national issue.

Piqué agreed, saying, 'The statute was handled with extreme frivolity, both by those who advanced it and those who opposed it, in a pretty coarse manner.'

The advancing of the statute also heightened political rivalries within Catalonia. After being drafted by a Socialist-led Catalan administration, the statute was later rescued by the right-leaning Convergence party. The party stepped in to negotiate some of its details directly with the Socialist prime minister in Madrid—José

Luis Rodríguez Zapatero—but not in the presence of the Social-ist leader of Catalonia, Pasqual Maragall.

'This created political turmoil and left Maragall marginalised by a Convergence party that had initially been on the sidelines,' recalled Antoni Zabalza, a former Socialist secretary of state. The fight over the statute ended up raising territorial tensions, as well as hurting Spain's two traditional parties in Catalonia. With hindsight, the clearest damage was suffered by the Social-ists, who most recently headed a coalition government in Cata-lonia in 2010.

'The Socialist party, which had been part of the solution in pushing for the statute, ended up being part of the problem, from a Catalan point of view, for not being able to produce solutions,' Batet declared. The Popular Party's visceral opposi-tion to the statute may not have hurt its election prospects, but it showed a conservative party 'unable to understand that Cata-lonia is essential,' she continued. 'If you really worry about what happens in Spain, you must also worry about Catalonia.'

What kind of referendum?

Even if politicians in Madrid and Barcelona somehow find a way to agree on holding a Catalan referendum, its constituent parts would themselves be subject to fierce debate.

For Inés Arrimadas, the regional leader of the Citizens party, which is firmly opposed to secessionism, Catalonia is heading for a collision. 'The more time we waste on the road to inde-pendence, the more time we will need to return to the path of sanity,' she told a group of foreign correspondents. The refer-endum demand, she argued, was used by Catalonia's inept governing politicians to deflect public attention from their cor-ruption and economic failures. Any Catalan referendum would encourage other Spanish regions to hold their own indepen-dence votes, she forecast, while Catalan separatists would seek a rerun should voters reject independence. 'Those who promote the referendum will hold as many referendums as are needed,' she said.

However, Roca, one of the fathers of the constitution, said it would be theoretically possible to set tough thresholds, like the qualified majority rules used in the independence referenda of Quebec. Whatever rules are set, he told me, 'I don't believe in independence if it is based only on 51 per cent voting for it.'

Catalan separatists also take Quebec as an example that secession need not be voted on forever. Joaquim Nadal, a former Socialist politician, commented that separatist politicians lost two referenda in Quebec, in 1980 and 1995. They have not suggested holding a third vote since. Like the Québécois, he said, 'Catalans are mature enough to understand that, if the result is not what some people would want, a reasonable amount of time would need to elapse' before reopening the debate.

Spain does not have a strong referendum tradition, but neither has it always shunned direct democracy. Since 1936, six national referenda have been held, including two spurious ones under Franco, which he won with over 90 per cent of the vote.

Yet Catalan demands for an independence referendum have taken place amid a broader debate about the instruments of Western democracy and the purpose of a referendum. (With the notable exception of my own country, Switzerland, where the referendum has long been the cornerstone of Swiss direct democracy.)

In 2016, David Cameron and Matteo Renzi, the prime ministers of Britain and Italy respectively, resigned after separately losing referenda. Countries like Greece and the Netherlands also broke with past practices by using referenda to resolve divisive issues—with mixed results.

This European track record has helped opponents of the Catalan referendum to argue that the referendum is an unsuitable and dangerous substitute for parliamentary governance. 'When you're deciding whether or not to install an elevator in a building, it makes sense to ask its residents,' said Zabalza, the former Socialist secretary of state. 'But it doesn't make so much sense for a democracy to use a referendum to decide whether or not to form a country.'

CIVIL DISOBEDIENCE AND THE RULE OF LAW

Before politicians consider holding a referendum, 'we have to raise the level of the debate,' argued Teresa Freixes Sanjuán, a professor of constitutional law at the Autonomous University of Barcelona, during a conference in June 2016. The problem, she said, is that 'the referendum simplifies the options so much that at the end it perverts them.'

Ahead of Scotland's referendum in 2014, however, 'British politicians went together to Scotland to defend a common British project,' which is the example that Spanish politicians should follow, Artur Mas told me when I asked him. Catalonia's future should be decided following a transparent campaign in which both sides try to convince voters with credible arguments, he said, rather than by wielding legal threats and relying on court sentences.

For many constitutional lawyers, the experience of 1978 demonstrates that a new constitution can be drafted if there is sufficient political consensus and urgency. According to constitutional law professor Albertí Rovira, the process might be slow and complicated, but 'it is a question of political will.'

When Spain last amended its constitution, in the summer of 2011, the country was sinking into a major economic crisis. Within a month, the main parties had agreed to introduce new limits on budget deficits within the constitution. 'The myth that the constitution is very hard to reform fell apart completely in 2011,' he continued.

A constitutional rebel

In 2015, Santiago Vidal, a judge, joined a group of separatist academics and lawyers working on a draft text for a new Catalan constitution that was then presented to Catalan lawmakers. It was an act of defiance that prompted the Spanish judiciary to suspend him as a judge. So Vidal switched to politics and got elected as one of Catalonia's representatives in the Spanish Senate.

Vidal has white curly hair and a goatee beard, but he speaks with the youthful and defiant tone of somebody keen to uphold his rebel image. He handed me an embossed business card that was written in Catalan, but had been issued by the Spanish Senate and came with the royal crown and other emblems of Spain. On the wall of his office, Vidal had pinned two flags side-by-side. One was a large Catalan separatist flag and the other an equally big Basque flag that was given to Vidal by Arnaldo Otegi, one of the most divisive figures in the Basque separatist conflict. Vidal received the flag on the day that he went to greet Otegi as he left prison in early 2016, after completing a sentence for rebuilding an outlawed party that had links with ETA, the terrorist group.

I asked Vidal whether he had always been an outspoken secessionist. His answer, as with that of many other separatists, was not straightforward.

Vidal explained that he came from a very conservative background. His father was a doctor and the last mayor appointed by the Franco regime in his town of San Sadurní de Noya, the heartland of cava, Catalonia's sparkling wine.

Vidal rebelled by starting his legal career on the other side of the political fence, among far-left militants, as the lawyer of the Confederación Nacional del Trabajo, or National Confederation of Labour, best known by its acronym of CNT. The CNT workers' syndicate epitomised the anarchist movement that took shape in Barcelona shortly before the First World War and ended up leading the fight against Franco during Spain's civil war.

'My youth experience was a bit bipolar,' said Vidal. 'There was a lot of order imposed by my parents at home, but I was also an extremely young lawyer for the CNT, discovering a world without any kind of respect for institutions.'

After the civil war, members of the CNT joined the clandestine resistance to Franco's dictatorship. But after Franco died, the organisation lost much of its credibility because some of its militants continued to advocate violence rather than embrace a democratic transition. In January 1978, CNT militants and other anarchists threw Molotov cocktails at the Scala banquet hall in Barcelona, setting it alight. Four people died in the fire.

Vidal stopped being the lawyer of the CNT the following year and eventually became instead a judge in Barcelona. The experience of the CNT, he said, made him decide to pursue a path somewhere between authoritarianism and anarchy.

'I felt revolutions had to be carried out peacefully and democratically, respecting the laws but also understanding that laws can and must be changed, because laws are there to resolve problems and conflicts,' he said. 'When they are obsolete, like the Spanish constitution that we have now, they have to be changed.'

Vidal's ambiguous relationship with the Spanish constitution is unsurprising. In the 1990s, he was among a group of judges who refused to apply the law that made military service compulsory in Spain, on the grounds that the law was unconstitutional. The Spanish government then ended up abolishing military service before the constitutional court issued a ruling on the issue.

'Civil disobedience is legitimate when it is done on behalf of the majority,' he explained.

However, in early 2017 his rebel streak took him a step too far. He resigned from the Spanish Senate and was put under court investigation, this time after making serious accusations against the Catalan government, in particular over its handling of secret tax data. Yet this roller-coaster ride seems more broadly to underline the conflicted feelings behind this secessionist conflict, often held by people who started out before Spain even had a democratic rule of law.

At the time of writing, the Catalan secessionist conflict appears to have turned into a war of attrition, with each side refusing to cede an inch.

Since starting to push for independence, the Catalan authorities have contemplated 'at least four different ways to hold an independence referendum—none of which appears likely within the framework of the Spanish constitution,' said Josep

Maria Castellà Andreu, another professor of constitutional law at the University of Barcelona. However, article 150 of the constitution, which sets the conditions under which Madrid can devolve power, could be used for Catalonia, much like Cameron, then Britain's prime minister, allowed Scotland to vote on independence in 2014.

Andreu Mas-Colell, a former Catalan finance minister, told me, 'The problem is one of trust. The Madrid view is that any concession to Catalonia means more demands the next day and the Catalan view is that there is no point negotiating any concession if Madrid never keeps its word.'

Mas-Colell seems, to my mind, to have hit the nail on the head. It has always amazed me how territorial disputes can get people to stop talking about their feelings and obsess instead about the fine print of the law. Constitutions and treaties are suddenly scrutinised to the point that they become household concepts, whether in Catalonia or Britain, where the once-obscure article 50 of the still-obscure Lisbon treaty was the key to triggering Britain's exit from the European Union.

Yet feelings endure. To Rajoy or anybody else hoping that Catalan secessionism will simply evaporate, de Miñón suggested taking a look at modern Basque history, following the removal of the '*foros*', or Basque autonomous institutions, in 1878. At that time, a leading Catalan politician, Francesc Pi i Margall, warned 'that the ashes would continue to burn—and he was proved right,' Herrero de Miñón recounted. A century later, Basque separatism returned as Spain's greatest and most deadly challenge. Even if it is impossible to predict Catalonia's future, 'Catalonia cannot be handled as a problem that will simply disappear,' he said.

17

PLAYING POLITICS IN CATALAN SPORTS

In Catalonia, football and politics are never very far apart.

In November 2010, Joan Laporta, an ebullient former president of FC Barcelona, faced two simultaneous challenges. On the one hand, Laporta and his newly-formed political party, Catalan Democracy, were preparing to compete in a Catalan election later that month. The party was committed to Catalonia's independence, and Laporta was hoping to benefit from his track record at the helm of Catalan football's powerhouse.

On the other hand, Laporta, a lawyer by profession, was facing an unprecedented lawsuit initiated by Sandro Rosell, his successor as president of the club. Rosell was accusing Laporta of fiddling the club's accounts in order to turn a loss of almost €80 million into a reported profit of €11 million during Laporta's last season in charge.

Sitting in his law firm office, a jittery Laporta wasted no time in explaining to me just how far matters of football and politics were interwoven at FC Barcelona. Here they had been brought together in a conspiracy to sink him. Laporta denied any wrongdoing and accused Rosell of 'indecent accounting manoeuvres' to sully his name, along with that of the club. 'These people are managing to cast doubt on my reputation, but they are also hurting Barça's image,' Laporta said. 'They are also the tools of powerful political, media and economic groups who don't want to see my political project to turn Catalonia into a European state flourishing.'

Ultimately, Laporta fell short of his political ambitions. But he turned the tables on Rosell in an unexpected fashion. In 2010, Laporta's party got only four seats in the regional vote. Two years later, a remodelled version of his party fared even worse, failing to win a single seat. However, Rosell was forced to make a shameful exit from the club in 2014 for accounting trickery. He was accused of signing Neymar, the Brazilian star, for far more money than the club disclosed. At the time of writing, the Neymar case was ongoing, with the prosecution seeking to sentence not only Rosell for fraud, but also his successor, Josep Maria Bartomeu, and Neymar, the player at the heart of the scandal. In May 2017, Rosell's problems got even more serious. He was detained by Spanish police as part of a separate fraud investigation involving matches played in Brazil.

In sports, owners are capable of selling teams, firing coaches and offloading players who have been described as indispensable a day earlier. Hence, the fallout between Laporta and Rosell is not unique. But it revealed a high level of boardroom discord within a club that prides itself on its unique capacity to unite a whole nation around a flagship team.

Swiss origins

Accounting played a significant part in the club's origins. The young Swiss accountant and football Hans-Max Gamper helped found FC Barcelona in 1899. Gamper, who had previously also lived in Lyon, turned what was meant to be a short stay in Barcelona into a lifetime passion for the place. He learned Catalan, spoke the language with his children and even adopted the Catalan version of his name, Joan Gamper.

Gamper put together a team made up mostly of foreigners living in Barcelona. He chose *blaugrana*, or blue-maroon, as the colors for FC Barcelona, which almost match those of FC Basel, the Swiss club for which he had previously played. He also oversaw the financing of Barcelona's first stadium. His mission was to lead Barcelona both on and off the pitch, first as team captain and prolific goalscorer, and eventually as club president.

His devotion to football, however, suffered as a result of the early intrusion of politics into his club's affairs. On 24 June 1925, Barça's fans booed the Spanish national anthem and then applauded the British anthem performed by a visiting British Royal Marine band. Miguel Primo de Rivera, Spain's then dictator, accused Gamper of using his club to promote Catalan nationalism and closed its stadium for six months as punishment. Five years later, Gamper committed suicide, after also suffering heavy financial losses in the 1929 Wall Street crash.

Under Gamper, the club became a major supporter of the Mancomunitat, the political project to build a stronger Catalonia, around a statute of autonomy, that also helped rebuilt a war-destroyed village in France. (See Chapter 9) *La Voz de Cataluña*, a Catalan newspaper, wrote in an editorial at the time that 'FC Barcelona has changed from being a club of Catalonia to being the club of Catalonia.'

When Gamper put down the first stone for the club's new stadium, in February 1922, he delivered his own defiant message to those resisting Catalonia's ambitions. 'We are making a homeland! We are doing sports! And above all, long live Barcelona!' he shouted.

A year later, Josep Puig i Cadafalch, the then president of the Mancomunitat, paid tribute to Gamper in the Catalan Parliament. 'Foreign by birth, you have imbued yourself with the feelings and ideals of our people and for this reason Catalans love you like a son of our land,' he said.

Not all of the club's subsequent presidents have followed the same line in their politics. In the early stages of Franco's dictatorship, some were even appointees of the regime. But all have presented themselves as standard bearers of Catalonia, even in periods of boardroom conflict.

'We have been converted into a flagship,' said Carles Vilarrubí, a director of the club, when we met in the VIP reception area of the stadium, ahead of a match. The importance of that flagship was demonstrated when our interview was cut short because Vilarrubí also had to greet a cohort of Catalan politicians, foreign officials, corporate sponsors and celebrity guests, including former players. He shook hands and patted people on the shoulder. His beaming smile was that of a man who knew his way around Catalonia's corridors of power. Before coming to the club, he held key positions with Catalonia's public broadcaster. Now he also works for an investment bank and sits on the board of several Catalan companies and associations.

Between 2003 and 2010, Laporta's tenure as president seemed to showcase the different facets of a club whose directors—at least on paper—form part of a tight-knit Catalan elite. But boardroom disputes spilt over into open rebellion, including one in 2008 that resulted in eight of the 17 directors resigning. An investigation was even launched into whether the club had hired detectives to spy on certain directors.

Still, the team regained its successful streak after a period of disappointing results before Laporta took charge. Barcelona not only won domestic and European trophies, including the coveted Champions League twice, but it also nurtured an exceptional generation of players who reached their peak under Pep Guardiola, a former Barcelona midfielder who had returned as a coach. Many of Guardiola's players also formed the backbone of the Spanish national team that triumphed for the first time in the World Cup, in 2010 in South Africa.

Since then, Barcelona has continued to accumulate silverware, but the club has arguably lost some of its uniqueness within a football world increasingly dominated by the power of money. In December 2010, Barcelona signed a deal worth €165.5 million with the Qatar Foundation to add its name to the team shirt. It was the first time in the club's century-long history that it had received payment to advertise on its team shirt. In doing so, it joined the ever broadening ranks of European clubs financed by Middle Eastern money. (The club had previously had a non-profit sponsorship deal with Unicef.)

'If we could have avoided it, we would not have sold the shirt,' said Vilarrubí, the club director. 'But to continue competing at the level that we have reached, to pay what is paid for the best players now, we had to.'

The Qatari sponsorship remains a sensitive issue. Xavier Sala i Martín, a former treasurer of the club, recounted how his management had opted for Unicef rather than accepting another sponsorship deal worth about €100 million from an online gambling company. The board rejected the idea of advertising the 'disease' of gambling, because it could hurt 'the image of Barça,' he said. In response, the gambling company simply offered its sponsorship to arch-rival Real Madrid, he said, and was accepted.

Barça's image, Sala i Martín argued, required staying committed to democratic values that could not be represented by Qatar. These were the values embodied in Josep Sunyol, a politician and president of the club, who had been killed at the start of the civil war. Sunyol had wanted to drive to the frontline outside Madrid to hand over money to Republican troops, but his driver got lost on the way and they ended up instead being detained and shot by Franco's troops. 'Barcelona is a club of democrats,' said Sala i Martín. 'You cannot have the name of a dictatorship on your shirt.'

Another indication of changing times is that Barcelona is no longer the homegrown team it was a decade ago, when it was heavily reliant on its own youth training academy, La Masia.

As recently as the 2012 season, Barça fielded a team composed entirely of players who had gone through the academy. In 2016, however, the proportion of La Masia-trained players was down to around one third of the team—still high by European football standards, but not exceptional. Barcelona continues to invest heavily in football education—to the tune of almost €30 million a year—but the return on that investment is less apparent. The club's most recent stars have instead joined for stratospheric transfer fees. They include the Brazilian superstar Neymar and Luis Suárez, the Uruguayan who previously played for Liverpool.

With La Masia, 'we all thought that there was a special formula, but we now see that if there isn't really the talent, it doesn't quite work like that,' said Ferran Adrià, the renowned celebrity chef and diehard fan of FC Barcelona. For Adría, having homegrown players on the team is 'important but not essential'—everything depends on the results. 'If we win the Champions League, it doesn't matter' who was playing, Adría said. 'But if we lose, then we will certainly be hearing that those who played weren't Catalans.'

La Masia was designed as 'a factory to create players who were different, but not necessarily Catalans,' Sala i Martin, the former treasurer, told me. Its main purpose, he argued, was to teach the Dutch philosophy of 'total football'—in which all players are trained to play any position—which Johan Cruyff learned as a player before passing it on as Barcelona's coach. In early 2017, shortly after Cruyff's death, the club announced that it would build a statue for its Dutch hero, as well as name an annex stadium after him.

Yet even with this Dutch legacy and more foreign players, Barça's role as Catalonia's ambassador has grown visibly. In September 2012, just after Catalonia celebrated its national day, the club announced that the red-and-yellow stripes of the Senyera, the Catalan flag, would feature on the team's second shirt. A year later, the club proudly announced that sales of its Catalan shirt had overtaken those of the normal *blaugrana* team shirt.

Booing for independence

Whenever Barça plays an important home match these days, a large section of its Camp Nou stadium starts chanting the word 'independence' after seventeen minutes and fourteen seconds of play. This commemorates 1714, the year that Barcelona fell under the control of Spain's Bourbon monarchy. Barça fans nowadays often also wave the Estelada.

In May 2016, the Madrid authorities turned the use of the Estelada into a courtroom dispute, following an attempt to stop

Catalan fans from bringing any Estelada flag to a cup final in Madrid's Vicente Calderón stadium. Two days before the final, however, a judge rejected the arguments of the central government's representative in Madrid, Concepción Dancausa. Dancausa had wanted to prohibit the Estelada on the grounds that 'football in particular should not be converted in a setting for political confrontation.'

The European football authorities, however, have taken a different stance towards the Estelada. In 2015 UEFA, the governing body of European football, imposed a fine on FC Barcelona after its fans waved the flags during a European match. UEFA said that using the Estelada breached European football rules that forbid 'any message that is not fit for a sports event, particularly messages that are of a political, ideological, religious, offensive or provocative nature.'

Rafael Martín Faixó is one of the fans who has regularly booed Spain's national anthem, as well as shouting for Catalonia's independence during Barcelona matches. In April 2014, Martín Faixó filed a lawsuit against Spain's national police, claiming that he had been beaten up by eight police officers during the half-time break of a King's Cup final played in Valencia. He said he had been grabbed by policemen as he made his way to the toilet draped in an independence flag. They allegedly took him down a side staircase and hit him repeatedly, while insulting him for being Catalan.

I met Martín Faixó by chance, while dining with friends in the family restaurant headed by his father. He was courteous and helped select our food and wine, advising on exactly which fish was the best catch that day. I found it hard to imagine such an affable person arrested for hooliganism.

'I played dead so that they would stop,' he said the next morning, having agreed to meet again over breakfast so that he could recount his police ordeal. 'Then they handcuffed me and threw me into a police van like a bag of rubbish.' Martín Faixó spent the night in police custody, but said that he was eventually taken to hospital to be treated for a haematoma and a split rib.

To support his claims, he also showed photos that he had kept of his battered face after his detention.

Spain's national police, however, filed a counter-suit against Martín Faixó. The police denied any wrongdoing and said that he had been detained because of his unruly behaviour, including throwing objects from the stands. Martín Faixó denies this. The police also said that his bruising came from accidentally hitting his face on the ground after he resisted the arrest.

At the time of writing, the case was yet to reach trial. But Martín Faixó's father, who is also called Rafael Martín, said the family had already spent about €24,000 on legal fees and was willing to go further to defend his son's honour. 'If I have to sell our house, I will,' he said.

Other Spaniards, Martín Faixó argued, should respect his right to boo the Spanish anthem, as a sign of his rejection of the monarchy and other Spanish institutions. 'There are people who feel pure hatred for any Catalan who wants to boo the Spanish hymn and wants to leave Spain,' he said. 'I believe it is in moments like this match that we can raise our voice and be heard.'

But Vilarrubí, the club director, insisted that FC Barcelona was 'an institution that will never take sides'. The club never allowed the display of political messages, he said, and the independence flags were distributed by people unrelated to the club, as well as outside the stadium.

'A lot of people would like us to steer completely clear of such issues, but we can't,' Vilarrubí said. Referring to the club's ownership by its thousands of members, he asserted, 'We are a club owned by nobody and owned by everybody.' He defended a decision the club had taken to open its Camp Nou stadium to pro-independence demonstrators, when they had formed a human chain across Catalonia in 2013. 'If there is a human chain that crosses the country and brings together two million people, should we close the stadium?' he asked.

For Vilarrubí, Barça is a victim of double standards, since several other clubs—from Real Betis in Seville to FC Valencia—wear shirt colours that mirror the flags of their regions, without triggering any controversy. Athletic Bilbao also uses the Basque flag, known as the Ikurriña, for its second shirt team.

'It seems to be fine for others, but when Barça wear the Catalan flag, it becomes a political issue,' said Villarubí. 'That doesn't make any sense—it's just crazy and unbelievable.'

The French passion for rugby

In the French city of Perpignan, where some residents speak Catalan, sports is also used to promote Catalan identity, but through rugby rather than football. Perpignan has two rugby clubs that are unabashedly proud of their Catalan roots. (See Chapter 5).

Bernard Guasch turned a family butcher shop into a slaughtering and meat processing company with €40 million of annual sales. By the time we shared a late-morning coffee at his rugby stadium, he had already worked almost a full day, having reached his factory at 3.30 am to supervise the first meat transports. In the afternoon, however, he planned to take a siesta, he said, 'like a real Catalan'.

Guasch used his business acumen and wealth to revive the practice of rugby league in Perpignan, merging two moribund local clubs and then investing enough money in the new club, the Catalan Dragons, to make it the only French team playing in the European Super League. The emergence of the Catalan Dragons coincided with the decline of the Union Sportive des Arlequins Perpignanais, or USAP, which had been one of the leading teams in French rugby union.

The two versions of rugby—union and league—differ in their rules as well as in the number of players. Where both of Perpignan's clubs see eye to eye, however, is in their defence of Catalan values. Before each match, fans of the Catalan Dragons sing the official Catalan anthem, *Els Segadors*. Those of the USAP sing *L'Estaca*, another emblematic Catalan song.

Perpignan's rugby teams have also made themselves ambassadors for Catalonia. In 2007, the Catalan Dragons played a European final at Wembley stadium in London, in front of 85,000 spectators. 'I think it completely stunned people in Barcelona to see that a French team could get a huge crowd to sing *Els Segadors* in England's most famous stadium,' said Guasch. Both the USAP and the Catalan Dragons have the red-and-yellow colours of the Catalan flag on their main team shirts. In the stadium of the Dragons, the stands are also painted red-and-yellow.

The Perpignan rugby clubs have been less successful in promoting their sport in what they call South Catalonia, because it lies on the southern side of the Pyrenees. In 2009 the Catalan Dragons played a match against Warrington, an English team, in Barcelona. The event itself was a success—18,000 spectators watched the game at the Montjuïc Olympic stadium—but Guasch's subsequent attempts to get entrepreneurs in Barcelona interested in investing in rugby went nowhere. 'Sadly we found that the South Catalans were real businessmen, worried about their money and not interested in risking any of it in order to develop our sport,' he said.

Even so, Catalan separatists have used the French rugby games held in Barcelona to promote independence. In June 2016, when Toulon and Racing, two other French teams, played a match in Barcelona, separatist militants distributed 40,000 souvenir postcards to French rugby fans with a clear printed message: 'Barcelona, capital of rugby today and tomorrow capital of a new state.'

At fifty-six, Guasch no longer has the physique that once made him a top-level rugby player. But he keeps his passion for his Catalan origins, including the town of L'Espluga de Francolí, where he spends his summer vacations.

In 1934, Guasch's grandfather was elected as the Republican mayor of L'Espluga de Francolí. But after the Spanish civil war broke out, he was arrested and put in prison in Barcelona. He eventually managed to escape and walk across the Pyrenees to safety in France. One of his sons, José Guasch, became a butcher as well as a star rugby union player. Yet he fell out with his club, the USAP, because he needed money to buy a new meat stand, at a time when rugby union's amateur clubs refused to make any payment to their players. However, Perpignan's main rugby league club, then called the Treize Catalans, stepped in, offering Guasch the money for his meat stand in return for him switching sport and club.

'I don't know if it is because of the failure of Europe or because of globalisation, but I defend an identity based on things very close to me that allow me not to feel lost in this world,' said Guasch. 'I'm administratively French, but deep down I'm Catalan, reaching for my family roots.'

A classic duel

French Catalans have struggled to spread rugby in Catalonia. But perhaps they can take heart from the fact that football also needed foreign input to gain popularity in Catalonia, after getting imported from England to a few other parts of Spain, like Huelva and Bilbao. When Barcelona's first clubs were established, their players were mostly defined by nationality. Gamper's FC Barcelona played its first game on Christmas Eve of 1899, fielding a team mostly made up of Englishmen and other foreigners working in Barcelona. As their name suggests, SC Catala, Barça's opponents on that Christmas debut, had mostly Catalan players.[1]

Barcelona then added another team, Espanyol, founded in 1900 and initially called *Sociedad Española*. The club sought players born in Spain, which helped attract civil servants representing the central government in Barcelona. (In a telling change, the club dropped the Castilian 'ñ' in its name in the 1990s.)

While SC Catala no longer exists, Espanyol has survived, albeit transformed and always in the shadow of Barça. A Chinese company now owns the team. In 2009, Espanyol switched to a new stadium built on the outskirts of the city. After the change in the spelling of its name, the club also reaffirmed its Catalan credentials by following Barça's example and turning the Catalan flag into its second team shirt in 2012.

The shirt similarity, however, has not reduced the rivalry between the two Catalan clubs. In April 2016, I watched Barça crush Espanyol 4–0, in a sold-out Camp Nou stadium. Barça's fans did not miss the chance to rub salt into Espanyol's wounds. They unfurled a banner that read 'Welcome to Barcelona,' in a jibe at Espanyol's move to an out-of-town stadium.

But the real test for FC Barcelona is always the *Clásico* match between Barcelona and Real Madrid, the other powerhouse of Spanish football.

This rivalry is also rooted in the history of Spanish politics. Under Franco, Real Madrid and the national team became the regime's perfect instruments for showing Spain off on the European stage. While Real Madrid dominated European football in the 1950s, Spain's national team beat the Soviet Union in the 1964 final of the European championship in Madrid, creating a symbolic victory for Franco over Soviet Communism.

After winning the civil war, Franco started to interfere in the affairs of FC Barcelona. He forced the club to tweak its name—from FC Barcelona to the Spanish initials of CF—as well as alter its crest because it featured the Catalan flag (though the club got back its original crest in 1949, to mark its fiftieth anniversary.) For many Catalans, the club therefore came to represent a counterweight to the Franco regime. It turned into 'the non-armed army of Catalonia,' a phrase coined by Manuel Vázquez Montalbán, a journalist and writer.

The resistance to Franco, however, was led from the stands rather than the directors' box. Franco initially selected the presidents of Barça. Many of the directors came from a textiles sector that was dependent on Franco for its production quotas and subsidies right until the end of his dictatorship, according to José Martí Gómez, a veteran radio presenter.

'The board cared about their textiles and made clear that anything to do with the club shouldn't interfere with their money issues,' he said.

Yet the club's officials tacitly endorsed the militancy of their fans, for instance during a tram strike in 1951. After watching their team win on a rainy Sunday, the fans walked home from the stadium, avoiding public transport to show support for the strike.[2]

The famous slogan 'more than a club' did not appear till 1968. It was spoken by Narcis de Carreras in his inaugural speech as president. 'Barça is more than a place where we see a team play on Sundays, more than all these things it represents a spirit that is ingrained in us, and wears colours that we esteem more than anything else,' the club's new president said.

To my mind the assertion that Barcelona is 'more than a club' is sometimes problematic. In cities like New York and Hong Kong, I have seen FC Barcelona turn into a global brand that transcends borders and sometimes even any real understanding of football and secessionism. There are fans who adore the players more than their sport. The children in Latin America, Africa or Asia who wear a Barça shirt in their playground would no doubt be stunned to hear that people living close to Barcelona's actual players and stadium are bickering over whether the club is dividing Catalan society.

Conversely Joaquim Coll, a historian and vice-president of the Societat Civil Catalana (an association opposed to secessionism) argued in a newspaper column in 2016 that Barcelona had become 'considerably less' than a club since its management sided with the separatists. Coll even accused the club and its security staff of allowing Catalan flags in the stadium and banning Spanish ones, contrary to the non-intervention policy explained by Villarubí.[3]

Imma Puig, a psychologist who has worked with Barcelona's players for fourteen years, described the stadium as 'the ragbag of Catalonia.' Catalans express 'all the feelings they don't seem capable of expressing elsewhere, perhaps because they have not always been allowed to.' Fans, she said, also display another Catalan trait, which consists of mixing high expectations with a sense of pessimism and apprehension.

The attitude of Barcelona fans, she said, can't be compared to the joy and optimism that can be found in other stadiums of Spain. Fans go the Camp Nou thinking 'let us see what we can do today, because of this fear that something bad could always happen,' Puig argued. She noted that some Catalan families had no qualms about going to court to dispute a club membership if it was left unassigned in a deceased parent's will. 'Having a seat in the stadium signifies a lot in Catalonia—it's like a family asset that defines your identity,' she said.

Indeed, for many fans, allegiance to Barça is an act of faith, shared by hundreds of thousands of migrants who settled in Catalonia. For migrants who did not learn the Catalan language, 'Barça has been an essential factor for social integration,' said Antoni Bassas, a journalist who presented a television series on the club.

Loyalty to Barça perhaps unsurprisingly often comes hand in hand with hostility towards Real Madrid. For many fans, any switch between the two clubs is a deadly sin. In 2002, when Luis Figo returned to Barcelona to play for his new team, Real Madrid, he was pelted with objects thrown from the stands, including a pig's head. Barça received a largely symbolic fine of €4000, even after its then president, Joan Gaspart, suggested Figo should bear some responsibility for the abuse. 'I don't like people to come to my home with the aim of provoking,' he said.

Even a fan shifting support is 'the greatest treason in football.' This was the headline of an opinion column written by David Jiménez for *El Mundo*, published shortly before he was ousted as editor in 2016. Spain is 'a country that could forgive a change of partner, continent or even sex, but never a change of football team,' he wrote.[4] In his piece, Jiménez accused Barça's boardroom of making the club 'another tool to widen the split in Catalan society and marginalise those who do not engage with the independence movement.'

When we met over coffee a few months later, Jiménez, who was born in Barcelona, recalled that this article was also his most read column, reflecting the passions generated by football and secessionism. The real treason, he argued, was not a fan abandoning his childhood club, but a club fracturing Catalan society and distorting its 'more than a club' slogan.

'Divisions are easy to create but much harder to repair,' he said.

18

PLEASURES AND TENSIONS AROUND THE TABLE

After starting from humble origins, Santi Santamaria and Ferran Adrià managed to conquer the world of haute cuisine in the 1990s by setting up two restaurants that became Catalonia's first three Michelin-star establishments.

The two chefs differed in their approach to cooking, but developed a close friendship—which made their eventual falling out even more astounding.

Santamaria was raised in the village of Sant Celoni, in a farming family with a strong sense of Catalan patriotism. His grandfather had been shot at the end of the civil war, when Franco's troops captured Sant Celoni. Later on, Santamaria's father had spent time in police custody for removing signs that had been posted in Castilian Spanish around his village.

Santamaria started working in different factories, including one that made plastic packaging, but then decided that he would convert his home into a restaurant. While cooking there, he also organised evening gatherings to discuss his two passions: food and politics.

Following in his family's footsteps, Santamaria became a fervent supporter of Catalan independence. According to his son, he pushed his activism as far as getting involved in Terra Lliure, the organisation that briefly tried to force Catalan independence through acts of terrorism. At soirées, 'he would be discussing mushrooms one night and independence the following,' said his son, Pau Santamaria.

His Catalan convictions came to the fore in his preaching of the concept of a 'zero kilometre' gastronomy, which stipulated that great food should be grown locally. In 1994, Santamaria became the first Catalan chef to receive his profession's highest accolade, when the Michelin guide awarded a third star to his restaurant, El Racó de Can Fabes.

Santamaria would go to extraordinary lengths to pursue his gastronomic curiosity, as well as to satiate his huge appetite. His son recounted a youth spent trailing after his father for hundreds of miles as they went in search of a special restaurant or food market in the silver-plated Mercedes belonging to Manolo, a local taxi driver. Metaphorically speaking, 'Manolo won the lottery when he came to work with my father, but he also liked using his money to play the real lottery a bit too much,' Pau said, with a smile.

Nothing related to good food was excessive for his father. Pau suffered from dyslexia and used to see a famous specialist in Barcelona. When he was sixteen, his father picked him up one afternoon from the specialist and asked where he wanted to eat. Pau selected a restaurant famous for its desserts. His father agreed, but then decided that they should first visit six other restaurants around Barcelona. Late that night, they reached the establishment chosen by Pau, to have their dessert. 'My father was crazy, I've never seen anybody eat so much,' said Pau. Santamaria was also very extravagant, willing to spend €500 on a tin of gourmet clams or €80,000 euros on a silver tray for his restaurant.

Santamaria and Adrià became close friends. Adrià would take Pau to watch matches in Barcelona's Camp Nou football stadium. After a full evening working in his own restaurant, Santamaria would regularly drive his whole family to El Bulli, Adrià's restaurant overlooking the Mediterranean. There they would share food and ideas with Adrià till the small hours. 'My father would take us all in our Renault 5, after putting us two children asleep in the back, and drive down to El Bulli even if it was already midnight,' Pau said.

Growing up, Adrià had not enjoyed studying and did not see any need to go to university. But he knew that he needed to earn some money in order to have fun, ideally partying in Ibiza. He found a temporary job washing dishes in a hotel restaurant in Castelldefels, a beach town near Barcelona. He had a good enough time there to extend his stay and make it the starting point of a career as a chef.

'I really liked partying, I liked the girls, so I stayed a lot longer washing dishes than the two months that I had planned,' said Adrià. "I really think I started out with less of a vocation than anyone in history who became successful."

After working at a club in Ibiza and preparing the food for his navy commander during his military service, Adrià eventually joined the kitchen of El Bulli, a small and isolated restaurant with wooden beams that had once served as the cafeteria of a mini-golf club. As other staff left, Adrià won promotion and then in 1987 took charge of a kitchen that also included his brother, Albert, who joined as pastry chef. Ten years later, in 1997, El Bulli received its third Michelin star, joining an extremely select group of Spanish three-star restaurants. As well as Santamaria, there was Juan María Arzak, the Basque owner of Arzak, in San Sebastián.

But while the 1990s put Adrià and Santamaria on the same pedestal as standard bearers for Catalan gastronomy, the two started drifting far apart in terms of their cooking. From 1994 onward, Adrià said he stopped doing traditional Catalan cuisine and focused instead on innovative ingredients and cooking techniques. He pioneered the use of chemical emulsifiers and additives such as liquid nitrogen, to achieve instant freezing, and methyl cellulose, a gelling agent. Adrià's push into so-called molecular cuisine was a major departure from the cooking of Santamaria and others.

'The avant-garde has no nationality. Picasso came from Málaga, lived in Barcelona and then moved to Paris, but Cubism has no country,' said Adrià. "I was perhaps informed by my Catalan identity up till 1994. In terms of the way I feel, I still cook like a Catalan. But I have been promoting an entirely different kind of cuisine, which is not something to do with Catalan culture or identity.'

In August 2003 Arthur Lubow, an American food writer, published an article for the weekend magazine of *The New York Times*, which put Adrià on the front cover. He argued that Spain—led by Adrià—was replacing France and its Nouvelle Cuisine as the hub of food creativity. 'While there are many exciting chefs throughout Spain, the name on everyone's lips, the man who is redefining *haute cuisine* into *alta cocina*, is a prodigiously talented, self-taught Catalan,' Lubow wrote. A visit to El Bulli, Lubow advised, is 'a gastronome's once-before-you-die mecca.'[1]

Adrià does not like discussing his fallout with Santamaria, not least out of respect for the memory of a great chef, since Santamaria died in 2011. But for those wanting to point a finger, he believed that the friction started essentially 'because of *The New York Times*—and I'm talking in earnest,' he said. "*The New York Times* decided who in Spain was shaping the revolution—and decided that it wasn't Santi."

The boundless praise from *The New York Times* was 'a shock for many,' Adrià said. It changed 'the image of Spain,' presenting the country as a modern cooking nation ready to surpass France.

Was Santamaria overcome with jealousy? 'To talk about jealousy always makes it sound childish, but I think it was about wanting recognition,' said Adrià. 'There is a part of everybody that needs outside recognition—I am not what I am because of what I say but because of what people say about me.' He told me, however, that he never took the criticism that followed as personal, even if he did not take kindly to suggestions that he should change his cooking, nor to accusations that he was poisoning diners with artificial food.

'I respect the right of every person to do things his own way. Nobody is here to tell me what I should be doing,' said Adrià. 'This became a confrontation between people who wanted change and those who did not. It occurred in Catalonia but it had worldwide repercussions.'

Pau Santamaria said his father was not trying to undermine Adrià but was instead defending his own ideas about healthy food and trying to curb Adrià's so-called molecular cuisine. 'My father believed that we have to allow the client to know exactly what he eats,' he said. 'If something has chemicals in it, it should be labelled as such.'

Yet though he remained very attached to his Catalan roots, Santamaria also pursued his ambitions across the world. He died of a heart attack in Singapore while presenting his most recent restaurant to journalists.

Pau Santamaria is the spitting image of his father, albeit a much svelter version. He also keeps a photo taken at a pro-independence demonstration as the screen shot on his cell phone. He did not join his father in the kitchen. Instead, he tenders a fruit and vegetable garden near Vic that supplies fresh food to about forty restaurants, mostly in Barcelona.

Pau described his father as a workaholic, but he himself is no slacker. On the day that we toured his vegetable field, he had got up around 6 am and planned to work past midnight, to prepare the next day's early-morning deliveries. Inside a shed, he had samples of the ten varieties of tomatoes that he was growing that month, including one that he was keeping because it was his father's favorite. He held it delicately to show off the dark colours of the 'black Crimea' tomato, originally grown on the Black Sea island of Krim.

Keeping the best food

In 2011, the same year that Santi Santamaria died (though the two events were not connected) Adrià stunned the world of gastronomy by closing his El Bulli restaurant. He said that he wanted to create a food research foundation instead.

Despite the concerns, El Bulli's closure did not lower Catalonia's gastronomic profile. In 2013, El Celler de Can Roca—an establishment run by three brothers in a working class neighbourhood of Girona—was voted the world's best restaurant.

The three Roca brothers—Joan, Josep and Jordi—still try to lunch most days on their mother's food, in the nearby restaurant where they learned about cooking while playing football among the tables and chairs. In the mother's establishment, local residents and workers get served a hearty lunchtime menu that costs €11. But those eager to sample the far more intricate and unique dishes prepared by her sons face an eleven-month waiting list for a table and then a bill that starts at €180 per person for the shortest version of the menu, excluding the cost of the wine.

Can Roca lies between El Bulli and Can Fabes, 'both in concept and geography,' since it is 50 kilometres away from both, Joan Roca told me. 'We have strived to be at the vanguard while preserving traditional aspects that are now rarely found in a kitchen like this,' he added, pointing to a firewood oven.

The Rocas decorated the back of their kitchen with a blown-up photograph of a cook running out of Can Fabes, Santamaria's restaurant. But they themselves also came under some criticism from Santamaria.

'When there has been a revolution, it is good to take some time to examine its impact. But Santi did it in a way that was perhaps too aggressive and unorthodox—and that led to conflict,' said Joan Roca.

For all of Santamaria's love of Catalan gastronomy, the Roca brothers noted his cooking had elements that were arguably strongly French, including signature dishes like '*ris de veau*' and '*poularde de Bresse.*'

'It's human nature, but it's a problem when you dress up jealousy as something more conceptual,' said Josep Roca, who is the restaurant's sommelier.

In the meanwhile, the Rocas have helped showcase the diversity of their own Catalan ecosystem. Most notably they have done this by cooking with 400 varieties of plants and herbs found within 40 kilometres of their restaurant, including wild chives, baby sage and red sorrel.

'We found plants that my mother ate because people were scavenging after the war, but that our generation then lost thanks to industrialisation and better times,' Josep told me.

The falling out between Adrià and Santamaria tested allegiances among the chefs' community. Nandu Jubany, a Catalan chef who now runs eighteen restaurants worldwide, was a 'disciple of Santi' at the start of his career. 'I wanted a restaurant like Can Fabes, which was run by a Catalan cook, pro-independence and defender of the Catalan culture,' Jubany said. 'But we reached a moment when Santi was saying that either you go with me or against me.' On the other hand, he said, Adrià kept his door open and "completely changed the concept of what a cook is."

Where the chefs were still united was in raising the status of gastronomy in Catalan society. "When I started working, businessmen came to see me because they were worried that their daughter wanted to be a cook, but now it's a source of family pride," Jubany said.

Restaurants in Catalonia have accumulated fifty-four stars in the Michelin guide for 2017. That's almost one third of the total awarded in Spain, as well as more stars than the three next regions combined (the Basque Country, Madrid and Andalusia.) Given the area's restaurant boom, some experts remain dumbfounded about why there needed to be any rivalry at all at the top of Catalan cuisine.

'Santi was wrong to pick a fight, because there was already room at that time for both,' said Pep Palau, who organises Fòrum Gastronòmic, an annual food fair in Barcelona.

Beyond Adrià himself, El Bulli's kitchen spawned an exceptional generation of chefs, many of whom are nowadays running award-winning restaurants.

Oriol Castro, who spent eighteen years at El Bulli, where he ran the kitchen, opened a Barcelona restaurant, Disfrutar, in 2014, along with two other former El Bulli colleagues. There, they use many of his cooking techniques, as well as maintaining his obsession with innovation.

"At El Bulli, Ferran would be happy with whatever we discovered for one day—then the next day we had to be looking for something else new," said Castro.

Once Adrià had established himself as the leader of a new haute cuisine, he encouraged others to join, promoting a culture of collaboration that first took shape across the Basque region, driven by veteran chefs like Arzak and Pedro Subijana. "While previously a special recipe would be kept in a drawer, Ferran taught us that to share is to profit. Those who don't share recipes are those who probably have very few of them," said Jubany.

Jubany is himself a member of a local association for chefs and restaurateurs around Vic. 'If I hear somebody speaking badly about somebody from the group, I defend him,' he said. 'You end up feeling as if you are in a family.'

Sharing onions

Sharing is certainly an important element in traditional Catalan cuisine, as showcased by the *calçotada*, the winter barbecue party of Catalonia. The *calçot*, a green onion, was probably born in the late nineteenth century in southern Catalonia. According to the legend, a farmer called Xat de Benaiges planted the sprouts of some of his onions and harvested them again the following season. Believing the outcome to have been a failure, he threw the onions in the fire. But when curiosity then made him try out some of the roasted remains, he was stunned by their sweet taste and soft texture, so the *calçot* soon became a local specialty of the farmers around Valls.

Nowadays, these Catalan onions have turned into the gastronomic feast known as the *calçotada*. In the province of Valls alone, it generates about €16 million every winter, as day-trippers from Barcelona and other tourists invade Valls to eat *calçots*.

Silvia Sans Molins, a twenty-five-year-old with a cheerful face, has extended the *calçot* from a winter obsession to a lifetime's pursuit. She has spent five years researching a variety of *calçot* developed around 2015 that almost triples production levels from a decade earlier.

Sans Molins knows all about how to produce the perfect *calçot*. 'You don't want it too fat, because then the inside stays raw, but nor do you want it too small because then it really burns,' she said. For her, the *calçotada* is special because of the convivial way in which it is eaten. 'You get together around the fire and you then get stuck in and get your hands really dirty, so that it gets pretty disgusting,' she said, flashing another smile.

In fact, she argued, the *calçot* loses part of its charm if eaten in a restaurant. 'The really special *calçotada* is when you are with your friends or family, sharing a meal in the countryside, having fun together outside in the fresh air,' she said.

During a summer weekend in the Terra Alta, the highlands of southern Catalonia, I joined Josep Maria Vaquer, an oenologist, as he prepared lunch for his family and friends in a small stone farmhouse, on the border between Catalonia and Aragón. The place can be reached by a dirt track and overlooks a vineyard whose grapes produce Garnatxa blanca, or Grenache blanc—a white wine with a low degree of acidity. There is no other house in sight, except for the ruins of a hermitage.

Behind the farmhouse, Vaquer lit a fire which was made from olive wood to help flavour the sardines and lamb. The lamb was the main course, but the special part of the meal was the starter, the *clotxa*, which turned out to be so filling that it made it hard to eat the main course of roasted lamb.

The *clotxa* is a loaf of bread where the crust is emptied before being filled with salted sardines and tomatoes, as well as with cloves of garlic and olive oil. The *clotxa* was also used as a carrier bag by field workers, which meant they had no need to bring a plate for their lunch break. Vaquer prepared the sardines carefully on the fire. 'I know about my wine, but I think I also know something about grilling,' he said, as he wiped the sweat from his brow and then readjusted his cap.

The *clotxa* is both an individual and a shared experience. Vaquer set the example, preparing his *clotxa* in no time flat. He then invited everybody to select their own ingredients to fill their own loaf. 'The *clotxa* is all about sharing, but each makes his own choices,' he said. 'Some like to add onion, but garlic is just fine for me.'

The origins of food

Catalonia was at the forefront of European gastronomy even in the fourteenth century. This is illustrated by the recipe book of Sent Soví, which was written in 1324 and was an extraordinary example of how advanced Catalan society already was, said Adrià. Like other innovative cooking societies, Catalonia then fell under what Adrià called "the creative monopoly of French gastronomy," which lasted from the seventeenth century well into the twentieth.

The meaning of Sent Soví, as well as its authorship, remains something of a mystery. It was followed by other cooking manuals that codified Catalan cuisine into a set of recipes and techniques unmatched in most other regions of Spain. Some of Sent Soví's recipes were also copied in cookbooks that then formed the cornerstone of fifteenth century Italian cuisine, including the *Libro di arte coquinaria*.

Catalan cuisine 'looks outward, toward Europe and the Mediterranean, rather than back into the Iberian interior,' wrote Colman Andrews, an American food writer, in his book on Catalan gastronomy. 'It is a real cuisine, distinct and elaborate in a way that the cooking of, say, Castile, Andalusia and Extremadura are not.'[2]

During the time of the Roman empire, Catalonia was also the first place in the Iberian peninsula to be planted with olive trees and grapevines, as well as leavened bread, chick peas, lentils and other produce favoured by the Romans. The Moors then brought eggplants, saffron, almonds and cane sugar, as well as a taste for sweet-and-sour flavour combinations that remain a hallmark of Catalan cuisine, according to Andrews. As trade and travel developed, people also started to exchange the recipes of the coast and the highlands, resulting in a sea-and-mountain Catalan cuisine that can be found in popular dishes like braised chicken with shrimp.

The debate over where food and recipes really come from is only relevant in as far as such knowledge can prevent political manipulation, argued Adrià. 'A country and an identity is always the sum of its parts,' he continued. 'Everything comes from somewhere. Take beer—which is not from Germany or Belgium, but originally from Mesopotamia and Egypt.'

In the case of Catalonia, Adrià argued that Catalans should be aware of their 'unique factors,' celebrating their specialities without reinventing their history. That goes equally for mainstay dishes like *pa amb tomàquet*, in which a grilled slice of bread is then rubbed with fresh tomato and seasoned with oil and salt.

The concept of spreading tomato on bread is nowadays part of the staple diet of Catalans, even if there are disagreements over how to make even such a simple dish. Ignasi Camps, who has a restaurant in the village of Cantonigròs, explained that mistakes can arise at every stage. The loaf of bread and tomatoes must first be cut down the middle, he argued, and the tomato must be spread starting from the edges of the bread slice. Then comes an issue that has 'split the country in half,' he said: to salt or not to salt? Camps stuck to pouring some olive oil on his bread slice, without adding salt.

Camps believes *pa amb tomàquet* has been at the heart of Catalan cuisine for at least 100 years, even if its origins are probably more ancient. It most likely reached Catalonia in the early twentieth century, brought by impoverished farmers who migrated from southern regions like Murcia, according to Salvador Cardús, a sociologist. These migrants then built Barcelona's metro and other parts of its infrastructure, on meagre salaries that only allowed them to lunch on dry bread, which they softened and made tastier by adding tomato.

If you go much further back in history, 'bread comes from Mesopotamia and tomato from Peru,' said Adrià. 'You must be fully aware of such origins to make sure you don't get manipulated.' When discussing Catalonia's traditional food, he said, 'Popular Catalan cuisine is very important, based on an incredible geographic and climate situation, but it is also an old culture that has been improved over time.'

Nationalism, in Catalonia or elsewhere, runs counter to the global culture of the internet, he argued. Japanese 'sushi is already Catalan as well as American. Tradition today is a very short concept, because we have moved from the first civilisation, which was Mesopotamia, to the latest, which is global.'

Castro, Adría's former right-hand man, gave the example of uncertainty over the origins of Catalonia's quintessential bread with tomato as a reason to wait before deciding whether Adrià was less faithful to Catalan cuisine than Santamaria. 'Ferran did something different, but perhaps in one hundred years his foams and airs will be considered to be just as much part of Catalan gastronomy as bread with tomato,' he said.

Since closing his restaurant, Adrià has had more time to explore food around the world. I once spoke to him by phone as he was descending a river deep in the Amazon forest, on the trail of indigenous plants and other foodstuff. One of Adrià's projects has been a gastronomic encyclopedia, dubbed Bullipedia, that compiles data about all the ingredients used in cooking. The project was launched in late 2015, in conjunction with about twenty university research centres. Adrià's intellectual pursuits are not tied to any political views, he said, but he has views on national identity.

'What I don't ever find useful is the belief that we are unique,' he said. 'We have to promote our identity, but realise that great people and great things also happen in other parts of the world. Catalonia has enough identity not to nitpick.'

A few chefs and restaurateurs, however, have been happy to mix cooking and politics. Ada Parellada, who comes from a restaurant-owning family, opened her own establishment when she was twenty-five. Almost twenty-five years later, she is running three restaurants, including Semproniana, in Barcelona's Eixample neighbourhood, a place with brightly-coloured walls and shelves filled with vintage objects. Parellada, who has published a dozen cooking books, said her restaurant was also prospering because much of her local clientele shared her views on independence.

'My father taught me that, being in the restaurant business, one should always be apolitical, but I decided to ignore that, because his belief was shaped during a different time, under Franco, when there was actual fear,' she said. 'Anybody who's in business of course should always worry about losing customers,' she added, 'but taking a stance on independence has actually helped my business.'

As to her father's advice, Parellada retorted, 'Actually, I think that I took my stance partly for my father. He would have deserved to live in a country like the one we want Catalonia to be.'

19

THE FACTS OF A GOOD NEWS STORY

Framed front pages of events that have marked Catalonia's road to independence are everywhere you look in the offices of the Girona-based newspaper *El Punt Avui*. Some celebrate Catalan achievements, others highlight the differences between Catalonia and the rest of Spain.

There's the front page published on the night of Mariano Rajoy's election as Spanish prime minister in November 2011. His Popular Party won the most votes across the country—except in Catalonia. *El Punt Avui* chose to ignore the overall result of the election. Instead, under the headline 'Catalonia is not Spain,' it told the story of how Catalans went against the nationwide tide of votes that swept Rajoy into power.

Catalonia has repeatedly been portrayed by the newspaper in terms of its resistance to the rest of Spain. Sometimes it has used cartoon maps resembling those in the famous comic books where Asterix and Obelix fight the mighty Roman Empire. Other maps show Spain in crisis. In May 2012, when Spain's banking system needed rescuing, Punt Avui printed a map of a fractured Spain on its front page, under the headline 'Spain is falling apart.'

'All newspapers have an ideology, but ours is perhaps clearer and more transparent than others,' said Xevi Xirgo, *El Punt Avui*'s editor-in-chief.

The polarisation of Spanish politics has been a dominant theme across the Spanish media. The division has been exacerbated not least because of the financial difficulties of a sector whose advertising revenues have dwindled, particularly for newspapers.

'The media has become so weak,' said Joan Vall i Clara, the chief executive of *El Punt Avui*. 'There is a widespread problem of media dependence on those who have political as well as economic power.' Those tensions are becoming ever more visible. Since 2014, two ousted editors of *El Mundo*, one of Spain's main conservative newspapers, have accused outsiders of interfering in their editorial decisions.

Catalan secessionism has also created a split in newspaper readership, at the same time as online media have provided access to more sources of information. Vall i Clara noted that the four main political newspapers printed in Madrid—*El País, El Mundo, ABC* and *La Razón*—sell less in Catalonia now than his own newspaper. 'Catalans these days hardly read the newspapers from Madrid,' he said.

In 2010 another daily newspaper, *Ara*, was launched in Catalonia for the separatist readership. Yet even this faced challenges in an era when Catalan language media are struggling. They receive public subsidies, but not enough to offset the dramatic fall in corporate advertising. In *Punt Avui's* case, said Vall i Clara, language-linked subsidies amounted to €800,000 out of a budget of €22 million.

Complaints over political interference have also risen in relation to public television networks that have been losing market share. 'One of the weaknesses of our democracy is that we have not managed to protect public media from political interests,' said Màrius Carol, the editor of *La Vanguardia*, the Barcelona-based newspaper. 'It makes no sense that a change in the Spanish government should mean a change of director of the national television—something which also happens in Catalonia.'

Television made a late arrival in Spain. The country was kept internationally isolated by Franco's regime for a long time, at a point when other European economies were recovering from the Second World War with huge financial aid from America's

Marshall Plan. As a result, until the 1960s, television had hardly made any inroads. By this time almost one quarter of British households already owned their own sets. Even after the television boom started in Spain's main cities, television remained a luxury in the countryside, where villagers instead would gather around a TV set located in the country's 6,000 'teleclubs,' which opened as municipal leisure centres. Wherever it was watched, Spanish television only showed the programmes that had got past Franco's censorship.

In the absence of free media, other ways of challenging the regime emerged. In Catalonia, a new generation of singers began defying the dictatorship in the 1960s by singing in the banned Catalan language. Their movement became known as the *Nova cançó*, or New song.

Lluís Llach was one of the main artists of the *Nova cançó*, whose popularity transcended Catalonia and eventually allowed him to sell a third of his records in France. Llach grew up in the village of Verges, in what he called 'a clearly pro-Franco family'. However, he left for France in the final years of Franco's regime. In 1973, he made his debut at the Olympia, the famous Paris concert hall.

'When I turned seventeen or eighteen,' he told me, 'I realised that I was in a repressed cultural community and that I belonged to a sexual as well as a linguistic minority, always living on the edge of danger. To defend a small language without a state and without any protection was for me as important as defending the right to sexual diversity.'

In 1968, Llach composed *L'Estaca*, a song about a rotting stick that made a thinly-veiled comparison with Franco's faltering regime. The song—to this day—remains the anthem of the Catalan independence movement. He declared, 'Catalan singers became reference points for society at a time when our media was almost non-existent.'

Some other artists also used their creative license to circumvent Franco's media censorship. Even though Franco's regime prohibited any private television project, in 1974 Antoni

Muntadas set up a local Catalan channel, in the resort of Cadaqués. His 'prototype', Cadaqués Canal Local, as Muntadas called it, lasted only one week. Then Franco's ministry of information sent a telegram from Madrid ordering its closure.

Muntadas was not trying to kickstart a political uprising but he did want to challenge Franco's control over information. The Cadaqués channel mixed interviews with short reports about local life, which residents could watch on television sets distributed around the bars of Cadaqués.

'I wanted to question the hegemony of television, because it is incredible to think that in 1974 Spain still had only one channel,' Muntadas said, sitting in his apartment, with one of the posters promoting his Cadaqués channel framed on his wall. 'It wasn't about raising our fists to protest, but about showing that television should mirror reality, life in a village as it really was.'

Once Franco's dictatorship ended, the return of free media helped transform Spanish society, reviving the dormant culture of debating everything, from politics to the arts. In Catalonia, the media also served the additional purpose of re-establishing the Catalan language.

Catalan readers were able to discover new or forgotten words in the newspaper *Avui*, which was started in 1976 as the first daily published in Catalan since the civil war. That same year, Joaquim Maria Puyal provided the first radio commentary for a FC Barcelona match in Catalan. 'He really created his own dictionary of football in Catalan,' said Carol, the editor of *La Vanguardia*.

Pooping for a laugh

In July 1983, a precocious radio presenter, Miquel Calçada, became the first person to speak on Catalonia's new public radio broadcaster. Calçada had first gone on air as a fifteen-year-old, on a local radio station in Terrassa. He was about to turn eighteen when his voice launched Catalonia's public radio.

Calçada continued his breakthrough by becoming the first person to convince Spain's national television to make a Castilian version of a Catalan talk show. The show was a hit in Catalonia, with Calçada conducting the interviews in the persona of 'Mikimoto'. On Spanish television, however, Mikimoto only survived one year. Somehow, the audience outside Catalonia did not bond with a character who mixed sarcasm and provocation and wore the clothing and sunglasses of a 'bad boy' rockstar.

'It was a once-in-a-lifetime experience, never to be repeated,' Calçada said, with a frown on his face. He remembered an uncomfortable Christmas dinner in Madrid, organised by Spanish television for its presenters. 'I really didn't belong there,' Calçada said. 'I didn't laugh at their jokes and it was very difficult for me.'

Was the problem that most Spaniards do not laugh at the same jokes as Catalans? Calçada claimed that it was 'scientifically proven' that the Catalan sense of humour was closer to that of Britain than that in the rest of Spain. In the 1980s, he said, Catalan viewers fell for British comedy series that got a much more lukewarm response in the rest of Spain, like *Black Adder*, *The Young Ones*, or *Yes Minister*.

Producers of Catalan comedy or political satire have struggled to export their work to Madrid, Calçada argued, because such programmes generally require a sense of self-mockery. Other Spaniards, he concluded, 'cannot stand laughing at themselves'.

The sociologist Salvador Cardús concurred, saying that for all the importance of Catalan flags and other symbols, Catalan society is distinguished by being 'incredibly irreverent'. Take the example of Jordi Roca, a famous pastry chef who launched an ice cream business in 2012 that sells a popsicle shaped like his protruding nose. 'I probably had a bit of a complex about my nose as a child, but I learnt to laugh at myself,' Roca told me. 'I really think that's one of our strengths' as Catalans.

Toni Soler, the director of *Polònia*, the main political satire show on Catalan television, said it was difficult to draw firm conclusions about why his show might not translate for a Spanish audience. But he noted that Catalan politicians did not complain about having his actors mimic them. 'Since everybody is inherently ridiculous, they accept that these are the rules of the game,' Soler said.

He pointed out that a striking aspect of Catalan humour is its scatological obsession, whether in jokes or in Christmas traditions. Catalan children search for the '*caganer*,' or pooper figurine, that is hidden somewhere in the nativity scene. Christmas presents are also traditionally next to the '*caga tió*,' a log with a painted smiling face which children are made to believe can poop their gifts out. Both traditions date to a time when human excrement was used to help fertilise fields and was therefore also a symbol of food and prosperity in the countryside.

Since the 1990s, the '*caganer*' figurines have increasingly been made to look like politicians and other celebrities, in workshops like that owned by Anna María Pla, a former ceramic artist, and her two sons, in the town of Torroella de Montgrí. 'For a Catalan politician, there is pride rather than shame in having his own *caganer*,' said Pla, as she sat before a table covered with some of the 450 hand-painted figurines of celebrities that her Caganer. com company makes. The likenesses range from Catalan sportsmen and politicians to foreigners like Donald Trump, whose figurine has also become a hit in the United States.

A public broadcaster

In the 1980s, Jordi Pujol, the founder of the Convergence party, helped reshape Catalonia's media, turning the launch of TV3, the public television channel, into 'the jewel in the crown' of his project for Catalonia, according to Carol, *La Vanguardia's* editor. 'Pujol believed that an essential part of his legacy would be to leave behind a broadcaster that restored and normalised Catalonia and its language,' said Carol.

TV3 certainly expanded viewers' vocabulary in Catalan when it started to dub *Dallas* and other foreign hit series. '*Dallas* had the first insults that I heard on television in Catalan,' Carol said. 'There were expressions that had to be created anew.' The 'bitch' insult repeatedly leveled at Sue Ellen, one of the *Dallas* characters, became '*pendó*' in Catalan.

But sometimes Catalan public media can be accused of pushing the promotion of Catalonia to the limit. In 2007, the public radio broadcaster was forced to issue an apology to Cristina Peri Rossi, a Uruguayan writer. It had announced her dismissal as a contributor because the broadcaster said it could no longer pay anybody who spoke on the radio in Castilian Spanish rather than Catalan. Peri Rossi responded with dismay, saying that she thought that she had been hired 'not for the language in which I express myself, but for what I say.'[1]

During the 2016 Olympic Games in Rio de Janeiro, TV3 also generated criticism in Madrid for displaying a Catalan flag rather than a Spanish flag next to the names of Catalan athletes representing Spain. When Mireia Belmonte, a swimmer, won Spain's first gold medal of the Rio games, TV3 also pointedly described her as a Catalan swimmer. Despite this, Belmonte celebrated her win by draping herself in a Spanish flag, handed over by her father from the stands.[2]

On the flip side of the coin, as secessionism has gained ground, so too have complaints in Catalonia about the Madrid-based media. In 2014, a group of Catalan lawyers set up an association, Drets, to identify and prosecute anti-Catalan defamation in the Spanish media and on social networks. In August 2015, Drets even targeted Felipe González, Spain's former Socialist prime minister, after he wrote an open letter to Catalans—published on the front page of *El País*, Spain's main newspaper—to warn that independence could turn Catalonia into the 'Albania of the twenty-first century.' González made free with his damning political metaphors, also comparing the secessionist plan to Europe's past experience of Fascism. 'It most resembles the German or Italian adventure' of the 1930s, González wrote.[3]

Drets accused González of violating 'the moral integrity' of Catalans, as well as rendering Nazism and Fascism banal. The public *prosecutor's office*, however, rejected the lawsuit.

Maria Vila, a lawyer from Drets, claimed that Spain's judiciary repeatedly sentenced citizens for defamatory online comments, as well as some deemed to incite and praise violence, but ignored similar attacks on Catalonia. 'There is an absolute and brutal difference in treatment,' Vila argued.

Covering Pujol

Even if the media have probably lost more of their independence since the financial crisis of 2008, the problem dates further back. In Spain, the return of a free press after Franco's dictatorship did not result in unfettered criticism of the political establishment. In Catalonia, this became even more apparent once Pujol took charge of Catalonia and became the key partner of successive governments in Madrid.

'The media mostly protected Pujol because he had such huge influence,' said Andreu Missé, who spent seventeen years reporting from Barcelona for *El País*, while Pujol ran Catalonia. 'But you have to understand the historical context, of Pujol as a national hero in Catalonia. He was also admired as a democrat throughout Spain, a man who was tortured during Franco's regime and who then founded a party that managed to gain back freedoms and a level of self-government for Catalonia never seen before.'

Missé was one of the journalists who investigated the problems of Banca Catalana, the financial institution founded by Pujol's father. In May 1984, *El País* broke the news that the state prosecutor was about to indict Pujol and other directors of the bank. As discussed earlier in this book, the scandal did not taint Pujol, since Pujol managed to 'wrap himself in the Catalan flag' and turned a story of corporate mismanagement and fraud into a political issue. He was later cleared of wrongdoing.

'The case was turned into an attack on Catalonia,' Missé recalled. 'Once economic issues become politicised like that, they get stuck in the middle—they are neither a classic financial scandal nor a real political conflict, which makes it very hard for citizens to get any clear idea of why things went wrong.'

As a Catalan writing for a Madrid-based newspaper, Missé found it almost impossible not to get caught himself in the middle of the political tensions. 'Whatever I wrote for *El País*, whether about Banca Catalana or later about issues of regional financing, I was always just seen as the one writing for Madrid,' he said.

José Antich, a newspaper editor, argued that the shortcomings in the coverage of Pujol and his banking problems needed to be analysed in their historical context. With hindsight, Pujol's decision to keep shares in Banca Catalana after his election could be labelled as a conflict of interest. But in the 1980s, Antich argued, it was a less serious issue, since there were no official rules on such conflicts of interest. On top of this the banking scandal occurred three years after an aborted Spanish military coup. 'The view then was that there was no conflict worth having if it could affect our democratic health,' said Antich.

Still, it seems to me that the political consequences of a failed coup should never have prevented journalists from properly investigating a failed bank. Antich acknowledged that Pujol found it easy to keep not only journalists at bay, but also other political parties, trade unions and interest groups that received loans from his father's bank. Banca Catalana was 'a bank in which a large part of the Catalan political class had been implicated,' Antich said. Catalonia's new public television also transformed the banking scandal into a political conspiracy. Thanks to TV3, 'this was immediately sold as a political operation against Pujol,' said Antich.

The flaws of the Catalan media were chronicled in depth by Jordi Pérez Colomé in a series of articles published in 2015 by *El Español*, a Madrid-based online newspaper. Pérez Colomé argued that Pujol convinced important journalists to work for his government, while ordering investigations into other reporters who would not switch sides. Pérez Colomé also pointed out the obstacles faced by anybody trying to probe Pujol's entourage, such as the three co-authors of a book on Banca Catalana, who ran into all sorts of problems to get their work published.

According to Pérez Colomé, the Catalan media had limited leeway for several reasons. First, public subsidies to Catalonia's private media have been higher than elsewhere in Spain. Second, the politics of Catalan nationalism added an element of 'emotional adherence' to the media coverage, Pérez Colomé claimed. Finally, a relatively small and tight-knit place like Catalonia could build more impenetrable networks of power than larger countries.[4]

Since January 2016, Catalonia has been led by a former newspaper editor, Carles Puigdemont, who was also once the founder of a Catalan news agency. According to Puigdemont, the accusations of political bias in the Catalan media come mostly from politicians with their own biased agenda, namely to prevent Catalonia's independence. The criticism from the Ciudadanos party and Madrid politicians ignores the plurality and diversity of the media in Catalonia, he said, including the fact that most Catalans watch Spanish rather than Catalan television channels. Indeed, TV3, the Catalan broadcaster, has seen its audience market share fall by about 10 percentage points between 2010 and 2016, mirroring a similar drop for Spain's national broadcaster.

'There is this toxic explanation that what is happening in Catalonia is the fault of TV3, media subsidies and language immersion,' said Puigdemont, referring also to the push to teach Catalan at school. 'The brainwashing theory is pretty insulting for the majority of Catalans who can read and watch what they want.'

For all the awareness of Spain's history of censorship under Franco, Puigdemont suggested that remarkably little attention was given to the news selection criteria applied from Madrid by Spain's public radio and television corporation, particularly in its political coverage. More than six months after his election as leader of Catalonia, Puidgemont said that he was surprised not to have received any interview request from Spain's national television, even though Catalan separatism was at the top of Spain's political agenda. 'Any voice in favour of independence just doesn't appear,' he said.

While the management of Spanish television has denied any editorial interference, the broadcaster's own ethics committee has regularly complained about political news items being purposely ignored or downplayed. Still, Puigdemont said that his main preoccupation was not the bias of the media, but the lack of truth in much of the information released both from Madrid and Barcelona. Inaccurate reporting stretched from politics to more personal matters, he argued.

Puigdemont listed some untruthful stories that had been written about him, ranging from the size of his salary to his 'mop top' haircut, which resembles the style made famous by the Beatles in the 1960s. Some in the media have claimed that the fringe was grown in order to hide a scar on his forehead. 'Such information is literally wrong,' he protested. Not such a big deal compared to the fake news spread about other politicians around the world. But, as Puigdemont is well aware, small inaccuracies can lead to bigger and more dangerous misperceptions.

CONCLUSION

I first went on a major trip just before turning eighteen, in the summer of 1989, travelling by train across much of Communist Eastern Europe.

The trip had needed the kind of planning that few such journeys now require, because the Communist countries only reluctantly gave visas to individual visitors who did not join tours organised by their official travel operators. With the help of some family friends working for international organisations in Geneva, I eventually managed to get the visas, while some friends of friends generously agreed to host me on the other side of the Iron Curtain.

I was initially due to travel with a close friend, but he had to drop out shortly before departure. My mother was not keen to see me travel alone and out of reach, long before the age of the smartphone. 'You can see what is behind the Berlin Wall next year,' she told me.

But since I had already put quite a lot of effort into preparing this trip, I ignored my mother's advice. In July, I arrived in Budapest—just in time to see East Germans climb over the walls of Western embassies to seek political asylum. I left East Germany two months later, just after the first street demonstration in Leipzig that would be the prelude to the fall of the Berlin Wall later that year.

The trip taught me how quickly the world can change. At the time of finishing this book, Catalonia's independence appears out of reach. But I no longer believe in labelling any political or social change as impossible.

At the start of this century, how many people thought that Americans would elect their first black president, followed by a political outsider like Donald Trump? How many thought Colonel Muammar Gaddafi would be killed by his own people in the midst of a popular uprising? Or that the British would vote to leave the European Union?

Every 11 September, I also think about the strange coincidence of watching Catalans celebrate their national day on what has become a day of mourning in America. When terrorists flew planes into the World Trade Center, they also changed America's concept of security in a way that nobody foresaw.

Thinking back to some of these monumental changes, the creation of a new Catalan state does not look like a pipedream. But neither, of course, does it seem inevitable, particularly since Catalan society has often shown itself to be more inclined towards pragmatism rather than hot-headed idealism.

'Catalans can feel that they have the moral high ground, talking about democracy, about our rights and how badly we are treated by Madrid, but we don't have an army, we don't have a treasury and we don't have anything except wishful thinking,' said José María Martí Font, a journalist and the president of an association of Catalan correspondents. 'Who is going to be the first Catalan really willing to risk major problems, in the name of independence?'

So far, Catalan secessionism has increased the split between the politicians in Madrid and Barcelona. But more open attitudes on both sides, or perhaps a changing of the political guard, could go a long way towards bridging the gap. At the time of writing, Mariano Rajoy, Spain's prime minister, had instructed his deputy, Soraya Sáenz de Santamaría, to reopen the dialogue with Barcelona and spend more time there in 2017. Rajoy then also promised billions of investment in Catalan transport infrastructure to help 'seal cracks, rebuild bridges and look ahead of us.'

In the meantime, Catalan politicians also need to consider the divisions that they have helped widen within a society that has always had its split personality, torn between what Catalans call their '*seny i rauxa*,' or sanity and rage.

This almost bipolar Catalan trait was perhaps best analysed by Jaume Vicens Vives, a historian who published an essay in 1954 that is still considered essential reading on Catalonia. Blending history with sociology, Vicens Vives also highlighted the dichotomy between the Catalans from the mountains and those from the sea. For all the efforts that Catalans have made to be portrayed as a people of sea merchants, it is mountain peasants who gave Catalans their most specific traits, according to Vicens Vives. 'In Catalonia, the shepherd and the siren, as in other countries of the Mediterranean, have rarely got on,' Vicens Vives wrote. 'The nerve of the Catalan mentality has been created in the mountain.'

A foreign visitor to the new 'mountain' bastions of secessionism, cities like Berga, might easily reach the conclusion that Catalonia's declaration of independence is only weeks away. But if this same foreigner then visited some of the cities around Barcelona, like L'Hospitalet de Llobregat, independence would seem only a remote possibility.

Finally, there is an important issue to consider, which is whether the passage of time favours or runs against secessionism. Part of the answer depends on events probably beyond the control of anybody either in Madrid or Barcelona. Another European financial crisis, for instance, could revive the kind of social tensions that surfaced around 2011, in the midst of record unemployment and soaring debt levels. Another major European political change could also send shockwaves as far as Catalonia, notably if the Scots were to hold another independence referendum, as their leader, Nicola Sturgeon, is demanding.

To explain why Catalonia will remain a thorny issue for Spain—whatever else happens in the rest of Europe—academics in Madrid often quote José Ortega y Gasset, the philosopher who studied extensively Spain's idiosyncrasies. In a famous 1932 parliamentary speech, Ortega argued that Catalonia 'is a problem that cannot be resolved, that can only be steered along.'

Of course, many separatists believe that they are steering Catalonia along a one-way road towards independence. Oriol Junqueras, the leader of the Esquerra Republicana party, told me that 'our desire for independence doesn't change if Scotland wants to be independent or gets independence.' Matters of national identity, Junqueras argued, transcend issues of time. 'Did the Irish, after three centuries of being British, get tired of being Irish?' he asked rhetorically. 'No'—and neither, he predicted, would Catalans suddenly abandon their efforts to stop being subjects of the Kingdom of Spain.

Junqueras belongs to a generation of Catalan politicians who are staking their careers on fulfilling their independence pledge, one way or another.

'It is by putting one foot after another that you make progress,' said Raül Romeva, the foreign policy chief of Catalonia. 'If we have to go back to base camp because of a storm and then climb via another mountain trail, we will.'

But it still seems to me that timing could prove important for Catalonia, particularly as two forces appear to be pulling in opposite directions.

One is political momentum. The prolonged bickering among politicians, both in Barcelona and in Madrid, has left citizens feeling profoundly disillusioned. Many of those who once thought that independence could be achieved swiftly now feel that political pledges have been broken. After all, Catalans have taken part in nine different votes since 2010 (including municipal elections), but their results have not led to any fundamental change in the relationship between Madrid and Barcelona.

Pere Vehí, the owner of a bar in Cadaqués, compared the situation to that of a restaurant manager who ends up confusing even his own staff about what kind of menu is on offer. 'I have believed in independence for the last two or three years, but this whole process has just become a synonym for confusion,' he said. 'I have got tired of how much useless talk there is.'

CONCLUSION

On the other hand, there is the demographic force of secessionism. I have met a generation of Catalan students who have been involved in an independence debate that their parents would not have had. Many have become deeply committed to the secessionist cause, without even necessarily living in Catalonia.

Take the example of Marc Blay, who finished his political studies at the Pompeu Fabra university in Barcelona and then started working in Amsterdam, just as Catalonia's separatist politicians were staging an informal ballot on independence, despite Madrid's opposition. On the day of the ballot—9 November 2014—Blay could neither vote online nor mail his vote to Catalonia. There was also no polling station in Amsterdam, so Blay paid for a day return train ticket to Brussels, the nearest city where Catalans could cast a vote, in a ballot box located within Catalonia's European Union representative office.

'We had to queue for four hours, but that at least gave me time to meet a lot of fun Catalans who had also travelled from all sorts of other places,' Blay said. 'I knew that my vote would change nothing legally and certainly wouldn't bring independence, but I felt it was an important gesture, at least to claim the democratic right to vote.'

Blay and many others have spent time and money wanting to get involved in a political process that they consider essential for their generation, however significant the obstacles.

During the Diada demonstrations, small children take to the streets, their faces painted in the red-and-yellow colours of Catalonia. They wave flags and clutch the hand of their parents to avoid getting lost in the crowd. It has reminded me of how my father once took me to Servette Geneva's special match against FC Barcelona.

These Catalan children will be the voters of tomorrow, fed on the exhilaration of the Diada, like young football fans who remember the excitement of their team's first big match. Few of us football fans probably remember exactly why we started to feel close to our team. But even fewer of us have later been swayed to change allegiance.

Shortly after taking office as Catalonia's leader in 2016, Carles Puigdemont delivered a speech in which he paraphrased a famous Spanish poet, Jaime Gil de Biedma. Gil de Biedma wrote that 'life is a serious matter, but that is something one only gets to understand later.' Puigdemont adapted the poet's words to say that 'independence is a serious matter that you will only understand when it is too late.'

There still appears to be time to defuse tensions between Madrid and Barcelona. What may be missing is the will. Prime Minister Rajoy and others seem to believe that the Catalan issue can be swept under the carpet, perhaps long enough for some institutional reforms, more public investments and a stronger Spanish economy to heal wounds or reduce secessionist aspirations.

But breaking political deadlock, in my limited experience, has generally required strong negotiation skills, of the kind that were sorely missing as I was finishing this book, in early 2017. If Spanish unity is to be preserved, politicians and ordinary citizens also need to spend more time forging mutual understanding and recognising the plurality of their nation.

I struggle to understand people who do not see the advantage of speaking several languages. Yet I am also dumbfounded by those who decry an opinion without first seeking to understand it. Sadly, I have hardly met a single fierce opponent of Catalan secessionism who has actually watched a Diada demonstration. Without at least trying to understand the feelings expressed by hundreds of thousands on the streets of Barcelona, any attempt to reunite the peoples of Spain will remain little more than a scramble in the dark.

APPENDIX

LIST OF INTERVIEWS

Abella, Susana — spokesperson for the association defending the Ebro delta

Abril i Abril, Amadeu — law professor and promoter of Catalan domain name

Adell, Joan-Elies — director of Catalan regional government office in Alghero

Adrià, Ferran — chef of El Bulli restaurant

Alberich, Jordi — director general of Cercle d'Economia, Catalan business association

Alivesi, Sara — journalist in Alghero

Álvarez Junco, José — historian

Alvesa, Hortensia — pensioner from Valderrobres

Antich, José — cditor of *El Nacional*

*Aragay, Ignasi — culture journalist and subdirector of *Ara* newspaper

Armengol, Manel — photographer

Arguera, José Antonio — former president of Maella's football supporters' club

*Arrimadas, Inés — Catalan regional leader of the Citizens party

Atxaga, Bernardo — Basque writer

Aznar, José María — former prime minister of Spain

Ballone, Francesco — language expert in Alghero

Bartolomé, Pere — recipient of family documents from Salamanca civil war archives

Bassas, Antoni	journalist at *Ara* newspaper
**Batet, Albert	mayor of Valls
Batet, Meritxell	Socialist member of Spanish Parliament
Bayén, Juanito	owner of Pinotxo bar in Barcelona
Bel, Ferran	mayor of Tortosa
Bel, Germà	Catalan lawmaker and professor of public policy
Bengoetxea, Joxerramon	Basque professor of jurisprudence
Bergaz Pessino, Juan	archivist of Bacardi drinks company
Bertrana, Eva	director of La Bressola school in Perpignan
Bes i Martí, Xavi	wine distributor
Blay, Marc	former student of political studies at Pompeu Fabra university
**Bonet Ferrer, José Luis	president of Freixenet, producer of cava
Bosch, Alfred	historian and politician of Esquerra Republicana
Boadas, Joan	head of the Girona archives
Boadella, Albert	playwright, theatre director and founder of Els Joglars company
Bonet, Jordi	architect of Sagrada Família
Bostyn, Christophe	Belgian consultant and political scientist working in Barcelona
Burzako Samper, Mikel	government official from Basque Nationalist Party
Cabarrocas, Jordi	director of the 1898 Company, Cuban asset recovery fund
Calçada, Miquel	television producer and media entrepreneur
Camps, Ignasi	restaurant owner in Cantonigròs
Camps, Òscar	lifeguard and founder of Proactiva Open Arms
**Carbonell, Xavier	chief executive of Palex, a supplier of medical devices

APPENDIX

Cardús, Salvador	sociologist
Carod-Rovira, Josep-Lluís	former politician and professor of social diversity
Carol, Màrius	editor of *La Vanguardia*
Cànovas, Alfred	honorary president of Atlètic–Barceloneta swimming club
Castellà Andreu, Josep Maria	law professor at University of Barcelona
Castro, Oriol	chef and restaurant owner
Catalán Barceló, Miguel Ángel	pensioner from Maella
Cendoya, Núria	director of El Rosal biscuit maker
Coixet, Isabel	film director
Colau, Ada	mayor of Barcelona
Colón, Cristóbal	founder of La Fageda yoghurt company
**Conesa, Ángel	judge of *castell* tournament in Tarragona
Costas, Antón	professor of economics at Barcelona University
Cruanyes, Josep	lawyer who has investigated Salamanca archives
*Cuixart, Jordi	president of Òmnium Cultural
*Culla, Joan B.	Catalan historian
Cuní, Josep	television and radio presenter
de Carreras, Francesc	professor of constitutional law, co-founder of Citizens party
De la Fuente, Ángel	economist and director of Fedea economics research institute
Di Francesco, Hugues	French singer and composer
Elzo, Javier	Basque professor of sociology
Expósito, Marcelo	member of the Spanish parliament for En Comú Podem
Fara, Maria Giovanna	official of Meta tourism foundation of Alghero
Fernàndez, David	lawmaker of the CUP party

Font, Sergi	president of the Verdi street association in Gràcia
Font, Jacques	cinema owner in Perpignan
Fontana, Josep	historian
**Forcades, Teresa	nun and co-founder of a separatist political movement
Fossas, Ignasi	prior of Montserrat monastery
**Fraga Iribarne, Manuel	senator and former minister under Franco (died January 2012)
Fuerte, Veronica	founder of Hey, Barcelona design studio
**García Albiol, Xavier	president of the Catalan branch of the Popular Party
Gasch, Manel	administrator of Montserrat monastery
Gendrau, Pere	journalist from Berga
Giménez, Xavi	Catalan cinematographer
Gimeno, Albert	journalist and media executive, former interior ministry spokesman
Giralt-Miracle, Daniel	art critic and exhibition curator
Goia, Eneko	mayor of San Sebastián
Guardans, Ignasi	former member of the European Parliament
Guasch, Bernard	chairman of Catalan Dragons rugby league club
El Hachmi, Najat	Moroccan-born Catalan writer
Homs, Francesc	Catalan spokesman of Convergence party in Spanish Parliament
**Hugh, Edward	British economist who lived in Catalonia (died December 2015)
*Iceta, Miquel	leader of the Catalan Socialist party
Jiménez, David	former Editor in Chief of *El Mundo*
Junqueras, Oriol	President of Esquerra Republicana party
Jubany, Nandu	Catalan chef

Keating, Michael	politics professor at the University of Aberdeen
Khalsa, Gagandeep Singh	representative of Sikh community
Lacueva, Miguel	pensioner from Maella
Lafontaine, Brice	deputy mayor of Perpignan, representing Unitat Catalana party
Borja Lasheras, Francisco de	director of Madrid office of European Council on Foreign Relations
Lago Peñas, Santiago	economics professor at Vigo University
Lamo de Espinosa, Emilio	sociologist and president of Real Instituto Elcano think tank
**Laporta, Joan	lawyer and former president of FC Barcelona
Legrais, Hélène	French writer from Perpignan
Lite, Marc,	co-founder of Firma, Barcelona-based branding consultancy
Llach, Lluís	songwriter and member of Catalan Parliament
Lobo i Gil, Ricard	writer and former Montserrat monk
Longo, Francisco	professor of public management at Esade University
López Burniol, Juan José	Catalan lawyer and notary
Madí, David	businessman and former chief of cabinet of Artur Mas
Majà, Marc	priest from Berga
Majó, Joan	former Spanish industry minister
Malé, Toni	civil servant in Barcelona
Manchón, Manel	editor of *Economía Digital*
Manzanares, Pere	promoter of Arels school in Perpignan
Martí Gómez, José	radio journalist for Cadena Ser
Martí Font, José María	president of the Association of Catalan Correspondents

Martin Faixó, Rafael	fan of FC Barcelona
Marín i Martínez, Núria	Socialist mayor of L'Hospitalet de Llobregat
Martín, Rafael	restaurant and vineyard owner in Cadáques
Martínez, Dolors	member of the Verdi street association
Mas, Artur	former leader of Catalonia
Mascarell, Ferran	Catalan historian and politician
Mas Collel, Andreu	former Catalan finance minister
Mas de Xaxàs, Santi	official from PAH association fighting housing evictions
Matabosch, Joan	artistic director of Teatro Real, Madrid opera house
Mayor Oreja, Jaime	former Spanish minister of the interior
Mayoral, Jordi	art gallery director
McCrone, David	professor at the Institute of Governance of Edinburgh University
Minoves Pujols, Ramon	town hall councillor in Berga
Missé, Andreu	business journalist, director of Alternativas Económica
Molina, Tomàs	Catalan television weather presenter
Molins, Cèsar	chief executive of Ames, maker of car parts
Muñoz, Ramon	mayor of La Galera
Muntadas, Antoni	artist and university professor
Nadal, Joaquim	historian and former mayor of Girona
Novoneyra, Branca	culture official in Santiago de Compostela's city hall
*Olid, Bel	president of the Catalan language writers' association

APPENDIX

Ollé, Àlex	artistic director of theatre company Fura dels Baus and opera stage director
Ortiz, Daniela	Peruvian born artist living in Barcelona
Palau, Pep	organiser of Fòrum Gastronòmic food exhibition
Pàmies, Sergi	writer and journalist
Parellada, Ada	restaurant owner in Barcelona
Pardo, Jordi	director general of the Casals music foundation
Pastor, Perico	painter and illustrator
Pausas Mas, Josep	priest of Sitges church
Perrot, Catherine	writer, widow of Dalí's former secretary John Peter Moore
Piqué, Josep	economist, businessman and former Spanish foreign minister
Pla, Anna María	ceramic artist and maker of *caganers*
*Playà Maset, Josep	culture journalist at *La Vanguardia*
Polanco, Joseba	director of the Confederation of Cooperatives of Catalonia
Portabella, Pere	film director and opponent of Franco's regime
Puigbert, Josep	director of Catalan office in Perpignan
Puig, Imma	psychologist and former professor at Esade University
Pujol, Jordi	founder of Convergence party and former leader of Catalonia
Raguer, Hilari	monk and historian of Montserrat
Ramoneda, Josep	philosopher and political columnist
Redondo Terreros, Nicolás	former Basque Socialist politician
Ribera, Francesc	musician and city official in Berga
Riquer, Borja de	historian
Rivera, Albert	leader of Ciudadanos party

Roca, Joan, Josep and Jordi	chefs of El Celler de Can Roca
Roca i Junyent, Miquel	lawyer who drafted Spain's constitution
Rodés, Gonzalo	President of Barcelona Global business association
Roig, Josep Maria	owner of La Colmena, pastry shop in Barcelona
Romeo, Mario	notary and president of Tercera Vía association
Romeva, Raül	foreign policy chief of Catalan regional government
Romeo, Mario	notary and president of Tercera Vía association
Rovira, Bru	Catalan journalist and writer
Rufián, Gabriel	member of Spanish Parliament for Esquerra Republicana
Ruiz, Meritxell Catalan	regional minister for education
**Rull, Josep	Catalan conservative lawmaker
Rusiñol, Pere	journalist and magazine editor
Sala i Martín, Xavier María Isabel	economist and professor at Columbia University
Salazar Bertran	recipient of family documents from Salamanca archives
Samaranch, Juan Antonio	financier and member of Olympic Committee
Sánchez, Policarpo	lawyer and historian who defends the Salamanca archives
Sánchez Serra, Toni	deputy mayor of Port Bou
Santamaria, Pau	market gardener near Vic
Sans Molins, Silvia	researcher into the *calçot* at the Polytechnic University of Catalonia
Segura, Cristian	journalist at *El País*
Serra, Narcís	former mayor of Barcelona
Solé, Tilman	partner in Mucho, design company

APPENDIX

**Solé Tarrago, Josep — former president of *castell* team in Valls

Soler Martínez, Pere — librarian in Altea

Soler, Oriol — political strategist and publisher

Soler, Toni — director of *Polònia*, television show of political satire

Soriano, Mònica — owner of a communications and branding agency

Subirats, Marina — professor of sociology at the Autonomous University of Barcelona

Suñe, Josep María — wine farmer in Batea

Surra, Ana — Uruguayan activist, Catalan member of Spanish Congress

Tarrida, Joan — owner of publishing company Galaxia Gutenberg

Tomàs, Manolo — spokesperson for an association defending the river Ebro's delta

Torra, Quim — book publisher and lawyer

Troya, Wilson — Barcelona homeowner facing eviction by his bank

Uriarte, Pedro Luis — former Basque economics minister and banker

Vall i Clara, Joan — chief executive of *Punt Avui*

Vaquer, Josep Maria — oenologist

Vaquer, Miquel — Catalan pensioner

Vehí, Joan — former carpenter and amateur photographer who worked for Dalí

Vehí, Pere — owner of Boia, bar in Cadaqués

Venturós, Montserrat — mayor of Berga

Vidal-Folch, Xavier — columnist for *El País*

Vidal, Santiago — judge and member of Spanish Senate

Vilà, Francesc — psychoanalyst and director of Cuina Justa association

Vila, Maria — lawyer for Drets association

Vila Santi — Catalan regional minister for culture

Villas, Gauden	Spanish consul in Perpignan
Vilarrubí, Carles	vice president of FC Barcelona
*Vinyes, Ricard	historian and Barcelona city hall official
**Vives, Xavier	professor of economics at IESE business school
Voltas, Eduard	publisher of *Time Out* Barcelona
Xirgo, Xevi	editor of *Punt Avui*
Zabalza, Antoni	former Spanish secretary of state and economics professor
Zarzalejos, Javier	secretary general of Faes, conservative political think tank

(*) denotes meetings held with a small group of foreign correspondents.

(**) denotes interviews conducted prior to this book project.

NOTES

1. CREATING STATEHOOD ON THE STREETS

1. Opinion polls show a draw, see Dani Cordero, 'El 'no' a la independencia se impone por la mínima en Cataluña', *El País*, 18 November 2016, http://ccaa.elpais.com/ccaa/2016/11/18/catalunya/1479465331_528329.html
2. Joan Planas, *España desde el bar*, Salamanca: Editorial Hispalibros, 2016, p. 108.

2. CELEBRATING A DEFEAT

1. George Orwell, *Notes on Nationalism*, 1945.
2. Carles Cols, 'Nadie defendió el Born en 1991', *El Periódico Barcelona*, 19 Octobe 2016, http://www.elperiodico.com/es/noticias/barcelona/nadie-defendio-born-1991–5574524
3. Garbiel Tortella, José Luis García Ruiz, Clara Eugenia Núñez and Gloria Quiroga, *Cataluña en España*, Madrid: Gadir Editorial, 2016.
4. Jordi Canal, *Historia mínima de Cataluña*, Madrid: Turner Libros, 2015.
5. Josep Llobera, *Foundations of National Identitty: From Catalonia to Europe*, New York: Berghahn, 2004.

3. CATALONIA'S HAZY BORDERS

1. Público, 'Tormenta en Catalunya por el mapa del tiempo de TV3', 3 April 2012, http://www.publico.es/espana/tormenta-catalunya-mapa-del-tv3.html

2. Study of where the Catalan language is spoken, Generalitat de Catalunya, http://llengua.gencat.cat/permalink/91192f76-5385-11e4–8f3f-000c29cdf219

3. *El Periódico*, 'El Gobierno de Aragón se compromete a derogar la ley del lapao', 2 September 2015, http://www.elperiodico.com/es/noticias/politica/compromiso-gobierno-aragon-derogacion-ley-lapao-4475002

4. 'Dispute in Matarranya: Noticies del Matarranya', local publication, August 2016.

5. Hélène Legrais, 'Dalí in Perpignan' in *Découvrir Perpignan: Son histoire, son patrimoine*, Baixas: Balzac éditeur, 2015.

4. REMEMBERING THE CIVIL WAR AND FRANCO

1. *El País*, '"Una guerra civil no es un acontecimiento comemorable", afirma el Gobierno', 19 July 1986, http://elpais.com/diario/1986/07/19/espana/522108013_850215.html

2. Jorge Semprún's handling of Dalí's will, from *Federico Sánchez se despide de ustedes*, Barcelona: Tusquets Editores, 1993, http://www.diarioinformacion.com/opinion/2014/01/19/sueno-dali/1459464.html

3. Laura Freixas, 'Una generación de catalanes', *El País*, 21 January 2014, http://elpais.com/elpais/2014/01/09/opinion/1389266138_094028.html

4. Josep Playà Maset, '...Y Dalí ayudó a Tarradellas', *La Vanguardia*, 17 April 2016, http://www.lavanguardia.com/cultura/20160417/401162758315/dali-josep-tarradellas-cuadro-eco-antropomorfic.html

5. Paul Preston, *The Spanish Civil War: Reaction, Revolution and Revenge*, London: William Collins, 2016, p. 93.

5. REVIVING A LANGUAGE AFTER DICTATORSHIP

1. Pilar Ortega, 'El Instituto Cervantes niega que censurara un acto del escritor catalán Sánchez Piñol, *El Mundo*, 5 September 2014, http://www.elmundo.es/espana/2014/09/05/54098f84e2704eaa1f8b4574.html

2. Genaumag.com, 'El idioma catalán en Alemania', 7 May 2014, http://genaumag.com/catalan-alemania/
3. Margit Knapp, 'Commerce Replaces Politics at the Frankfurt Book Fair', *Der Spiegel*, 9 October 2007, http://www.spiegel.de/international/germany/a-controversial-homage-to-catalonia-commerce-replaces-politics-at-the-frankfurt-book-fair-a-510291.html
4. Europa Press, 'Más de 70 personalidades de la cultura reivindican el doblaje de películas al catalán', 22 November 2016, http://www.europapress.es/catalunya/noticia-mas-70-personalidades-cultura-reivindican-doblaje-peliculas-catalan-20161122202809.html
5. Manifest, 'Per un veritable procés de normalització lingüística a la catalunya independent', http://llenguairepublica.cat/manifest/

6. CATALONIA'S GREAT MELTING POT

1. US State Department Bureau of Democracy, Human Rights and Labor, 2011 Country Reports on Human Rights Practices, 24 May 2012, http://www.state.gov/documents/organization/208582.p
2. Joaquima Utrera, 'El hombre que apedreó a Pujol', *El País*, 10 November 1988, http://elpais.com/diario/1988/11/10/espana/595119611_850215.html
3. Jordi Canal, *Historia mínima de Cataluña*, Madrid: Turner Libros, 2015.

7. A CONSERVATIVE DIVORCE

1. Mariano Rajoy, *En Confianza: Mi vida y mi proyecto de cambio para España*, Barcelona: Planeta, 2011.
2. Aznar's praise of Catalan https://www.youtube.com/watch?v=9Sgty4Cey08
3. Amanda Figueras, 'Zapatero hace vibrar al Palau Sant Jordi con un discurso por la pluralidad', *El Mundo*, http://www.elmundo.es/elmundo/2008/03/06/eleccionesgenerales/1204831825.html

4. Jordi Pujol, *El caminante frente al desfiladero: Cuando todo es difícil. Y necesario*, Barcelona: Ediciones Destino, 2013, p. 287.
5. Jordi Pujol, *El caminante frente al desfiladero: Cuando todo es difícil. Y necesario*, Barcelona: Ediciones Destino, 2013, p. 295.

8. THE SHARED DISEASE OF CORRUPTION

1. Ponç Feliu, 'El nostre', *El Punt Avui*, 19 August 2014, http://www.elpuntavui.cat/article/7-vista/8-articles/769773-el-nostre.html
2. Lluís Bassets, *La Gran Vergüenza*, Barcelona: Ediciones Península, 2014, p. 111.

9. A DIPLOMATIC BATTLE ACROSS EUROPE

1. Artur Mas, 'Artur Mas gastó 18,5 millones en 'embajadas' en plena crisis', *El País*, 2 August 2016, http://politica.elpais.com/politica/2016/08/01/actualidad/1470066880_944583.html
2. Adam Ramsay, 'Scottish voters have spoken out against Brexit—and even without independence they could rejoin the EU', *Independent*, 24 June 2016, http://www.independent.co.uk/voices/brexit-scottish-referendum-scotland-eu-remain-nicola-sturgeon-snp-a7100736.html
3. Lluís Bassets, *La Gran Vergüenza*, Barcelona: Ediciones Península, 2014, p. 46.

10. BARCELONA, A CITY BEFORE A NATION

1. Jordi Canal, *Historia mínima de Cataluña*, Madrid: Turner Libros, 2015, p. 41.
2. Robert Hughes, *Barcelona*, London: Vintage, 2001.
3. Enric Juliana, 'Barcelona, la pionera', *La Vanguardia*, 20 July 2012, http://www.lavanguardia.com/magazine/20120720/543 27079811/barcelona-la-pionera-juliana-magazine.html
4. Sara De Diego, 'Ada Colau responde a la dura carta de la PAH: 'Yo haría lo mismo en vuestro lugar'', *El Confidencial*, 3 December 2015, http://www.elconfidencial.com/espana/cataluna/2015-12-03/ada-colau-carta-pah-desahucios_1112815/

11. THE SYMBOLISM OF A TOWER AND A TREE

1. José Ángel Montañés, '¿Cuántos años tiene la estatua de Colón y dónde señala su dedo?', *El País*, 28 September 2016, http://ccaa. elpais.com/ccaa/2016/09/28/catalunya/1475056077_833339. html
2. Jesús Laínz, *España contra Cataluña: Historia de un fraude*, Madrid: Ediciones Encuentro, 2014.
3. Antoni Tàpies, *A Personal Memoir: Fragments for an Autobiography (Complete Writings. Volume I)*, Bloomington, IN: Indiana University Press, 2009, p. 90.
4. Jordi Canal, *Historia mínima de Cataluña*, Madrid: Turner Libros, 2015, p. 41.

12. THE DECLINE OF CHURCH AND CROWN

1. *La Vanguardia*, 'El Govern no se da por aludido por la carta del Rey', 18 September 2012, http://www.lavanguardia.com/politica/20120918/54349722499/govern-no-aludido-carta-rey.html
2. P. Marcos, 'La afirmación del Rey de que 'nunca se obligó a hablar en castellano' provoca una tormenta política', *El País*, 25 April 2001, http://elpais.com/diario/2001/04/25/cultura/988149601_850215.html

13. FINANCING SPAIN'S ECONOMIC POWERHOUSE

1. *Delta del Ebro: La Guía*, Tarragona: Magazín Parcs, 2009.
2. La opinion de Murcia, 'Pujol asegura en su último libro que vio ´el cielo abierto´ con el PNH de Aznar', 16 February 2012, http://www.laopiniondemurcia.es/comunidad/2012/02/16/pujol-asegura-ultimo-libro-vio-cielo-abierto-pnh-aznar/385761. html
3. Xavier Vidal-Folch, *¿Cataluña Independiente?*, Madrid: Los Libros De La Catarata, 2013, p. 8.
4. Ara.cat, 'Francesc de Carreras afirma que l'estat català seria com Sicília, ple 'de màfies, gàngsters i 'vendettas'', 12 October 2012, http://www.ara.cat/politica/Ciutadans-Albert_Rivera-Francesc_

de_Carreras-Juan_Carlos_Girauta-Arcadi_Espada_0_790
721025.html

5. Modest Guinjoan, Xavier Cuadras Morató and Miquel Puig, *Com
Àustria o Dinamarca: La Catalunya possible*, Barcelona: Editorial Pòr-
tic, 2013, p. 22.

6. Josep Borrell and Joan Llorach, *Las cuentas y los cuentos de la independencia*, Catarata, 2015, p. 92.

14. THE BUSINESS OF SHARING

1. Cooperatives in Spain, see Ministerio de Empleo Y Seguridad
Social, 31 December 2015, http://www.empleo.gob.es/es/sec_
trabajo/autonomos/economia-soc/EconomiaSocial/estadisticas/
SociedadesAltaSSocial/2015/4Trim/AVANCE_TOTAL.pdf

15. THE VIOLENCE OF BASQUE SECESSIONISM

1. ETA Interviews by Lourdes Garzón, published on 7 June 1998 by
La Revista de El Mundo, http://www.elmundo.es/larevista/
num138/textos/eta1.html.

2. Lluís Visa, 'Atentado mortal de Terra Lliure en vísperas de nacional catalana protagonizada por los independentistas', *El País*,
11 September 1987, and Paul Delaney, 'American Sailor Dies in
Barcelona After U.S.O. Blast That Hurt 10', *New York Times*,
28 December 1987, http://www.nytimes.com/1987/12/28/
world/american-sailor-dies-in-barcelona-after-uso-blast-that-
hurt-10.html

16. CIVIL DISOBEDIENCE AND THE RULE OF LAW

1. *La Vanguardia*, 'Fallece Tarradellas, guardián de la legitimidad
democrática', 10 June 2013, http://www.lavanguardia.com/hem-
eroteca/20130610/54374539775/josep-tarradellas-catalunya-
politica-generalitat-provisional-exilio-retorno.html

2. Ibid.

3. Xavier Vidal-Folch, *Cataluña Ante España*, Madrid: Los Libros De
La Catarata, 2014.

4. Conference on 'Constitutional reform and territorial organisation', organised by Unidad Editorial in Madrid, 29 November 2016.

17. PLAYING POLITICS IN CATALAN SPORTS

1. Jimmy Burns, *Barça: A People's Passion*, London: Bloomsbury, 2009.
2. FC Barcelona website: http://arxiu.fcbarcelona.cat/web/castellano/club/club_avui/mes_que_un_club/mesqueunclub_historia.html
3. Joaquim Coll, 'Lo que la 'estelada' esconde', *El País*, 25 May 2016, http://elpais.com/elpais/2016/05/23/opinion/146399 1681_094924.html
4. David Jiménez, 'Por qué cometí la mayor traición del fútbol', *El Mundo*, 22 May 2016, http://www.elmundo.es/opinion/2016/0 5/22/57409e87268e3eff0c8b45f1.html

18. PLEASURES AND TENSIONS AROUND THE TABLE

1. Arthur Lubow, 'A Laboratory of Taste', *New York Times*, 10 August 2003, http://www.nytimes.com/2003/08/10/magazine/a-laboratory-of-taste.html
2. Colman Andrews, *Catalan Cuisine: Europe's Last Great Culinary Secret*, London: Grub Street, 1997, p. 4.

19. THE FACTS OF A GOOD NEWS STORY

1. 'Catalunya Ràdio pide disculpas a la escritora Cristina Peri Rossi', *El País*, 7 October 2007, http://elpais.com/diario/2007/10/07/catalunya/1191719254_850215.html
2. 'El PP denuncia que TV3 identifica a los deportistas olímpicos catalanes con la senyera', *El Mundo*, 7 August 2016, http://www.elmundo.es/cataluna/2016/08/07/57a70a75268e3e0b298b4 5cc.html
3. Felipe González Márquez, 'A los catalanes', *El País*, 31 August 2015, http://elpais.com/elpais/2015/08/29/opinion/1440863 481_811526.html

4. Jordi Pérez Colomé, 'El libro negro del periodismo en Cataluña: un epílogo con datos', *El Español*, 23 September 2015, http://blog.elespanol.com/libro-negro/

INDEX

INDEX

INDEX

INDEX

INDEX

INDEX

INDEX

INDEX

INDEX

INDEX

INDEX

INDEX

INDEX

INDEX

INDEX

INDEX

INDEX

INDEX

INDEX

INDEX

INDEX

INDEX

INDEX

INDEX

INDEX

INDEX